Swift's Poetic Worlds

Swift's
Poetic Worlds

Louise K. Barnett

Newark: University of Delaware Press
London and Toronto: Associated University Presses

© 1981 by Associated University Presses, Inc.

Associated University Presses, Inc.
4 Cornwall Drive
East Brunswick, N.J. 08816

Associated University Presses Ltd
69 Fleet Street
London EC4Y 1EU, England

Associated University Presses
Toronto M5E 1A7, Canada

Library of Congress Cataloging in Publication Data

Barnett, Louise K.
  Swift's poetic worlds.

  Bibliography: p.
  Includes index.
  1. Swift, Jonathan, 1667–1745—Poetic works.
I. Title.
PR3728.P58B35   821'.5   80-54538
ISBN 0-87413-187-1   AACR2

Printed in the United States of America

for my husband

The Caesars in my heart
Tell me how all infamy is possible,
And certain treacheries extremely probable!

Delmore Schwartz, "Swift"

Contents

A Note on Texts and Abbreviations 12
Acknowledgments 13
Introduction 15

PART I: *Ordering the Self: The Poetry of Fictive
        Self-portraiture*

1. Strategies of Self-defense 47
2. The Vulnerable Self 91

PART II: *Ordering the World: The Satiric Poetry*

3. The Verbal Universe 112
4. "Foppery, Affectation, Vanity, Folly, or Vice":
   The Disordered World of the Gentlewoman 150
5. Poetry of Excess: The Body and the Body Politic 171
   Conclusion 194

Notes 198
Works Cited 214
Index 221

A Note on Texts and Abbreviations

The editions of Swift's writings used throughout, together with abbreviations used to refer to them, are listed below.

Corres.	*The Correspondence of Jonathan Swift.* Edited by Harold Williams. 5 vols. Oxford: Clarendon Press, 1963–65.
Journal to Stella	*Journal to Stella.* Edited by Harold Williams. Oxford: Clarendon Press, 1948.
Poems	*The Poems of Jonathan Swift.* Edited by Harold Williams. 2d ed. 3 vols. Oxford: Clarendon Press, 1958.
Prose Works	*The Prose Works of Jonathan Swift.* Edited by Herbert Davis. 14 vols. Oxford: Clarendon Press, 1937–68.

Wherever dashes in the Williams edition of the poems indicate the omission of names or vulgar expressions, I have filled these in from *Swift's Poetical Works,* ed. Herbert Davis (London: Oxford University Press, 1967).

Acknowledgments

I have known no more splendid and inspiring teacher than Clifford Earl Ramsey. What I learned from his graduate seminar in eighteenth-century poetry was the beginning of this study that made the rest possible. To Terry Jones I am indebted for a thoughtful reading of my first draft and many valuable discussions. For encouragement and good will I am grateful to David M. Vieth, Donald C. Mell, and Richard Quaintance, while to John Irwin Fischer, for his more than generous contribution of time and criticism, I owe a special debt, acknowledged here with gratitude. In recognition of Robert J. Barnett Jr.'s general support and specific suggestions I am happy to dedicate this book.

Parts of this study originally appeared in somewhat different form in *Contemporary Studies of Swift's Poetry, Concerning Poetry,* and *Review.* I wish to thank the editors of the University of Delaware Press and the two journals for permission to reprint this material. I also wish to thank Doubleday & Company for permission to reprint lines from "Swift," copyright 1959 by Delmore Schwartz, which appeared in *Summer Knowledge: New and Selected Poems 1938–1958* by Delmore Schwartz.

Introduction

A writer seldom masters two genres equally, and when he is widely acclaimed for excellence in one, his achievement in the other is apt to suffer by comparison. This has been the case with Swift: his prose satires have overshadowed the poetry and preempted critical attention.[1] Almost every aspect of Swift's life and work except his poetry has now been extensively studied; while scholarly treatment of the prose satires proliferated between 1950 and 1976, the same period produced only one volume entirely devoted to the poetry—Maurice Johnson's *The Sin of Wit*.[2] Until quite recently only a small group of poems, the "scatological" poetry, was commented upon with any frequency, but this attention tended to be morally judgmental and critically negligible. A few other poems continued to be anthologized, but the body of Swift's poetry was ignored by scholarly criticism or often, on the basis of the notorious poems, dismissed. As late as 1971 the distinguished Swift scholar Irvin Ehrenpreis could write: "Swift survives as the author of half a dozen prose satires and a few humorous or complimentary poems. Who reads more?"[3]

The failure to give Swift's poetry the same kind of critical attention that the prose has commanded seems to be attributable to two quite different attitudes toward it. Beginning with Dr. Johnson's assertion that "in the poetical works of Dr. Swift there is not much upon which the critic can exercise his powers,"[4] the aesthetic argument has maintained that Swift is only a "man of rhymes" who writes "upon trifles."[5] Explaining why she omits Swift from her book on Augustan poetry, Rachel Trickett characterizes Swift's poetry as "informal and casual to an extent which

15

seems to cast doubt on the whole serious art of verse-making."[6] She concludes:

> It is this which prevents us from considering him in detail as representative of the main tradition of Augustan poetry, and which, perhaps, has inhibited his most friendly critics from doing more than noting the importance of his verse, and the neglect into which it has fallen.[7]

The occasional nature of much of Swift's poetry and his own offhand remarks about it have undoubtedly contributed to the view that Swift, in Oswald Johnson's words, "simply is not interested in 'being a poet.' "[8] The poetry itself, its mockeries and burlesques of traditional genres and conventions combined with an open contempt for certain kinds of poetic diction, has led Herbert Davis to call Swift "the most extreme example that we have ever had in England of reaction against the historic or romantic view of the poet's function and art."[9] Such a view accords with the preeminence of the prose to foster a dichotomized approach to Swift as a writer of serious prose and light verse, a "verse man," as W. R. Irwin calls him.[10]

Traditionally, another reason for dismissing the poetry has been that it is morally or philosophically deficient. This prevalent nineteenth-century view was given new currency in the twentieth century by such well-known figures as D. H. Lawrence, Aldous Huxley, and F. R. Leavis.[11] Here, too, a significant difference in attitude toward the poetry and the prose obtained. What was disturbing in the prose could be comfortably distanced from Swift the man and discussed critically. The poetry, in contrast, tended to be interpreted more as direct personal statement, evidence of Swift's own deficiencies rather than art. For Lawrence, the references to excrement in "Cassinus and Peter," not those of *Gulliver's Travels,* demonstrate that Swift is a "mental lunatic."[12] Because the poetry often uses a character or speaker named Swift, or an unidentified speaker not so readily separable from the author as is the speaker of *A Tale of a Tub*, it has been inviting to assume that Swift speaks in his poetry in his own voice. At the same time as certain critics have found the poetry morally reprehensible, they have also been attracted by its power. Leavis refers to Swift's "great force," and Huxley attributes greatness to his intensity.[13] Oswald Johnson, while assailing Swift for his "abuse" of the pastoral in "The Description of a City Shower," remarks that "the pleasure of reading the poem comes from the outrageous ways in which Swift makes fun of the poetic language he pretends to be using."[14] Bonamy Dobrée, who regards Swift's two descriptions as "defiantly anti-poetic," also finds that "much of what he did is individual, unmatched."[15] More sympathetically, in his perceptive reappraisal of 1934, Edmund Wilson writes: "There is nothing else quite like this in literature. The curses and sneers of Swift created a new kind of lyric."[16]

Among friendly critics, this singularity, rather than lack of consequence, accounts for the poetry's long neglect: it is a body of work difficult to categorize and discuss. Just as "pastoral" connotes what is least interesting in "A Description of the Morning," so the most obvious handles to many of the poems are equally unrewarding or misleading. Swift's "scatological" poems have been widely known since their appearance, but as Aubrey Williams remarked at the 1977 MLA seminar on Swift's poetry, scatology enters into only about five percent of the entire canon. Given the violation of rhetorical expectations and the resistance to conventional rubrics that characterize Swift's poetry, it is understandable that past generations were tempted to eschew critical examination and read the poems as tokens of madness, misogyny, coprophilia, or "insane egotism" (Leavis). Swift's foremost biographer, Irvin Ehrenpreis, has almost singlehandedly demolished such extreme explanations in *The Personality of Swift* (1958) and in *Swift: The Man, His Works, and the Age* (vol. 1, 1962; vol. 2, 1967). These books, in conjunction with Harold

Williams's edition of the poems, now make it possible as never before to examine what is perhaps the greatest body of English poetry that criticism has heretofore misvalued and neglected.

In this poetry Swift stands revealed as an impressive virtuoso of language, a poet whose accomplishments are original, wide ranging, and at times strikingly modern. He can overwhelm a satiric target with *saeva indignatio,* mimic and parody any number of styles and dictions, and reproduce the rhythms of vernacular speech at any social level. His delight in poetry as an autonomous world of words is exhibited in numerous puns, riddles, and feats of rhyming and by verbal fantasies that make no claim to be pictures of reality but succeed through their witty and imaginative use of language. Like no other poet of his time, Swift is sensitive to misuse of language ranging from artificial diction to political propaganda; he asserts a relationship between political and linguistic corruption that has become a preoccupation of twentieth-century thought. Swift's greatest poems—"Verses on the Death of Dr. Swift," "The Legion Club," and "On Poetry: A Rapsody"—belong with the best of English poetry of their length and scope, while those deliberately rational tributes written for Stella, the birthday odes, are as eloquent a testimony of deep affection as any similar group of poems.

During the past decade Swift's poetry has become the focus of a growing critical interest and the subject of a number of excellent studies of individual poems and aspects of poetic technique. Most recently, several books have appeared: Nora Crow Jaffe's *The Poet Swift,* a comprehensive introduction; John Irwin Fischer's *On Swift's Poetry,* a specialized study of a small group of poems; and Peter J. Schakel's *The Poetry of Jonathan Swift: Allusion and the Development of a Poetic Style.*[17] My work is intended to be still another kind of investigation, one that approaches the poetry as a coherent whole structurally and thematically. Having found that customary rubrics and chronological organization are both inadequate to my discussion of recurrent concerns and techniques of Swift's poetry, I treat such traditional categories as the early odes, the poems to Stella, and the poems of Market Hill within more inclusive groupings intended to reveal a Swiftian poetics. The poems of fictive self-portraiture, for example, have in common the presentation of a character identifiable as Swift, who is portrayed either as successful in overcoming threats to the self or, in a smaller number of poems, unsuccessful. These different outcomes embody the ongoing tension in Swift's poetry between the power of art to provide a shaping vision for the world and the forces of chaos and entropy that oppose the ordering process.

The heterogeneous nature of the poetry not primarily concerned with self, which I have called the poetry of the world, demands a less schematic treatment. The poems I have begun with in this section notably lack the emotional intensity of so much of Swift's poetry because, whatever their subject and occasion, they remain within the verbal universe. Unlike Swift's other satiric poems they depend upon assumptions about language and literature more than rules of conduct; the sins committed are within a world of words less threatening than the world of men and events. Much of this poetry is playful, like the many riddles, epigrams, and verse exchanges with friends that show Swift's pleasure in poetry as language. But even when serious examples of folly and vice enter in, they tend to be eclipsed or transformed by imaginative wit into issues of language. The poems satirizing the faults of gentlewomen can be paired with the poetry of the verbal universe in terms of artistic control. Swift achieves success in both instances because his poetic stance lacks the ambivalence and violent feelings found elsewhere in his poetry; his notable skills are in harmony with the encompassing of the poems' standard satiric objectives.

These first two groups of poems constitute worlds of comic satire in which the poet's resources are more than equal to the follies he treats. These are poems of distance and control, but not *saeva indignatio*. That is to be found in the poems of excess, where satire verges on tragedy. When Swift considers the body and the body politic, his feelings of outrage tend to overwhelm the poetic design, and the order asserted is ambiguous or tentative. Under the rubric of excess I consider the scatological and political poems, poetry that is both powerful and flawed. The first group is marred by Swift's failure to see his subject clearly: there can be no total resolution because his satiric target expands from moral degeneracy to include the givens of physicality. The same result is produced by different circumstances in the political poetry. While Swift's vision of his satiric targets is unclouded, his rage often seems too extreme to submit to the requirements of poetic expression. Here, too, there is a sense of going beyond the province of satire into that of tragedy—the inescapable terms of existence, beyond what can be reformed or amended and equally beyond what the satirist finds bearable.

To discuss the structure of Swift's poetry I have adopted the useful idea of Claudio Guillén that "a process of expansion occurs within the order of the poem and as a product of that order."[18] The order of the poem, its "principle of unity," is thus challenged by a principle of expansion; the result is a "dynamic and dialectical relationship" that Guillén suggests is "one of the distinctive features of the verbal work of art."[19] Because it is always adversary poetry, even when it is not satire, Swift's poetry seems particularly suited to a critical approach that emphasizes dialectical movement without formulating it in the simplistic terms of polarized alternatives—terms all too easily applied to satire. The adversary may be an individual like Sir Robert Walpole or William Wood, a social evil like the public malfeasance of a group of identifiable persons in "The Legion Club" or the anonymous slander of "The Life and Genuine Character of Dr. Swift," or an impersonal force—time in the poems for Stella's birthday. Whoever or whatever the adversary, it is understood to be a powerful threat to the positive values the poet represents, yet one that can be contained (if not defeated in actuality) within the verbal universe created and shaped by the poet. This is the essence of the dialectic in Swift's poetry: a definition of the adversary, often the creation of a satiric fiction, becomes the principle of unity, which is expanded upon—reduced, enlarged, transformed, destroyed, or even, in the case of Partridge the astronomer, apotheosized—through the resources of poetry. The containment of the adversary within a verbal construct is an aesthetic triumph, but Swift often incorporates within his poetic world an awareness of the power of the enemy as it continues to exist outside the poem. The shifting strength of poet and adversary can be thought of as a spectrum with complete control at one end (such poems as the early birthday odes for Stella), and at the other, the vulnerability of "Holyhead. Sept. 25. 1727," and the thematic incoherence of "Strephon and Chloe."

The Poetry of Fictive Self-portraiture

1

In his discussion of Pope's epistles Maynard Mack provides an approach to the problem of biography in poetry with his suggestion that a first-person speaker identified with the author be regarded as a rhetorical strategy, necessary to establish a "satirical ethos."[20] If the satirist does not appear to be a particular kind of person, exhibiting—as Pope claims for himself—the strong antipathy of good to bad, his satire will lack credibility. Useful as this model is for many satiric speakers, it cannot be applied to the major part of Swift's poetry of fictive self-portraiture. From the earliest ventures on, Swift's depiction of self lacks the single-mindedness essential to the satiric speaker, the dichotomized presentation of good opposing bad. The self is both exalted and ridiculed within a full spectrum of character possibilities, which include the satirist-hero at one extreme and the unscrupulous opportunist at the other. In Swift's poetry self tends to be its own end rather than a strategy for presenting something else.

From first to last, Swift's poetry exemplifies what Maurice Johnson has called "the biographical presence."[21] Even in the early panegyrics, officially committed to the praise of others, self often displaces the putative subject. In the chronological development of Swift's poetry, poems that are primarily or totally concerned with a fictive Swift assume increasing prominence; with growing maturity and skill, the poet evidently felt less hesitant to admit that he was his own best subject and more engrossed with the possibilities he discovered in fictive self-portraiture.

Although Swift is a poet who responds to occasions furnished by the external world, from national issues like the Wood's Patent controversy to events of personal significance like Stella's birthday, underneath the specific impetus is an ongoing desire to create self-portraits. References to himself as "dean" appear in his poetry an extraordinary one hundred and sixty-two times.[22] When Swift is not writing about Swift third person or speaking as Swift first person, he is devising other ways of making himself the subject, most commonly by inventing some other character—often a fictive version of a real person—whose theme is Swift. Thus a "Lady in the North" (Swift's friend Lady Acheson) writes "A Panegyrick on the Dean," while Harley's secretary, Erasmus Lewis, is one of the speakers to describe Swift in "Horace, Epistle I. VII." Reporting other people's opinions of himself rather than allowing *them* to speak is another of the poet's favorite techniques for introducing the subject of self. "The Author upon Himself," whose title suggests that it will be Swift on Swift, is actually a report of the judgments of others about him. Purportedly external comment, often made by unidentifiable speakers, ranges from extravagant praise through neutral statement to scorn and condemnation. The credentials, if any, of these disembodied voices (and hence the reliability of their pronouncements) are difficult to determine.

These multiple self-portraits are partial views that add up to a total, multifaceted view: Swift's relations with women, disciples, servants, ministers, friends, enemies, public opinion, and posterity. When Swift constructs heroic portraits of himself, even such astute and friendly readers as Pope have been made uncomfortable; when instead he becomes a figure of fun in his poetry, there is less puzzlement, for we conventionally approve the man who can laugh at himself.[23] Negative portraits also exist, one drawn so convincingly that it was anonymously published by an unfriendly printer as an authentic libel.[24] Behind the profusion of perspectives on self in Swift's poetry lies a modern sense of the mosaic of personality, motivation, and perception—an awareness of the complexity of the self. In his poetry of fictive self-portraiture Swift focuses upon the closest and yet the most intractable of materials—his own experience and psyche, the most available and compelling example of that problematical entity, human nature.

Since role tends to determine the kind of portrait or portraits Swift constructs in a given poem, a useful approach to Swift's poems of fictive self-portraiture is to group them according to the role the character of Swift plays. Most of the Market Hill poems, for example, originate in Swift's violations of the role of guest. Although he is portrayed only in relation to one other person in the poems written for Stella's birthday, Swift plays a dual role combining dominance and subordination: as an artist he celebrates Stella in poetry, and as a man he depends upon her care and friendship. In contrast to these private versions of self other poems present Swift as writer, politician, churchman—in other words, as a public man. These poems work with the disparate views that make up the reputation of a well-known figure and are consequently more complex than the poetry of the private self.

2

What sustains tension and interest in the poetry of fictive self-portraiture is a generally interfused sense of connection between Swift as author and Swift as character. Whatever their distance from the reality of Swift's life, his fictive selves assume the guise and authority of biography.

The identity of author and character in "The Author upon Himself" and "Horace, *Lib. 2 Sat.* 6," and the common biographical basis—that the man described is a real person who did associate with Harley and Bolingbroke— give the poems a certain degree of credibility. The use of recognizable biographical materials is a strategy to gain the reader's confidence, but where the poems diverge in their treatment of Swift's political role—real power versus sham—art, not biography, must provide the resolution.

The abiding concern of Swift's poetry of fictive self-portraiture is not to lead back to biography through the expression of a "real self," but to refract and thus meditate upon the world's perceptions and misperceptions of this self. As Swift wrote to Bolingbroke and Pope, he wanted "to be used like a Lord by those who have an opinion of my parts; *whether right or wrong, it is no great matter.*"[25] Views of the self are almost always filtered through other imagined consciousnesses because Swift is not writing confessions but constructing fictive portraits that are always to some degree public and external. That the portraits cannot be reconciled among themselves or with historic Swift not only underscores their fictive character but calls to our attention the diverse materials that contribute to a public image: the polarized assessments of interested parties—friends and enemies; or of different vantage points—cynical outsider or sympathetic insider. Labeling conflicting portraits *Swift* is a compelling dramatic device to provoke these reflections and to insist upon the epistemological issue: the same set of facts, the general public knowledge of Swift's career, can yield—and in Swift's poetry repeatedly does yield—radically different interpretations. Swift's use of multiple self-portraits in his poetry is similar to the procedure he recommended for pursuing political truth: "Whoever has so little to do as to desire some Knowledge in Secrets of State, must compare what he hears from several great men, or from one great man at severall Times, which is equally different."[26]

The biographical data in Swift's poetry include identifiable fact, half-truth, untruth, conjecture, and fantasy. Nonetheless, however the data are classified, in the poetry they become fictive statement, part of a created context rather than history. Swift's most characteristic use of biographical materials is neither a straightforward presentation of truth nor a mechanical reversal of fictive to true. It is subtle, ambiguous, ultimately impossible to categorize precisely because no one formula of relationship is sustained for long.

The poetry of fictive self-portraiture is generally posited upon the kind of knowledge of Swift that an average contemporary reader might be expected to have, or it contains enough conventional clues to guide the reader. Even such personal versions of Swift as the Market Hill poems construct are accessible without their implicit biographical *donnée,* the close friendship of the Achesons and the Dean. Lady Acheson's praise of Swift in "A Panegyrick on the Dean" for serving as butler would be correctly read as ironic even without the note that Swift supplied to George Faulkner informing the reader that "he sometimes used to direct the Butler."[27]

The poems undoubtedly contain private biographical jokes designed for limited audiences, but when these are discovered they invariably enrich rather than alter the poetic statement. Knowing that Swift could be cantankerous transforms an inert detail in "Verses on the Death of Dr. Swift" ("was cheerful to his dying Day") into a joke, but by this point in the poem the reader should already suspect that the extravagant absolute claims made for Swift signalize an ironic treatment.

3

"It is allowed, Swift wrote, "that the Cause of most Actions, good or bad, may be resolved into the Love of our selves."[28] Clearly, one form that Swift's own self-love takes is making poetry about himself, although not necessarily flattering poetry. Swift's choice to make poetry out of the possibility of the world's abuse of himself is an act of defiance and domination that asserts his strength by out-doing and thus disarming his real critics. It gives the poet control, even over negative versions of self and, paradoxi-cally, serves to punish Swift for even a fantasied commerce with evils attributed to him by the world or by his own conscience.

Perhaps the most significant of Swift's reasons for writ-ing his poetry of fictive self-portraiture is the desire to leave a record of himself to combat what he described in the "Ode to the Athenian Society" as "Careless and Ignorant Posterity." In some part Swift may have wanted "to turn private crisis into public example,"[29] as Geoffrey Hill suggests, but in the main his self-absorption seems more personal, more a question of mastering private crisis and public misrepresentation by establishing his own version. Robert C. Elliott's investigation of the primitive origin of satire in the utilitarian practices of magic and ritual suggests exactly this function of art: "These rites spring from one primordial demand—a demand that out of the fears and confusions engendered by a hostile world man shall be able to impose some kind of order."[30] Swift's poetry of fictive self-portraiture may be viewed as a response to the demand for overcoming, through ordering and controlling within the verbal universe of his art, those fears and confusions inspired not only by the self's troubling encounters with the external world but by the confrontation with its own spirit.

The pattern of frustration discernible in Swift's life has its counterpart in the major body of poems of fictive self-portraiture, poems that exhibit what I call strategies of self-defense directed against threats to the self. Almost all of these poems employ some version of a basic situation, that of a man at odds with others, usually attacked by persons or groups who hold superior status or power. Through this adversary's ridicule or misunderstanding, Swift appears foolish or guilty, but on a less obvious level, or sometimes in a companion poem, he is vindicated. The diverse fictive Swifts who are ridiculed, slandered, or made sport of by the powerful in these poems have in common the underlying idea of a man who is misunderstood and misvalued, invariably more sinned against than sinning.

A simple paradigm of self-defense is found in the short poem "Drapier's Hill," where a threatening situation is introduced, expatiated upon, and then overcome. The tone of "Drapier's Hill" is not solemn, and on the surface the allusion to Denham's ambitious poem only makes Swift's poem seem slighter. In contrast to Denham's grand disquisition on perception, the first part of "Drapier's Hill" is humorously mundane, a catalogue of expected expenditures and income from the property. Halfway through the poem the introduction of the name "Drapier's Hill" serves as a turning point: the light tone of the earlier financial arithmetic continues to color the remainder, but the joking triviality is gone. Listing the tokens of his greatest public triumph is both a loving commemoration and a fearful encounter, for Swift imagines the worst, the total obliteration of all these gratifying memorials:

> That when a Nation long enslav'd,
> Forgets by whom it once was sav'd;
> When none the DRAPIER's Praise shall sing;
> His signs aloft no longer swing;
> His Medals and his Prints forgotten,
> And all his Handkerchiefs are rotten;
> His famous LETTERS made waste Paper.
>
> (11–17)

Characteristically in Swift's vision, time and ingratitude join forces to consign him to oblivion. Anticipating these evils, Swift prepares to counter them in advance by making his property a monument, which in turn is preserved in poetry:

> This Hill may keep the Name of DRAPIER:
> In Spight of Envy flourish still,
> And DRAPIER's vye with COOPER's Hill.
>
> (18–20)

Time, ingratitude, and now envy: Swift's enemies typically multiply, but he exorcises these threats to the self by preserving his cherished victory in land and in poetry, his own poem linked to literary tradition by the reference to Cooper's Hill.

Swift's greatest work of fictive self-portraiture, "Verses on the Death of Dr. Swift," makes essentially the same statement. Like Yeats in "Sailing to Byzantium," Swift escapes from the present not only through the process of making poetry, but through identifying the self with the artifact it has created. Yeats wishes to become the perfect aesthetic object, the golden bird. Swift cannot relinquish the self so completely, although he, too, wants to encompass "what is past, or passing, or to come" by becoming the monument he has himself constructed for posterity—the poetic memorial to self.

The Satiric Poetry

1

Swift's satire begins in rage, the famous *saeva indignatio* whose laceration of his heart is memorialized in his epitaph. "I am raging every moment against the Corruptions in both kingdoms," he wrote to Pope, and to Bolingbroke he envisioned himself dying in Ireland "in a rage, like a poisoned rat in a hole."[31] The image is an effective reminder of the negative effects of rage not transformed into satire: it can imprison and poison, remain bottled up in speechlessness and revenge fantasies, or find antisocial expression in expletives and blows. In satire it is not foolishly dissipated against inanimate objects or taken out on innocent bystanders (the familiar hierarchy of anger handed down from employer to employee to spouse to child to dog), but transformed into art, "a permissible release for the maddest energies of poetic impulse."[32]

Swift's annotations of Lord Herbert of Cherbury's *Life and Raigne of Henry VIII* (1649) reveal in its purest form the rage out of which satire is made. Most of Swift's brief comments are ejaculations of pure rage. Where Cherbury reports the King's command to execute Sir John Neville, he writes: "Dog, Villain, King, Viper, Devil Monster."[33] Swift refers to Henry as a dog eight times and as a monster, brute, beast, hell-hound, tyrant, rogue, and villain. When Cherbury concludes his book with "I wish I could leave him in his grave," Swift continues with his own notably less restrained conclusion: "And I wish he had been Flead, his skin stuffed and hangd on a Gibbet, His bulky guts and Flesh left to be devoured by Birds and Beasts for a warning to his Successors for ever. Amen."[34] Swift's rage has already transformed the King into a number of nonhuman shapes; the climactic image is a revolting bodily desecration of majesty. In the context of the other marginal notes such treatment of Henry has clear personal satisfaction for Swift. He was, after all, annotating for his own private purpose rather than preparing an essay for publication or even circulation among friends. Yet the last and lengthiest comment contains a satiric rationale: the gruesome spectacle would not only answer Swift's sense of Henry's crimes, and thus pacify his rage, but would also warn "his Successors for ever." These results, which cannot be achieved in reality, remain the dual aims of satire: the symbolic exposure of the body of vice may both punish the guilty and enlighten the innocent.

Brief and unorganized jottings, Swift's notes nevertheless vividly communicate his intense feelings against Henry. Rather than a posture of distance and noncommitment or disinterested evaluation, satire requires a stance of concern, a presentation of folly and evil as felt realities coupled with a desire to effect some change, however minimal, in behavior or awareness. The posture may be part of the fiction, but it must not seem to be; satire is a special case, a genre that has more direct and necessary ties to the world than other kinds of imaginative literature. The relationship tends to be circular: to begin with an occasion offered by the world, a departure from some standard of behavior, and to return to the world with an appeal for action to correct the deviation from the norm. Satire assumes a community of accepted values that is not only recognizable, but also subscribed to and, ideally, acted upon. Satiric exposure could motivate someone to right a wrong, but if this is unlikely—Swift wrote in the *Examiner*—it may still have the salutary effect of alerting the community at large to wrongdoing:

> It is very plain, that considering the Defectiveness of our Laws, the variety of Cases, the Weakness of the Prerogative, the Power or the Cunning of ill-designing Men, it is possible, that many great Abuses may be visibly committed, which cannot be legally punished. . . . I am apt to think, it was to supply such Defects as these, that Satyr was first introduced into the World; whereby those whom neither Religion, nor natural Virtue, nor fear of Punishment, were able to keep within the Bounds of their Duty, might be with-held by Shame of having their Crimes exposed to open View in the Strongest Colours, and themselves rendered odious to Mankind. Perhaps all this may be little regarded by such hardened and abandoned Natures as I have to deal with; but, next to taming or binding a Savage-Animal, the best Service you can do the Neighbourhood, is to give them warning, either to arm themselves, or not come in its Way.[35]

The function of satire in terms of the general public is to perform the valuable service of arousing the unaware to a danger in their midst. In terms of those who are culpable, Swift had no illusions; as he wrote to Charles Ford, satire may serve "to vex Rogues, though it will not amend them."[36]

The drubbing of satirists by enraged victims that punctuates the history of the genre is an indication that satire can indeed vex its targets. Walpole's response to "On Poetry: A

Rapsody" was to consider having Swift arrested,[37] while the Dublin politican Richard Bettesworth reacted to Swift's mockery by threatening to cut off the writer's ears. Swift retorted in poetry that keeping his ears and being forced to listen to Bettesworth harangue would be a far worse punishment.[38] According to Harold Williams, Swift "pursued Bettesworth with further ballads . . . and made [his] life a misery,"[39] an eighteenth-century vestige of Archilochus's power to drive his satiric targets to suicide.

2

Swift's most sustained poetic stance is that of the satirist-hero, to use Mack's term, but like most of his fictive self-portraiture it contains multiple perspectives.[40] Although the issue of what kind of poet he would be was resolved in the 1690s, the struggle between opposing values reappears whenever Swift writes of himself as satirist. The penalty for his choice of satire was one that he was always conscious of paying and never entirely resigned to. Retrospectively viewing his life in "Verses on the Death of Dr. Swift," he wrote: "Had he but spar'd his Tongue and Pen, / He might have rose like other Men" (355–56). Never aiming at the career rewards Swift coveted, Alexander Pope could glory wholeheartedly in his ability to discomfit the great: "Yes, I am proud; I must be proud to see / Men not afraid of God, afraid of me."[41] Where Pope's satiric posture is single-minded, Swift's is more apt to be ambivalent, an assertion of power which at the same time—with characteristic duality—acknowledges that the satirist must renounce the possibility of worldly success. This is a grudging theme of Swift's poetic representation of his own history from the earliest mention of it in the "Ode to Sir William Temple" to his last pronouncements in "An Epistle to a Lady" and "Verses on the Death of Dr. Swift." For Swift, the truth-telling that his satiric perspective demands is suited neither to the hack world of politics nor to the church. Militating against the worldly success of the satirist-genius is the envy

of inferiors, the outrage of satiric targets, and the disincli-
nation of the majority of men to listen to unpleasant truths
about themselves.

In spite of his consciousness of the price exacted, Swift
describes the world in terms that admit of no compromise:

> Must I commend against my conscience
> Such stupid blasphemy and nonsense?
> . . . .
> Or, shall the charms of wealth and power
> Make me pollute the MUSES' bower?
>> ("A Dialogue between an eminent Lawyer and
>> Dr. Swift Dean of St. Patrick's," 37–38; 45–46)

The questions are rhetorical, matching the antithetical
extravagance of the lawyer's counsel to turn false into true
and extol the ungodly; nevertheless, there is a noticeable
undercurrent absent from Pope's imitation of the same
poem, which is one hundred lines longer and a richer,
more complex poem. Pope chooses to deflect the issue
metalinguistically by eschewing the offending labels
"Libels and *Satires"* and substituting "grave *Epistles* . . . /
Such as a *King* might read, a *Bishop* write / Such as Sir
Robert would approve—."[42] The real world in which the
poet is an enemy of the official powers is thus transformed
into an ideal world in which the heads of church and state
confirm and participate in the poetic vision.

Predictably, Swift's version of the conflict between an
imperfect world and his art does not end like Pope's with
an ironically playful reconciliation by linguistic fiat. Given
oracular weight by the reference to Apollo's tripod, the
lawyer's concluding speech in Swift's imitation of Horace
1.2 sharply distinguishes between the two worlds:

> Some by philosophers misled,
> Must honour you alive and dead,
> And such as know what *Greece* has writ
> Must taste your irony and wit,
> While most that are or would be great,

Must dread your pen, your person hate,
And you on DRAPIER's *Hill* must lye,
And there without a mitre dye.

(49–56)

Under the aegis of Apollo the balanced presentation of
alternatives in simple and regular couplets, and the reiterated *must,* suggest truth, thoughtfully and directly conveyed. Through the clear compartmentalization of *some*
and *most,* and the climactic summing up of the two worlds
in the symbols of hill and mitre, the oracular voice asserts
that no reconciliation is possible; the appreciation of the
first four lines is inevitably conjoined with the penalties set
forth in the last four. Yet this last quatrain sustains the
positive thrust of the first part of the lawyer's speech. Swift
is accorded the power of satire to inspire strong negative
feelings in the implicitly unworthy holders of worldly
power, and if his choice of satire precludes a bishopric and
leads to a lonely grave, it also carries all of the heroic
associations of the Drapier. Syntactically, the phrase that
ends the poem merely modifies this positive invocation, but
its meaning has a greater weight. The mitre is itself a potent
symbol of value, and for a devout believer and career
churchman to die without it is a measure of loss and failure,
a tangible price paid for the pursuit of truth and art. That
final lingering phrase—"without a mitre dye"—reminds us
that, unlike Pope—who was always, as he described
himself, "unplaced, unpension'd, no Man's Heir, or
Slave"—Swift had enough worldly ambition and prospects
to make his choice of satire real rather than merely rhetorical.

Swift's fullest exploration of his role as satirist, "An
Epistle to a Lady," clarifies the actual process of making
satire. The initial situation, a woman protesting Swift's
criticism of her, simply creates a context for self-vindi-
cation that allows Swift to discuss the motivating force of
his satire—his own nature: "From the Planet of my Birth, /
I encounter Vice with Mirth" (140–42). Early in his career

as a poet Swift had despairingly referred to fate as the cause of his choice of poetry as a vocation: "Me she [nature] has to the Muse's Gallies ty'd" and "In vain to quench this foolish Fire I try" ("Ode to Sir William Temple," 191, 206). Now he can acknowledge his own kind of poetry as suited to his character, an internally generated necessity expressing itself in aggressive humor and satire rather than in the "Heroick Strain" the lady has desired. Decorum and harmony obtain in the relationship between Swift and the world because mirth and scorn are appropriate responses to vice and wickedness: "And I find it [my character] answers right" (147). This is Swift's formulation of the standard rationale invoked by satirists: *difficile est saturam non scribere*.

As Swift describes his satiric posture, it is a curious blend of power and impotence that is, perhaps, the key to satire as a genre:

> In a Jest I spend my Rage:
> (Tho' it must be understood,
> I would hang them if I cou'd:).
>
> (172–74)

Jest is the satirist's art, purposeful and controlled, not necessarily funny but jesting in the sense that it is not part of the world's serious business.[43] Rage is provoked first by the existence of evils and second by the satirist's lack of power to affect them. He knows that he cannot act literally against the world's malefactors but can only act symbolically by writing satire. "Drown the World," Swift confessed to Pope, "I am not content with despising it, but I would anger it if I could with safety."[44] Satire is therefore a substitute for action, which for various reasons, such as the danger Swift's letter suggests, cannot be carried out.

The vivid image that caps Swift's presentation of his feelings is an uncomfortably sadistic fantasy embodying both the satirist's rage and his impotence:

Let me, tho' the Smell be Noisom.
Strip their Bums; let CALEB hoyse 'em;
Then, apply ALECTO's Whip,
Till they wriggle, howl, and skip.

(181–84)

At this point, when violence is fully indulged, the lady—a voice of reason and civilized behavior—interrupts to criticize Swift for his display of passion. What follows seems to be a non sequitur: Swift asserts that his emotion, inspired as it is by the spectacle of public ruin, is legitimate, but he continues to describe his satire as light: "a little gentle Jerking," "merriment," "raillery," "a fling." None of these terms properly applies to the image of scourging backsides; on the contrary, it is a clear example of the storming and raging Swift has specifically abjured, and rather vicious work for the man whose greatest fault, he tells us, is tenderness. The image of lashing remains sharply defined and insufficiently accounted for, although the poem espouses and exemplifies a humorous and restrained treatment of vice for almost another hundred lines. As C. J. Rawson observes: "It has a unique disturbing effectiveness."[45] Moreover, all of Swift's talk of the best method of reforming ill suits the expressed desire to hang the malefactors he castigates.

These contradictory views can be understood as a characteristically satiric form of the tension between art and nature. What Swift advocates throughout is a utilitarian transformation of rage into jest because humorous chiding is a more persuasive strategy than bitter vituperation: "I may storm and rage in vain; / It but stupifies your Brain" (215–16). The key phrase is *in vain*. If Swift wants his satire to effect changes in people's behavior or attitudes, he must not express anger baldly in the alienating form of Juvenalian raging.[46] As the image of scourging proves, to do so is satisfying to the writer, but contrary to his purpose of gaining his victim's or his audience's cooperation. Righteous indignation may justifiably move the satirist and elicit the reader's approval, but hatred and sadism are ignoble. By briefly dropping the mask of the ideal, the distanced and controlled, Swift does not repudiate it; rather, he emphasizes the contrived, that is, artistic nature of his laughter. For a moment the raw material of passion threatens to overwhelm the aesthetic construct; by dramatizing both the strength of this passion and its atavistic nature, Swift makes us aware of the effort needed to channel it in a positive way and the desirability— indeed, the necessity— of doing so.[47]

Janus-like, satire makes both an official, conscious appeal and a subversive, unconscious one: when it denounces and flays in the name of order, it also taps the springs of disorder, the instinctive rage and aggression that all societies must deflect away from the body politic into harmless or useful expression. Rage is the enemy within, but it is also the source of satiric energy, emotion that can and must be transformed by art:

> [I] Thought no Method more commodious,
> Than to shew their Vices odious:
> Which I chose to make appear,
> Not by Anger, but a Sneer:
> As my Method of Reforming,
> Is by Laughing, not by Storming.

> (225–30)

Every line attests to the poet's choosing, ordering, and controlling. Laughter and storming are opposed responses, but by showing himself doing both, Swift dissects the satiric process more profoundly than in any other place in his writings. To read Swift's satire correctly, it must be kept in mind that an intense rage underlies his strategic laughter. At times completely mastered, at times only imperfectly transmuted into jest, this rage is the initial impetus of and driving force behind Swift's satire, which must nevertheless be ordered and controlled to achieve transmutation into art.

"To Doctor Delany, on the Libels Writ against him" formulates this same conflict in slightly different terms. Swift is not discussing satire specifically, but instructing his friend on the writer's proper response to unfair criticism. He offers his own experience in conclusion:

> On me, when Dunces are satyrick,
> I take it for a Panegyrick,
> *Hated by Fools,* and *Fools to hate,*
> Be that my Motto, and my Fate.
>
> (169–72)

The first recourse, the conversion of blame to praise, suggests a restrained and philosophical posture, able to put the criticism of fools into proper perspective. In the second couplet the speaker immerses himself in the satiric universe of hatred and folly, whose bleak circumscription is intensifed by the ironic balance of *"Hated by Fools* and *Fools to hate."* This concluding pronouncement reveals a split between the principle of unity the poem officially embraces—a stance of detachment and rational control—and the principle of expansion, an underlying turmoil of bitter feeling that to some extent escapes control. Swift's satire moves between these two poles, mastering the provocation of the world or being overwhelmed by it.

3

Whatever the particular manifestation, the underlying subject of Swift's satire is always a violation of the universal principle of unity—order. As Swift wrote to Stella, "Method is good in all things. Order governs the world. The Devil is the author of confusion."[48] What makes man susceptible to confusion is a propensity for self-deception that is constantly substituting false forms for true. According to the hack writer in *A Tale of a Tub,* the attractions of the various kinds of illusion far outweigh those of reality:

'Tis manifest, what mighty Advantages Fiction has over Truth; and the Reason is just at our Elbow; because Imagination can build nobler Scenes, and produce more wonderful Revolutions than Fortune or Nature will be at Expence to furnish. . . . How fading and insipid do all Objects accost us that are not convey'd in the Vehicle of *Delusion?* How shrunk is every Thing, as it appears in the Glass of Nature? So, that if it were not for the Assistance of Artificial *Mediums,* false Lights, refracted Angles, Varnish, and Tinsel; there would be a mighty Level in the Felicity and Enjoyments of Mortal Men.[49]

Genuine order, the principle that "governs the world" and is the implied antithesis of Swift's satiric thesis, depends upon an acceptance of the human condition as it actually is. The satirist's purpose is therefore to strip away all "artificial *Mediums*" and ideal versions; for Swift, the orthodox Christian satirist, these illusions are all efforts of presumptuous man to avoid confronting his sinful existence.

Swift's pervasive animal imagery and his insistence on the excretory function and on physical deformity and decay are standard strategies of satire, designed to dispel the illusions that man's vanity engenders and force him to accept the imperfect state of his material condition. Ronald Paulson makes the point that in satire "a certain disgust, a certain physical involvement of the reader is always necessary."[50] This calling attention to the body, and to those bodily functions that are traditionally regarded as embarrassing and private, communicates Swift's traditional religious message that the body is always in some sense the enemy of the spirit, capable of miring it in appetite, uncleanliness, temporality, and sin. Henri Bergson characterizes this idea of the body's encumbering the spirit as a basic mechanism of humor:

Let us suppose that instead of sharing the lightness of the principle that animates it, the body in our eyes is no more than a heavy and embarrassing exterior which holds to the earth a soul impatient to break away. . . . The impression of the comic will be produced when we have a distinct awareness of this overlay. We will experience it especially when we are shown the soul *tormented* by the needs of the body—on one side the moral personality with its intelligently varied energy, on the other the stupidly monotonous body, intervening and interrupting with the stubbornness of a machine.[51]

Because Swift wants to produce satiric rather than purely humorous effects, his disparities tend to be extreme; shock overshadows humor. Where Bergson uses the example of a public speaker who sneezes at the most touching point of his speech, Swift's characters are more likely to let fly a rouser. His foolishly romantic lovers illustrate the same principle when their search for physical perfection un-covers bodily sweats and streams in the beloved. The poems about streetwalkers stretch the disparity to its greatest limits, for the ravages of venereal disease more dramatically expose the body as tormenting the spirit than a sneeze does.

However powerfully presented, the orthodox moral stance of Swift's scatological poetry is not so compelling as an unacknowledged source of energy—another manifesta-tion of the twofold appeal of satire. The overt condemna-tion of vice coexists with a subversive vision, an inescap-able sense of the poet as voyeur. In the name of satire Swift graphically describes privies, minutely examines the para-phernalia of toiletry, and observes—not the sexual, but the excretory contretemps of a wedding night. These violations of the common decorum about the privacy of intimate functions, in which the reader is implicated both as object and as voyeuristic participant, contribute to the peculiar effect and effectiveness of the scatological poems. There is a felt tension between the satiric attack on vice officially embraced by these poems and an unvoiced but compelling concern with aspects of existence outside the legitimate province of satire. As C. J. Rawson comments, "It is sentimental of the critics to say that Swift resolved the dilemma by some kind of 'compromise' or middle way; it is the fact that he never resolved it at all which gives his work its particular urgency and truth."[52]

If Swift's rage impelled him to write satire, and his religion provided the framework of values directing it, his temperament supplied a third and at times unassimilable element—despair over the unalterable terms of human existence. At times this attitude produces serious difficulties of meaning, especially in the scatological poems, but our experience as readers of these poems suggests that Swift's failure to separate the vicious from the merely human is not entirely idiosyncratic. He encapsulates and gives arresting expression to cultural attitudes of ambivalence and repressed feelings about the body.

Elsewhere, the impossibility of achieving victories in the world, the numerical superiority of his satiric targets, and their unjust abuse of himself all combine to consume the satirist.[53] Walpole and Bettesworth were annoyed by Swift's poetry, but their real power was unaffected; as the satirist constantly reminds us, the devil is legion and he is one man fighting alone against enormous odds. Disheartened by the apathy of those he would save and harassed by the hostility of those he condemns, who are beyond reformation, the satirist-dean is described in "Traulus, Part I" as engaged in a war of attrition unworthy of his heroic expenditure of self:

> The Dean hath felt their Stings before;
> And must their Malice ne'er give o'er?
> . . . .
> Yet still the Dean on Freedom raves,
> His Spirit always strives with Slaves.
> 'Tis Time at last to spare his Ink,
> And let them rot, or hang, or stink.[54]
>
> (85–86; 99–102)

As Swift wrote to the Earl of Oxford in 1730, "The zeal of Liberty hath eaten me up, and I have nothing left but ill thoughts, ill words and ill wishes."[55] Like other men, the satirist is in danger of being overwhelmed by the negative forces imprisoned within his aesthetic construct but for all that still busily at work in the world.

Swift's Poetic Worlds

PART I

Ordering the Self: The Poetry of Fictive Self-portraiture

> Because, alas, when we all dye
> Careless and Ignorant Posterity,
> Although they praise the Learning and the Wit,
>   And tho' the Title seems to show
> The Name and Man, by whom the Book was writ,
>   Yet how shall they be brought to know
> Whether that very Name was *He,* or *You,* or *I?*
>   "Ode to the Athenian Society"

1
Strategies of Self-defense

MOST of Swift's poems of fictive self-portraiture effectively employ strategies of self-defense in order to defend the self from a multitude of real or imagined threats. Typically, the self is shown under attack by a powerful opponent, often anonymous libelers or an individual with some kind of superiority to Swift. Although Swift professed himself indifferent to the misrepresentations of libelers, telling Knightley Chetwode that "men must take distinction as they do land, *cum onere*," the poetic energy expended upon this subject in addition to the references in his correspondence suggests that he was more sensitive to being "torn to pieces by pamphleteers and libelers" than he cared to admit.[1] Having failed to receive the preferment he felt he deserved, Swift saw the distortions of his actions and motives that libels contained as yet another way that the world denied him his due. In a letter to Pope that is actually a document of self-defense, Swift's frustration is evident:

> I am not ignorant how idle a thing it is for a man in obscurity to attempt defending his reputation as a writer, while the spirit of Faction hath so universally possessed the minds of men, that they are not at leisure to attend to anything else. They will just give themselves time to libel and accuse me, but cannot spare a minute to hear my defence.[2]

The defense is heard in the poetry of fictive self-portraiture, where a libelous version of Swift is typically countered by a

47

positive portrait. Swift also becomes a ridiculous figure in the eyes of such people as Lord Harley and Lady Acheson but is similarly vindicated by a favorable version of self. Although both Harley and Lady Acheson were Swift's friends, his sense of family inferiority combined with his pride to humorously exploit the potential for humiliation in his relations with these social superiors.

To describe Swift as responding in his poetry to threats against the self is not to judge him to be an excessively fearful person. The physical and moral courage he demonstrated on a number of occasions is in keeping with the principle of fearless action advocated in his poetry:

> What's to be done? shall wit and learning chuse,
> To live obscure, and have no fame to lose?
> By censure frighted out of honour's road,
> Nor dare to use the gifts by heav'n bestow'd;
> Or fearless enter in thro' virtue's gate,
> And buy distinction at the dearest rate.
>> ("To a Friend who had been much abused
>> in many inveterate Libels," 7–12)

As the satirist-hero speaking here, Swift acknowledges the conditions imposed by the world. In his poetry of fictive self-portraiture, however, his concern is to preserve and defend the integrity of the self from whatever enemies assail it.

The characteristic structure of this poetry is a dialectical clash between opposing versions of Swift, one of which embodies the principle of unity. This primary portrait is expanded upon, usually by another self-portrait that challenges the first. Techniques of indirection work against both positive and negative portraits, although not to the same degree: overt ridicule and condemnation may be countered by implicit admiration or by the subtle discrediting of an anti-Swift speaker, while praise may be undercut by irony or called into question by flagrant hyperbole. As Robert C. Elliott has defined the problem, "In all the cacophony issuing from the throats of these spokesmen the task of the interpreter is always to try to distinguish the true voice, the one that speaks authentically for the author."[3] There may not in fact be a single "true voice" in the most complex poems of fictive self-portraiture, but the assumption of self-defense as strategy permits us to posit a basic principle upon which the poems are developed. Invariably, the dialectical movement of the poetic structure is toward the revelation of Swift as a sympathetic figure. However powerful in the world may be the voices raised against him, in the poetry they are, after all, subservient to Swift's design.

Swift's first treatment of the self, in his earliest poetry, shows a struggle to find his own poetic voice within the constraints of his chosen medium, the Pindaric ode. His ambivalent feelings, split not only between poetry and a worldly career but between more elevated genres and satire, are expressed in the form of a quarrel with his muse. Although the odes are intended to be panegyrics, they are chiefly memorable as the record of Swift's developing self-discovery. By the final ode Swift is able to renounce the subterfuge of the muse because he has clarified his attitude toward poetry and is now willing to assert a preference for fictive self-portraiture and satire.

The next stage is to treat different versions of self in separate poems, some of which use the same occasion to construct dissimilar portraits, as if Swift is trying out different interpretations of the same data. "The Author upon Himself" portrays a politically influential Swift, an image that is then exploded by "Horace, *Lib.* 2 *Sat.* 6." "My Lady's Lamentation and Complaint against the Dean" criticizes the same behavior extolled in "A Panegyric on the Dean."

The poetry of fictive self-portraiture culminates in "The Life and Genuine Character of Dr. Swift" and "Verses on the Death of Dr. Swift" with the presentation of conflicting portraits within the same poem. These are Swift's most ambitious ventures and greatest achievements in fictive self-portraiture, attempts to construct a fictive self for posterity by reworking the diverse materials that constitute public opinion. Assimilating widely differing views of himself within his poetic construct is the familiar mechanism of mastering threats to the self, in this case the anticipated threats of misrepresentation and neglect at a time beyond his death.

Swift and His Muse: A Prelude to Fictive Self-portraiture

The odes written between 1690 and 1693 are readily separable in form, in content, and in their consistent failure as poetry, from what follows in Swift's career.[4] They are uncertain and uncontrolled, torn apart by conflicting forces that Swift can scarcely admit, let alone channel into a coherent structure. On the one hand, the odes attempt to memorialize various kinds of virtue—civic, literary, ecclesiastical; on the other, an awareness of the opposition to virtue in the world creates a satiric counterthrust that usually overwhelms the panegyric and blurs the poem's focus. Since the expansive impulse toward self-portraiture must similarly contend with the poetic principle of unity, the announced panegyric intention, rather than appearing straightforwardly as a concern of the poetry the self is depicted clandestinely in the form of a preoccupation with the poet's muse. Ostensibly committed to the praise of others, the odes are subverted by self and satire, interrelated concerns that destroy these particular poems but in the process define Swift's true poetic voice and attitude.

The displacement of energy and attention from panegyric to satire and from purported subject to self occurs in all of these early odes as an abrupt and awkward deflection of resources in an unexpected and unjustifiable direction.[5] Of the two departures from the praise of the poetic subject that panegyric requires, the shift into satire is potentially more assimilable than the sacrifice of subject to self. An acceptable technique for enhancing the merit of virtue is to show it as part of a context that dramatizes its notable singularity. Provided satire does not dominate the poem, it can thus serve as a "strategy of praise"[6] by emphasizing the value and the rarity of virtue.

When an accomplished panegyrist like John Dryden employs this strategy, the satiric subject is firmly subordinated to the panegyric and, in addition, precisely delimited within the world itself. The condemnation of modern doctors in "To my Honour'd Kinsman, John Driden" intensifies the praise of John Driden's natural medicine; on the level of the world the practices of the doctors do not engulf and obscure all virtue but are seen as specific, limited, and remediable evils:

From Files, a Random-*Recipe* they take,
And Many Deaths of One Prescription make.
Garth, gen'rous as his Muse, prescribes and gives;
The Shop-man sells; and by Destruction lives:
Ungrateful Tribe! who, like the Viper's Brood,
From Med'cine issuing, suck their Mother's Blood!
Let These obey; and let the Learn'd prescribe;
That Men may die, without a double Bribe:
Let Them, but under their Superiours kill;
When Doctors first have sign'd the bloody Bill:
He scapes the best, who Nature to repair,
Draws Phisick from the Fields, in Draughts of Vital Air.[7]
(105–16)

Momentarily sharp though the satire may be, it does not permeate and energize the totality of the poem, but remains neatly compartmentalized, enclosed within the certainties of Dryden's ordered vision of the world, and within his tone of calm assessment as much as within the form of the heroic couplet. Having called attention to the doctors in order to celebrate his kinsman's natural care of his health, Dryden gracefully brings the poem back to its subject.

This is exactly the kind of discipline Swift's panegyric odes lack because his interests tend to be more complex

than Dryden's interweaving of subject and pattern. Characteristically, Swift's treatment of his subject, a subject that
opens out to encompass increasingly large areas, is predicated upon pessimistic assumptions of uncertainty and
fluidity, the shifting sands of man's nature that menace the
systems of order and value espoused by Dryden's panegyric. What generally happens when Swift refers to the
larger world is not the emergence of his subject but its
engulfment. Once the counter-world of disvalue has been
introduced, the poet seemingly cannot resist abandoning
panegyric and giving the poem over to satire:

> Ill may I live, if the good SANCROFT in his holy rest,
>   In the divin'ty of retreat,
> Be not the brightest pattern Earth can shew
>   Of heav'n-born Truth below:
> But foolish Man still judges what is best
>   In his own balance, false and light,
>   Foll'wing Opinion, dark, and blind,
>   That vagrant leader of the mind,
> Till Honesty and Conscience are clear out of sight.
>   ("Ode to Dr. William Sancroft," 50–58)

Sancroft is quickly eclipsed by "foolish Man," whose
errors are expatiated upon with growing satiric fervor for
another forty-eight lines. Then Swift interjects an apology
for his "ill-govern'd zeal" and resumes, not the panegyric
job of work but his satiric attack. Whatever its applicabil-
ity to the times, the rationale of Swift's apology does
express his own attitude toward panegyric:[8]

> And Poetry has lost the art to praise,
>   Alas, the occasions are so few.
>   (111–12)

If, as Swift suggests, panegyric is no longer a tenable
poetic genre because the world is more bad than good,
logic would dictate its abandonment in favor of satire,
and, in fact, the odes all illustrate this process. Swift's

attempts at praise are always overwhelmed by a stronger impulse to censure.

When he wrote the ode to Sancroft, Swift had already presented himself in an earlier poem addressed to Sir William Temple as constrained by nature to be a poet. His acceptance of the role of satiric poet is less forthright. The compulsion is presented as entirely external, a necessity imposed by a corrupt age that offers few opportunities to praise. A further mark of Swift's ambivalence about satire is, of course, his persistence in attempting panegyric while proclaiming and exemplifying its unfeasibility. What we have of "Sancroft" ends with an abruptly introduced self-admonition:

> Check in thy satire, angry muse,
> Or a more worthy subject chuse:
> Let not the outcasts of this outcast age
> Provoke the honour of my Muse's rage.
>
> (259–62)

The movement from satire to apology and abjuration typifies the odes. Swift cannot yet reconcile his preference for satire with the concept of "poetic greatness" promised by his muse. Forced into forms uncongenial to Swift's talents and checked by periodic resistance, the satire of these panegyric odes is generally unimpressive. Unfocused and diffuse, it lacks the sharp particularity of Swift's later satiric poetry.

What is significant in the odes is the working out of a poetics to unite the impulses of Swift's nature with the requirements of the world, a compound of literary tradition and vocational respectability. The issue does not take shape as a simple polarity between conventional behavior and individual assertion, external versus internal forces, because Swift is himself ambivalent over the choice, first between worldly and poetic expectations and then between "higher" kinds of poetry and satire. Capping a list of unpalatable career choices in the "Ode to Sir William

Temple,"[9] poetry is described as a fated bondage that frustrates more rational possibilities:

> In vain all wholsome Herbs I sow,
>   Where nought but Weeds will grow.
> Whate'er I plant (like Corn on barren Earth)
>   By an equivocal Birth
> Seeds and runs up to Poetry.
>
> (208–12)

Although this conclusion is couched in the self-deprecatory style of the poem's entire discussion of Swift, it reverberates oddly against the earlier description of Temple: "You strove to cultivate a barren Court in vain,/Your Garden's better worth your noble Pain" (175–76). Throughout the poem Swift's representations of Temple's accomplishments have been infused with painful anxieties about his own unresolved future; panegyric is displaced not only by the customary satire but by an embarrassingly extravagant self-castigation. Swift's muse is "humble," his verse "worthless," perhaps in response to a real expectation on the part of Temple or as a projection of Swift's own conflict about his vocation. In contrast to the gulf between successful patron and abject dependent that the poetic statement asserts, the imagery of cultivating barren ground suggests an underlying identity. Panegyric cannot thrive when there is nothing to praise, nor could Temple's virtue flourish at a corrupt court; the condition of the macrocosmic world is the common denominator that forces a retreat to a more circumscribed context—for Temple, his estate, and for Swift, ultimately, satire.

To examine the issue in the odes Swift divides the self into poet and muse, a strategy that allows him to entertain another stance without fully claiming it and to avoid responsibility for satiric divagations. Like the alternation between satire and panegyric, the treatment of the muse is testimony to Swift's ambivalence. First an abstract "Spirit of Exalted Poetry," then a nebulous "Dove-Muse"—more

bird than woman—and finally a vague feminine presence
who only gradually emerges as a woman, the muse is a
shifting entity both in form and in function. In the ode "To
Mr. Congreve" she first refuses to appear, then lectures the
poet for writing satire, and yet is implicated in the satire
that subsequently dominates the poem:

> Perish the Muse's hour, thus vainly spent
> In satire, to my CONGREVE's praises meant;
> In how ill season her resentments rule,
> What's that to her if mankind be a fool?
>
> (175–78)

Although the muse initially protested the poet's choice of
satire, their roles are now reversed: Swift distances himself from the perceived failure of the poem by protesting
the muse's abandonment of the panegyric intention, but
the inconsistency tends to reduce the muse to a rhetorical
device, an example of elegant variation that avoids the
first-person form without altering the substance. Most
often the muse is just such a rhetorical expedient whereby
Swift obliquely acknowledges defects in his poetry:

> Forgive a young and (almost) *Virgin-Muse,*
> Whom blind and eager Curiosity
>   (Yet Curiosity they say,
> Is in her Sex a Crime needs no excuse)
>   Has forc't to grope her uncouth way
> After a *mighty Light* that leads her wandring Eye.
>
> ("Ode to the Athenian Society," 62–67)

Defining curiosity as a specifically feminine foible needing
no apology enables Swift to offer a rationale for his poetic
stance while at the same time partially dissociating himself
from it.[10]
Only in the final ode, "Occasioned by Sir William Temple's Late Illness and Recovery," does Swift feel confident
enough to pronounce the muse a creation of his own brain
and to repudiate her as a delusion of the wayward femi-

nine part of his nature. Discouraged by this time with his failure to launch a promising worldly career, Swift is also ready to give over the kind of poetic aspiration foreign to his own genius. Putting aside the views embodied in the muse, her fantasy of poetic greatness and rejection of satire, he has completed the first stage of his ordering of the self. What began as a hesitant groping for a poetic voice ends with vocational self-discovery and affirmation—Swift's firm commitment to the kind of poetry he can write best.

Swift as Family Intimate

Swift's poetry of self-defense actually begins with Swift playing the role of family intimate within a circle of social superiors in three poems written in 1701 and 1702 when he was a member of the household of Lord Berkeley. In two of the three Berkeley household poems, "A Ballad on the Game of Traffick" and "Lady Betty Berkeley," the transformation of real into fictive Swift has no subtlety or complexity. Known to be witty, Swift portrays himself as a dullard in order to compliment Lady Betty on her cleverness:

> Even so Master Doctor had Puzzled his Brains
>   In making a Ballad, but was at a Stand,
> He had mixt little Wit with a greal deal of Pains,
>   When he found a new Help from Invisible Hand.
>   Then Good Dr. *Swift*
>   Pay Thanks for the Gift,
> For you freely must own you were at a Dead lift.
>   ("Lady Betty Berkeley," 23–28)

The third poem of the group, "The Humble Petition of Frances Harris," is somewhat more complicated, although true and false versions of Swift are still clearly distinguishable. Swift is portrayed as the household chaplain, a role he actually filled, and as Mrs. Harris's sweetheart, a fiction.[11] The poem's effects are fairly simple, but in several ways it foreshadows the more complex portraiture of Swift's later poetry. The presentation of self is indirect; Swift does not speak for himself but is the victim of Mrs. Harris's onrushing verbal energy, while she herself is satirized by Swift the poet.

The description of Swift through Mrs. Harris's eyes as a somewhat pompous figure—and as conjurer and true love to boot—is an obvious joke for the intimates of the Berkeley household, a truly fictive self-portrait safely removed from the reality of Swift's position and character. But it can also be read as a response to his actual feelings of pride and sensitivity to appearing foolish to others, a situation that frequently recurs in his poetry of fictive self-portraiture. As part of Mrs. Harris's narrative, the detail "he hates to be call'd *Parson*, like the *Devil*" is a casual observation made in Mrs. Harris's natural idiom. Further, it contributes to her comic characterization by Swift: she knows he detests the appellation but blunders twice anyway. On another level the positioning of the words suggests a relationship between *parson* and *devil*: Swift is pridefully emulating the devil in rejecting the title of parson. By writing of himself as a ridiculous figure Swift can administer a corrective to his pride and also exorcise the derogatory opinions others may hold by ordering and controlling them within his poem.

In a more elaborate form the role of family intimate within a household of social superiors is treated in Swift's Market Hill poems. The body of poetry associated with Market Hill, the country estate of Swift's friends Sir Arthur and Lady Acheson, illustrates the complete strategy of self-defense: a speaker portrays Swift as a ridiculous figure, but this portrait is then undercut so that the final result is a triumph over Swift's enemies—that is, friends turned into enemies within the poetic fiction. Under the guise of "these family verses of mirth,"[12] Swift confronts and exorcises various ridiculous postures in which his friends *might* see him.

Those Market Hill poems in which Lady Acheson supposedly discusses Swift take as their principle of unity the decorum of hospitality predicated upon their respective roles of hostess and guest. The basic fiction that Lady Acheson constructs is generated by a clash between her confinement within her prescribed role and Swift's refusal to be circumscribed by his: she portrays herself as a put-upon hostess plagued by an unwanted and meddlesome guest. The consciousness of another person, one of Swift's favorite points of view for fictive self-portraiture, combines in this instance the intimacy of personal knowledge with the distance of a third-person perspective. Lady Acheson is an unreliable speaker, however. Swift's portrait of an unfriendly speaker portraying himself is the mechanism for an elaborate joke in which the speaker, manipulated by the poet, insists upon a wrongheaded interpretation of Swift that underscores her own crudity and lack of good faith. While Lady Acheson energetically and self-righteously mocks a fictive Swift, she is in turn made foolish in the reader's eyes by the poet.

Although the principal technique of fictive self-portraiture in the Lady Acheson poems is a mechanical inversion of fictive to real, the portrait of Swift as unmannerly guest acquires depth through the framing device of the unfriendly and unreliable speaker. As revealed in Browningesque monologues, Lady Acheson's consistently ungenerous interpretation of Swift's behavior is more a key to her own character than to his.

"Lady Acheson Weary of the Dean" develops the conflict between host and guest in terms of their differing perceptions of time:

> His Manners would not let him wait,
>   Least we should think ourselves neglected,
> And so we saw him at our Gate
>   Three Days before he was expected.
>
>   (5–8)

In Lady Acheson's narration, of course, *Manners* is ironic; her interpretation of Swift's early arrival is lack of proper manners. Yet her own phrasing suggests the alternative possibility that good manners, Swift's desire to be attentive—"least we should think ourselves neglected"— may be responsible for his early arrival. Without the implicit biographical *donnée* that Swift was a valued guest whose hosts were happy to have him make long visits,[13] it is still unlikely that the poem would be misread; comic conventions of rhyme, meter, and hyperbole clearly operate to question the portrait's seriousness. More significantly than the comic details of Swift, his puppies, and his horses eating and swilling while the Achesons watch their mounting household bills, is Lady Acheson's fantasied assault on the Dean. In response to his epithets disparaging her appearance—"skinny, boney, snip and lean"—she imagines a violent revenge:

> Oh! if I could, how I would maul
>   His Tallow Face and Wainscot Paws
> His Beetle-brows and Eyes of Wall,
>   And make him soon give up the Cause.
>   (37–40)

Within the fiction that the speaker creates, she is the innocent victim of a rude and overbearing enemy who deserves the physical attack she fantasizes. But Lady Acheson stands exposed by the poem as a disingenuous narrator, whose account is shortsighted and reductive. In her eyes the Dean's affectionate and solicitous behavior is insulting and tyrannical, an ungenerous construction that displays her own lack of breeding and pettiness. Completing the strategy of self-defense, the putative victim emerges as the victor. Certainly, the playful tone of "Lady Acheson Weary of the Dean" softens this serious meaning; nevertheless, the aggressiveness of the humor that breaks through the comic complaint when the recital of minor aggravations gives way to Lady Acheson's musings on a vengeful attack must be taken as a subtle indication of this underlying seriousness.

The companion pieces, "My Lady's Lamentation and Complaint against the Dean" and "A Panegyrick on the Dean in the Person of a Lady in the North," continue Lady Acheson's attack on Swift as a presumptuous guest. The stated purpose of each poem would suggest that they convey opposite views of the subject, but in reality the methods of praise and blame produce the same ridiculous but well-intentioned figure. "My Lady's Lamentation" is Lady Acheson's description of Swift's pedagogic impulses run amok and her own recalcitrance as a pupil.[14] The extravagance of the lady's protest, a hyperbolic embroidery on the most ordinary events, creates the comedy:

> By the worst of all Squires,
> Thro' bogs and thro' briers,
> Where a cow would be startled,
> I'm in spite of my heart led.
>
> (45–48)

The ragged rhythms of the short, choppy lines and jouncing feminine rhymes like *startled/heart led* capture the difficulties of the expedition and the victim's unwillingness, all intensified by the sweeping character of each statement. Appreciating the work of comic exaggeration for each of Lady Acheson's wrongs entails recognition of the unvarnished particular: in this case the Dean's desire that they take a walk together. At the end of the episode the speaker reveals her unreliability by confessing her determination to oppose the Dean's projects, no matter how salutary:

> For I'd rather be dead,
> Than it e'er should be said
> I was better for him,
> In stomach or limb.
>
> (55–58)

A comic formulation of dialectical movement thus works throughout the poem in the interplay between the speaker's account and the Dean's unstated but readily ascertainable version.

Lady Acheson depicts Swift as a stern taskmaster and a carping critic, both of which ill accord with the role of guest, even if his demanding posture is assumed with the laudable intention of improving his hostess. While Lady Acheson is put to toil on Swift's recommendation, however, he is depicted as hypocritically absorbed in activities that further violate decorum. Fraternizing with and indistinguishable from the estate workmen, Swift is seen in another false position:

> Find out if you can
> Who's master, who's man;
> Who makes the best figure,
> The Dean or the digger.
>
> (167–70)

Swift's sins proceed in both directions along the social scale, the very offenses Swift warns against in his essay *Good-Manners and Good Breeding:* "One principal point of this art [of good manners] is to suit our behaviour to the three several degrees of men; our superiors, our equals, and those below us."[15] By presumptuously seeking to instruct his hostess, and at the same time lowering himself to the level of a workman, Swift has contravened the prescribed behavior for a guest and a clergyman and usurped Sir Arthur's prerogatives as husband and property owner.

Swift's foolishness is encapsulated for the speaker in the bower or "green seat" he has contrived, a pastoral retreat that is invaded and despoiled by both people and animals. Situationally, the tables are turned: rather than victimizing his hostess, Swift is victimized; rather than lamenting her ill-usage, she savors the befouling of Swift's creation. The vulgarity of the description and her malicious relish of

Swift's pain are examples of bad breeding that all but efface
Swift's social blunders. Thus the poet indirectly discredits
his speaker and turns into mirthful verse those aspects of
his behavior as a guest and friend which, viewed unsympa-
thetically, could produce the portrait drawn by Lady
Acheson.

The bad-tempered and overexacting tutor of the "Lamentation" becomes the good-tempered and gentle instructor of
the "Panegyrick," but just as the extreme portraits of the
"Lamentation" are undercut by the speaker's unreliability,
the assertions of the "Panegyrick" are qualified by irony. It
would be difficult to mistake the "Panegyrick's" heavy-
handed praise for genuine compliment:

> I THUS begin. My grateful Muse
> Salutes the Dean in diff'rent Views;
> Dean, Butler, Usher, Jester, Tutor:
> *Robert* and *Darby*'s Coadjutor:
> And as you in Commission sit,
> To rule the Dairy next to *Kit*.
>
> (37–42)

This mechanical survey parodies the methodical catalogue
of a serious panegyric, not only in form but in content.
Once more, Swift's violation of a prescribed role is Lady
Acheson's theme, but here he is commended rather than
condemned, for performing the tasks of various servants.
The order is essentially anticlimactic, but *tutor* appears
mixed in with the various serving positions, perhaps both
to negate the idea of order and to comment upon the value
generally accorded to such a job in aristocratic house-
holds—lower than the butler, but higher than the dairy-
man.

Details of the "Panegyrick" rebound off corresponding
details of the "Lamentation," but they also deepen in
significance when measured against the Swift who was a
close friend of the Achesons. The lavish praise of Swift's
preaching, for example, is comically heightened by the

information contained in Faulkner's note: "The Author preached but once while he was there."[16] The description of Swift's manners is still another exemplification of biographical data creating comic irony:

> With such Address, and graceful Port,
> As clearly shows you bred at Court!
>
> (83–84)

For Swift courts are invariably associated with false manners of insincerity and outward show. As he wrote in *Hints on Good-Manners*, "Courts are the worst of all schools to teach good manners."[17]

For the various serving positions Swift occupies, he is damned with lavish praise and ironic parenthesis. After describing in detail how he fills the lowly office of butler's helper so admirably, Lady Acheson concludes:

> With *Dennis* you did ne'er combine,
> Not you, to steal your Master's Wine;
> Except a Bottle now and then,
> To welcome *Brother* Serving-men;
> But, that is with a good Design,
> To drink Sir *Arthur*'s Health and mine:
> Your Master's Honour to maintain;
> And get the like Returns again.
>
> (97–104)

Swift is accused of doing what he humorously recommended in *Directions to Servants:* "If you serve a Country 'Squire, when Gentlemen and Ladies come to dine at your House, never fail to make their Servants drunk, and especially the Coachman, for the Honour of your Master; to which, in all your Actions, you must have a special Regard. . . ."[18] The description is a superb example of ironic accretion where each detail, masquerading as praise, only deepens the blame. From the initial absolute, with its emphatic repetition of *you,* the descent is skillfully managed to seem to save, but in reality to damn Swift.

Immediately after the insistence on his probity in matters of wine comes the devastating exception, followed by its venial justification, only transparently disguised as a duty of hospitality. Further, the "good design" of drinking the Achesons' health, expatiated on for three lines, is easily penetrated. The climactic detail exposes the real motive in all its comic shabbiness: Swift simply hopes to be treated to a glass of purloined wine when he visits the servants of other houses.

After lauding him as a house servant and tutor, offices that at least serve the people of the house directly, the panegyric takes Swift away from the Achesons and into more and more menial occupations, from master and mistress to pigs, rats, and poultry—and finally to butter. The sections that follow are comically linked by similarity of process: the squeezing of butter out of milk suggests the squeezing of a lampoon out of the brain and then, the final obsessive concern of the poem—the action of the bowels. The ironic panegyric on Swift becomes a mock-heroic panegyric on the goddess *Cloacine* in which the clerical title "Your Reverence" is itself transmuted into a euphemism for excrement. Paralleling the elevation of subject in a serious panegyric, Swift's reduction by the "Panegyrick" is complete.

In "The Grand Question Debated" Lady Acheson is not the speaker, but the same characterization of Swift as an insufferable and unwelcome guest is advanced by several speakers. The alternatives of the debate, whether to turn the property known as Hamilton's Bawn into a malt house or a barrack, are both presented as ways of liberating the Achesons from Swift's domination:

> First, let me suppose I make it a *Malt-House:*
> Here I have computed the Profit will fall t'us.
> . . . .
>
> And you and the *Dean* no more shall combine,
> To stint me at Night to one Bottle of Wine;
> . . . .

With *Parsons,* what Lady can keep herself clean?
I'm all over dawb'd when I sit by the *Dean.*
But, if you will give us a *Barrack,* my Dear,
The *Captain,* I'm sure, will always come here;
I then shall not value his Deanship a Straw,
For the *Captain,* I warrant, will keep him in Awe.
(7–8, 15–16, 29–34)

Where Lady Acheson is unpleasantly "dawb'd" by the Dean, the imagined Captain is described as "all dawb'd with gold Lace." Where Swift is shabby, the Captain is a resplendent hero of romance who flourishes a sword and rides a prancing charger. In contrast to the Dean's presumption and his assumed airs, the Captain is full of poetic compliment. Nevertheless, the disparagement of parsons, and the Dean in particular, is increasingly challenged by the evidence that for all his superficially fine appearance, sufficient to take in the eager servant Hannah, the Captain is a crude and obnoxious man. As part of Swift's self-portrait, the observations on parsons may be accepted as both amusing and accurate—more amusing because they are accurate, and made, ultimately, by a parson. As part of the Captain's characterization, however, they are rude remarks that point up the Dean's well-mannered forbearance. The liberal use of oaths reveals how thin a veneer the courtly compliment exchanged earlier with Sir Arthur was and, by extension, how false all such language is. By the end of his speech the Captain stands revealed to the reader as an inferior of the Dean, while his professed admirers seem frivolous and undiscerning.

The telling of Hannah's daydream is brought to an abrupt end by the appearance of the Dean, who banishes the specter of the Captain with his respectful inquiry, *"Will your Ladyship walk?"* Already discredited to the reader, the fantasy is now demonstrated to be impotent, a mere "chimera" in contrast to the flesh-and-blood Dean. Although both crown and army have conspired against him, the Dean is triumphant at poem's end.

In all the Market Hill poems ostensibly presented from the point of view of the Achesons, the fictive self-portraits are constructed by the same technique of simplistic reversal: historic Swift, the esteemed friend and welcome guest of the Achesons, is transformed into a fictive opposite. Hostile speakers or characters react to Swift's behavior with indignation and mockery but are always revealed to be unreliable. The caricatures of ill-behaved guest and mean-spirited hostess are broad comic types, but they also raise a serious epistemological issue: is the reported behavior of Swift unmannerly and officious, as the speakers claim, or helpful and considerate? Swift's use of biographical materials in these fictive versions of self diminishes its factuality and stresses the importance of the evaluative process rather than the data: "Human consciousness depends disconcertingly upon one's point of view."[19] That Swift enjoyed taking on projects around the estate and instructing Lady Acheson are facts that, depending on point of view, may be interpreted as gestures of friendly interest or presumptuous usurpations. The negative constructions placed upon Swift's actions by Lady Acheson are all possibilities that could be actualized within the real Swift-Acheson friendship or within any friendship through a failure of communication or a difference of opinion. Fictive Swift embodies those characteristics that the poet may also see as exaggerations of his real tendencies or unfriendly misconstructions of his behavior by others. By naming these deficiencies himself, turning them into jokes, he demonstrates power over them and exorcises their threat. More significantly, it is only on the surface that Swift is mocked. Those who see him critically are themselves subtly discredited, for while the poems show that he has tried to help the inhabitants of Market Hill in numerous ways, they have resisted his good intentions and relished thoughts of his humiliation. The revelation of Swift as morally superior to his antagonists completes the strategy of self-defense.

The conflict of host and guest repeatedly elaborated by the Market Hill poems has both social and personal meaning.

From his earliest days in London when he assiduously sought dinner invitations, Swift was a professional guest, well aware of the mutual obligations of hospitality and the need for good manners to order social relations. Friendship transforms the social roles of host and guest so that the duties of hospitality become a pleasure, and seeming officiousness becomes a token of affection.

The Poet as Careerist

In a number of poems Swift portrays himself as a political figure, not the disinterested satirist but the partisan. Because the public image is compounded of a wider range of materials, these poems are technically more complex than those presenting Swift in the restricted private role of family intimate and guest. Swift's role as a public man is presented through multiple perspectives, often of uncertain provenance. Mocked by people who are either his social superiors—as the Berkeleys and the Achesons were—or by the public, whose power proceeds from its size and anonymity, Swift is shown in ridiculous postures. This portrayal of self functions as it does in the family intimate poems as a strategy to disarm the powerful. Operating as a subtext beneath the level of professed submission and inferiority is the poet's ridiculing of those who make sport of his fictive self within the poem and hold power over him in reality.

While the poems about Swift's political career employ the strategy of self-defense, they also reveal what Thomas R. Edwards has called "the imagination's troubled recognition of its own involvement in the spectacle of power."[20] The conflicting perspectives of Swift's double vision as critic and participant are never fully reconciled, for while Swift shows the well-intentioned man struggling within a system that will necessarily defeat him, he also presents the attractions of power with such poetic vigor that there is no total repudiation. The best that can be done in the political

world, Swift claims, is to maintain an artificially divided
judgment, to "hate the Vice-roy, love the man," as he
writes of John Carteret, Lord Lieutenant of Ireland. The
idea is frequently expressed elsewhere in Swift's writings.
A letter to the Earl of Oxford states: "In your publick
Capacity you have often angred me to the Heart, but, as a
private man, never once."[21] Swift's "Character of Mrs.
Howard" asserts the same separation: "In all offices of life,
except those of a courtier, she acts with justice, generosity,
and truth."[22]

Like the poetry of fictive self-portraiture portraying Swift
in the role of guest, but to an even greater extent, the
political poems raise the epistemological issue. In the
earliest, "Part of the Seventh Epistle of the First Book of
Horace Imitated" (1713), Swift is seen by different observ-
ers, most of whom remain unidentified and consequently
beyond accurate assessment. He is first described as an
unknown parson brought to Harley's attention by a casual
glimpse: "Of Size that might a Pulpit fill, / But more
inclining to sit still" (12–13). The suggestion of physical
inertia resonates humorously against the Swift whose passion for brisk exercise was known to all his friends, but in
any case the portrait is presented as a superficial and
uninformed view, based upon a mere glance. The second
description of Swift, the result of Harley's inquiries about
him, is offered as generally held opinion. A portrait of
ambitious but ineffectual mediocrity, it damns with faint
praise:

> No Libertine, nor Over-nice,
> Addicted to no sort of Vice;
> Went where he pleas'd, said what he thought,
> Not Rich, but ow'd no Man a Groat;
> In State-Opinions *a-la-Mode*,
> He hated *Wharton* like a Toad.
>
>   (31–36)

This view of Swift has a certain plausibility both as received opinion and as accurate biography, but Swift's use of biographical materials is habitually both revealing and concealing. Each assertion could be considered biographically valid, yet the sum total might be any undistinguished party man who holds all the politically correct opinions and carefully avoids extremes of behavior that could damage his career. The portrait is a distanced public view, appropriate to its source, superficially correct, yet leaving the unique individual Swift undefined.

Assuming one of Swift's favorite couplet patterns, the intelligence report now adopts a tightly antithetical structure in which the first line of a couplet augurs well while the second deflates this promise:

> His Works were hawk'd in ev'ry Street,
> But seldom rose above a Sheet:
> Of late indeed the Paper-*Stamp*
> Did very much his Genius cramp;
> And, since he could not spend his Fire,
> He now intended to Retire.
>
> (41–46)

Within the rigid couplet structure each hopeful initiative is comically curtailed. Swift's "Works," a word charged with importance, are short, with counterconnotations of lack of substance and impermanence. The passage can be read as a compressed version of the later poem "The Author Upon Himself": Swift follows a subtly declining curve from seemingly admirable character and successful action to the anticlimactic final revelation that the writer is on the verge of abandoning his efforts—*fire* leads only to *retire*. Reduced to impotence in a laughable fashion, his genius made dependent upon a petty tax, this Swift is a ridiculed and trivialized figure. Like the earlier portrait, this view of Swift has biographical verisimilitude, a surface veracity without corresponding depth. It is true to what it purports to be in the poem—a public image of Swift constructed from generally available information.

Each succeeding portrait overlays, rather than materially changing, what has gone before. Now a narration that seems to be objective reportage becomes the poem's dominant voice. Although the character Swift speaks on two occasions within the narrative, in each instance his speech is introduced by a description that indicates how it should be read. Swift is seen to bungle Harley's dinner invitation and then to appear equally foolish in his attempt to explain his rudeness. Both the objective narration of the episode, which calls Swift's apology a "lame Excuse," and the dialogue itself establish his awkwardness:

> My Lord—The Honour you design'd—
> Extremely proud—but I had din'd—
> I'm sure I never shou'd neglect—
> No Man alive has more Respect—
>
> (67–70)

Swift's "lame Excuse" is a comic mixture of insincere servility and ingenuous desperation.[23] The dashes separating the phrases suggest snatches of conversation overheard, but also pauses indicative of confusion. In contrast to Swift's stammering, Harley's reply is relaxed and courteous. When the joke has gone too far and Swift feels thoroughly victimized, he begs for his release with humorous resignation: "Then since you now have done your worst, / Pray leave me where you found me first" (137–38). Only by joining in the laughter can a powerless man survive the humor of the powerful, against whose caprices it's "a Folly to Contest." This serious charge completes the pattern of subtle reversal, which is Swift's most characteristic strategy of self-defense. As Peter J. Schakel writes, "Since Harley, at his own initiative, brought Swift to the highest levels of social and political life, led Swift to expect much and others to expect much for him, he has a responsibility to provide for him in a way commensurate with his abilities, dignity, and new expectations."[24] "Poor Swift," as he is twice referred to, is truly deserving of pity, while Harley, with his lofty amusement at his victim's plight, is urbanely cold-blooded. And if Swift's stammerings are ludicrously awkward, they are also genuine, while Harley's glib ease masks insincerity and cruelty. At the same time, Swift's susceptibility to the flattery of ministers and the rewards of power has made Harley's sport possible.

The same fictive situation, Swift at the mercy of ministers or the vagaries of politics, is portrayed again in two poems written in 1714, "The Author Upon Himself" and "Horace, *Lib*. 2 *Sat*. 6." The same period in Swift's life is drawn upon to construct what at first glance are radically different portraits, one heroic, the other faintly ridiculous. Such a sharply defined compartmentalization is uncharacteristic of Swift's fictive portrayal of the public self, and in fact both poems are informed by a mixture of true and false data that produces more complicated effects than a neatly dichotomized rendering of personality.

What is most significant is the use Swift makes of paired poems. Like the different (but not conflicting) voices of "Horace I.VII," the pairing here enlarges the scope of the portraiture and makes the choice among possible Swifts more difficult. Ordinarily, in the poetry of fictive self-portraiture when polarity is established by direct and indirect means, the underlying or indirectly expressed usually seems to be the more authoritative. In these poems, however, the competing views are both stated directly, and we must look to the overall strategy of self-defense for a means of discriminating between them.

The title of "The Author Upon Himself" obviously invites an assimilation of the character Swift to the poet, although the discussion of Swift is in the third person. Reduced to a structure of events, the poem could be a continuation of Swift's prose autobiography into a later period of his life: the same sentiments of bitterness and betrayal permeate the chronicle of another promising start that has ended in failure. The idealized nature of the Swift character introduces a recurrent difficulty in reading

Swift's poetry on the self—the reader's acculturated
repugnance toward self-praise. It is reasonable to assume
that Swift was equally aware of this conventional attitude
and is exploiting it; the idealization of the self-portrait is
calculated, not ingenuous. What keeps the poem from
being merely an exercise in self-admiration is the way in
which Swift curbs and undercuts the flattering portrait:

> *Swift* had the Sin of Wit no venial Crime;
> Nay, 'twas affirm'd, he sometimes dealt in Rhime:
> Humour, and Mirth, had Place in all he writ:
> He reconcil'd Divinity and Wit.
> He mov'd, and bow'd, and talk't with too much Grace;
> Nor shew'd the Parson in his Gait or Face;
> Despis'd luxurious Wines, and costly Meat;
> Yet still was at the Tables of the Great.
>
> (9–16)

The theological and moral terminology applied to Swift
is an immediate source of both serious and comic disparity. The labeling of wit as sin, "no venial Crime," is
humorously excessive, as is the claim of reconciling
divinity and wit; that Swift was actually criticized for
violations of clerical decorum and suspected to be irre-
ligious gives the statement its serious dimension. To
those whose vices are of the ordinary sort, the Popean
catalogue of "Tobacco, Censure, Coffee, Pride, and
Port," the superiority represented by wit, and also by
personal grace—another pun—is indeed a sin. The sin-
gular individual is again contrasted to an implied common run in lines 15–16, this time by disliking fancy food.
Swift's intimates would be amused here by their knowledge that he did in fact enjoy excellent wine.[25]

Because a part of the basic strategy of self-defense—
merit unjustly attacked—is overt rather than hidden, the
poem is an undisguised moral exemplum. On another
level the image of power and influence can be probed to

reveal a tissue of appearances without definite substance:

> And, *Harley,* not asham'd his Choice to own,
> Takes him to *Windsor* in his Coach, alone.
> At *Windsor Swift* no sooner can appear,
> But, *St. John* comes and whispers in his Ear;
> The Waiters stand in Ranks; the Yeoman cry,
> *Make Room;* as if a Duke were passing by.
>
> (31–36)

Swift manipulates particulars, always one of the great strengths of his poetry, to create a convincing testimony of power. While he does nothing, the behavior of *others* bespeaks his influence: first, the prime minister selects him as his sole companion on the journey to Windsor; then, another minister whispers in his ear while waiters and yeomen corroborate Swift's importance through their actions. The tableau is impressive, but on closer examination the evidence is only circumstantial. What is striking about the picture of Swift is the distance: although the title implies confession, the portraiture throughout is external and public. Rumor, suspicion, conjecture report Swift powerful, but while creating an aura of influence the poet abstains from specific documentation:

> Now *Finch* alarms the Lords; he hears for certain,
> This dang'rous Priest is got behind the Curtain:
> *Finch,* fam'd for tedious Elocution, proves
> That *Swift* oils many a Spring which *Harley* moves.
>
> (37–40)

An author discussing himself could give us the truth about his role rather than Finch's suspicions; he could report the particulars of his conversations with Harley and St. John. Instead, Swift gives us a world of appearances—what any onlooker might observe and deduce.

Throughout the poem Swift is a passive figure, the object of others' actions: *pursu'd* by the Duchess of Somerset, *invited* by Harley, left a victim by the Queen, then

applied to by the Scots. The conclusion is an abrupt
surprise, for up to this point—although beset by enemies—
Swift has appeared to be innocent and successful. The
whirl of foes and insincere friends around Swift suddenly
stops; power and strength are stripped away to reveal a
particularly extreme version of the strategy's familiar
figure, the man more sinned against than sinning. Like so
much else in the poem, the conclusion has often been
regarded as the heartfelt utterance of Swift the man, with
the concomitant assumption that while the politician ha-
rangued, the artist nodded. That the final speech can be
taken as true to Swift's view of his actions at the time is not
evidence of artistic negligence, however; Swift's poetry of
self-portraiture commonly utilizes such material for fictive
ends. What is aesthetically significant about the conclusion
is the shock value of the abrupt cessation of motion and the
new and unexpected portrait of Swift. The dangerous
priest, too talented to be a parson, loyally supported by
powerful friends and sought out by favor seekers, is exposed as vulnerable. In view of the picture drawn before,
the conclusion is a sharp reversal: not the victory anticipated, the rewards of ability and influence, but the unexpected and undeserved defeat that effectively dramatizes
the tenuous nature of political power. What differentiates
"The Author Upon Himself" from those poems where the
self is ultimately defeated is the heroic dimension of fictive
Swift. Performing "what Friendship, Justice, Truth require" (73), he retires with a dignity that salvages spiritual
rewards from a material defeat. Such an outcome completes the strategy of self-defense, for like the poet himself,
fictive Swift typically finds his victories in the intangible
realm of integrity, courage, and truth— not in the imperfect
world reflected in his satire.

In "Horace, *Lib.* 2 *Sat.* 6" the same period of Swift's life
yields a superficially different view. Throughout "Horace"
Swift is a gently ridiculed figure, preoccupied by such
mundane matters as his expenses and his lack of real
power. Where "The Author Upon Himself" describes him

treated like a duke, this poem shows him rebuked for pushing in front of a duke. Where important figures swarm around Swift to seek his favor in weighty matters in the first poem, here a host of anonymous petitioners besiege him for their own petty private business. Similarly, the treatment of the journey to Windsor in the first poem implies that Harley and Swift use their time alone to talk of state affairs; the details of the ride given in the second poem deflate such an idea: "Where all that passes, *inter nos,* / Might be proclaim'd at *Charing-Cross*" (79–80).[26] Yet there is a common bond between the two presentations, the prominent use of other voices to assess Swift's position. In "The Author Upon Himself" these voices attribute great influence to Swift and the speaker does not contradict them. We are therefore not prepared for the sudden confession of helplessness and defeat that concludes the poem. In "Horace" the humorous disparity between the power that the unidentified speakers attribute to Swift and the powerlessness he himself admits prepares for the concluding abjuration of the political scene.

The paired portraits of Swift's political role in Harley's ministry can each be considered alone, but their sum is a more complex entity than any single view, a Swiftian comment on the problems of perception and judgment, both of men and events. The fictive Swift of "The Author Upon Himself" may be self-deluded in assessing the strength of his influence; in "Horace, *Lib. 2 Sat. 6*" he is never so deluded. The pairing of these divergent portraits of Swift's political role emphasizes the difficulty of measuring the kind of unofficial behind-the-scenes position he held; there may be no definitive judgment possible. In spite of seemingly sharp differences, both poems penetrate the appearance of power to reveal powerlessness, and both portray a Swift whose victory must be in terms of the spirit rather than the flesh.

The two versions of self promulgated by "The Author Upon Himself" and "Horace, *Lib. 2 Sat. 6*" resonate against the historical public figure of Swift to form a triptych—multiple versions that demonstrate Swift's desire to play all roles, his way of shaping and controlling the many possible versions of self.[27] Swift achieves a multi-faceted vision that exorcises certain threatening realities, the vagaries of political power and the versions of himself irresponsibly created by common gossip.

Posthumous Self-defense

The two poems whose point of departure is the La Rochefoucauld maxim on friendship and its limitations—"The Life and Genuine Character of Dr. Swift" and "Verses on the Death of Dr. Swift"—are Swift's greatest poems of fictive self-portraiture. Reputation, especially as it is affected by death, constitutes the burden of Swift's presentation of self in both, and although they are structured differently, the poems have the same objective: to create a portrait of Swift designed to preserve his reputation after his death. Anticipating the evil that men will say when he is gone, he can strip it of harmful power by placing it within a context controlled by himself—his poem. At the same time, he offers a counterimage, Swift as he would like to be remembered by posterity. The natural and even necessary character of this procedure, predicated upon egotism, is upheld by the authority of the maxim: "In the misfortunes of our best friends we find something which does not displease us."[28] Because friends are ultimately motivated by self-interest, Swift concludes, a man must sing his own praises. Even the best of friends will be unequal to the task.

That Swift magnifies the grain of egotism contained in La Rochefoucauld's maxim is in keeping both with his own sense of self and his idealistic conception of friendship. The division of character into public and private behavior that he insists upon for Harley, Carteret, and Mrs. Howard enables him to ignore actions on the part of friends that would otherwise violate the spirit of friendship. As for his own behavior toward friends, he "solemnly affirmed" to Richard Steele that "with relation to every friend I have, I am as innocent, as it is possible for a human creature to be."[29] Swift expresses his sense of the importance of friends in a number of financial metaphors, as if to translate his own values into those more prevalent in the world. The death of friends is "the necessary tax of long life" which transforms Swift into "a man of desperate fortunes [who] . . . never aim'd at any other fortune than in friends."[30] Referring to the deaths of Gay and Arbuthnot, Swift writes to Pope: "Their living would have been a great comfort to me, although I should never have seen them, like a Sum of Money in a Bank from which I should receive at least annual Interest."[31] Another variation on the metaphor also occurs in a reference to Gay's death: "I would endeavour to comfort my self upon the loss of Friends, as I do upon the loss of money; by turning to my account-book, and seeing whether I have enough left for my support?"[32] The representation of friends as a financial resource suits the kind of ego-gratification they provide: their continuing concern for Swift from year to year enhances his self-image as annual interest enriches the purse.

Perhaps the most unbearable aspect of Swift's life in Ireland, as his letters document, was his separation from close friends and his sense that no one in his present surroundings could replace them. Time and again Swift's letters to his friends in England describe his existence as that of a hermit or monk and remark the small number and indifferent quality of his company. Swift was clearly bothered by the lack of genuine concern that he felt or imagined in his acquaintances in Ireland. After a bout of illness in 1727 he wrote to Mrs. Howard: "I bore the whole load my self, nobody caring threepence what I suffered, or whether I was hanged or at ease."[33] A comment in a letter to Pope is equally typical of the depiction of friends in both poems on his own death: "It is perfectly right what you say of the indifference in common friends, whether we are sick or well, happy or miserable."[34] Just as Swift seeks to exorcise those threats to the self of a malicious or forgetful posterity, so too does he attempt to overcome the limitations of friendship within his poetry.

In approaching this unpalatable subject in "The Life and Genuine Character of Dr. Swift," Swift is notably cautious. The poem's first reference to the maxim identifies malice as one of its components, a motive not found in La Rochefoucauld. Next, Swift suggests that the maxim may simply be a joke, but he goes on to pronounce a tentative judgment: "I fancy, there is something in it." At the end of the introductory section of the poem, lines 1–67, the ideas developed from the maxim have become "Truths." Moreover, Swift's way of rendering the maxim significantly departs from the original. Where La Rochefoucauld had said only that in the adversity of our best friends we find something that does not displease us, Swift intensifies the selfishness and adds elements of duplicity and sadism:

> He says, "Whenever *Fortune* sends
> "Disasters, to our *Dearest Friends,*
> "Although, we *outwardly* may Grieve,
> "We oft, are *Laughing in our Sleeve.*"
>
> (7–10)

In contrast to the open cynicism that he finds in the maxim, and in keeping with his hesitancy in giving it allegiance, the speaker's voice is that of the disillusioned idealist, whose view of the nature of friendship is not borne out by the practice of the world:

> My *Friend* should have, when I complain,
> A *Fellow-feeling* of my *Pain.*
>
> Yet, by *Experience,* oft we find,
> Our *Friends* are of a *diff'rent* mind;
> And, were I tortur'd with the *Gout,*
> They'd *laugh,* to see me make a *rout,*
> Glad, that themselves cou'd *walk* about.
>
> (45–51)

Throughout this introductory section the exemplification is far more cynical than La Rochefoucauld's maxim would warrant. Friends are portrayed as either sadistically delighted by the speaker's misery or completely unmoved—inquiring for show rather than sincere concern. Such couplings as *manners/grief, tortur'd/laugh* demonstrate the gulf between the ideal and the world. Mismatched reactions further emphasize the unnaturalness of the friends' attitudes:

> To lose a *Guinea* at *Picquet*,
> Wou'd make him *rage*, and *storm*, and *fret*,
> Bring from his Heart *sincerer* Groans,
> Than if he heard you *broke your Bones*.
>
> (27–30)

The extravagant but heartfelt response to the loss of a guinea at cards is as disproportionate as the lack of any feeling for the speaker's mishap. Paired, they are even more anomalous.

So far the voice has been that of a general satiric speaker, who uses "I," "you," and "we" for intimacy and complicity without specific personal application. After establishing the prevailing egotism of humanity, even in friendship, the poet abandons his generalized mode of address to present the case as his own. In keeping with the maxim he too is most interested when personally involved. At the same time, his own voice is replaced by a welter of anonymous voices, one of Swift's favorite techniques of fictive self-portraiture. Here the inconsistency of "The Life and Genuine Character" becomes apparent, for La Rochefoucauld's maxim and Swift's elaboration upon it concern friends, while the poem that follows this introduction advances views of Swift held by people not personally acquainted with him. Nor is the idea of another's adversity provoking satisfaction in our own well-being illustrated by the antiphonal voices.[35] What Swift does instead in the remainder of the poem is to construct through dialogue portraits of himself that show the kinds of reputation a public figure may have. If any maxim is illustrated by the exchange of opinions about Swift, it is not La Rochefoucauld's so much as Hamlet's: "For there is nothing either good or bad but thinking makes it so."

After the confusion of voices making brief remarks, the expression of views of Swift settles down into a debate between two opponents. The debate structure is misleading, however, for there is no difficulty in determining that the pro-Swift speaker makes the stronger case. A situation is set up in which the image of an ideal Swift wins out handily over an inimical portrait.[36] It rapidly becomes clear that the pro-Swift speaker is passionately committed and high-minded; his challenger is a cynic who seeks low motives everywhere and delights in denigrating the powerful and the famous. Further, the unknown critic of Swift is an ardent supporter of Walpole, exactly the sort of person who could not understand or approve of Swift. Consequently, many of the charges can be interpreted as favorable to Swift. What seems to him to be indiscriminate satire, for example— attacking *"Court, City, Camp"* and fellow clergymen as well—may be read as Swift's fearless impartiality in condemning vice wherever it is found. Swift's defense of Oxford and praise of Queen Anne, cited against him, would also be admirable from a Tory point of view.

Beyond the possible difference in interpretation represented by the two speakers, their differing techniques point up the superiority of the pro-Swift man. Where he is cogent and vigorous, his opponent flails around foolishly, meeting strong arguments with non sequiturs and vague generalizations. When the first speaker offers the *Drapier's Letters* as a concrete example of Swift's worth, the other can only reply with windy bluster:

> He shou'd have left them for his *Betters;*
> We had a Hundred *abler Men,*
> Nor need *depend* upon his *Pen*—.

(98–100)

This tends to be the pattern of the dialogue: when Swift's champion scores a point, his opponent either makes a feeble rejoinder or changes the subject altogether. Given the character that Swift's attacker reveals, the hearsay flavor of his remarks, and the opposing force of Swift's partisan, these undocumented accusations appear to be only the mouthings of a chronic malcontent, insubstantial and unconvincing. At times his argumentative ineptitude is comical, as when he concludes an attribution of the most venial motives to Swift with an expression of restraint: "I say no more—, because he's *dead*—" (143). Since he has already said the worst t at he can on this particular issue, the phony piety and sham renunciation are both outrageous and funny. The anti-Swift speaker is an excellent example of the irresponsible slanderer Swift warns against in such poems as "To Doctor *Delany,* on the Libels Writ against him," "To a Friend who had been much abused in many inveterate Libels," and "On Censure."

Swift's partisan finally brings the argument to a dignified conclusion. Recognizing their differences, he firmly reiterates the truth of his own position and suggests that, inasmuch as Swift is dead, the subject should be closed: " 'Then, since you *dread* no further *Lashes,* / 'You freely may *forgive his Ashes'*" (201–2). The imputation is hardly favorable to the opponent, who stands accused of the same kind of base motive he attributed to Swift.

Reading the debate on Swift in the light of the poem's seemingly irrelevant introduction reveals further meaning. Wrapped in their own egocentricity, friends cannot be counted upon to give you your due; therefore, you must do it yourself. The anonymous champion is transparently Swift himself, anticipating and countering what a detractor might say on the occasion of his death. Unable to defend himself then, and unable to rely on friends, the poet presents in advance a disarming apologia within the fictive world of his poem.[37] This is the familiar ritual of Swiftian exorcism, the imposition of aesthetic order on a threatening experience beyond the poet's control in reality. When

Swift's voice is audible behind his champion's, the last lines take on a poignant resonance.

The other poem occasioned by La Rochefoucauld's maxim, "Verses on the Death of Dr. Swift," is Swift's most accomplished effort to impose order on the materials of posthumous reputation and a worthy culmination to his poetry of fictive self-portraiture. Commentators ranging from Swift's contemporaries to twentieth-century scholars have been preoccupied with separating the fictive from the true, or more accurately, have been misled by Swift's use of biographical data into disregarding the poem as an imaginative creation. William King, who had been entrusted with supervising the poem's London publication, submitted "Verses" to Pope and other friends of Swift.[38] Pope set the tone for much later criticism in writing to Orrery, who had apparently acted as an intermediary in conveying the poem to him: "I return the verses you favored me with, the latter part of which is inferior to the beginning, the Character too dry, as well as too Vain in some respects, and in one or two particulars not true."[39] In defending the changes and excisions that he allowed, King followed Pope's opinion. His letter of March 6, 1739, to Mrs. Whiteway comments that "the latter part of the poem might be thought by the public a little vain, if so much were said by himself of himself."[40] As late as 1967 Ronald Paulson similarly protested that the eulogy "is an error of strategy, an overplaying of cards in the traditional apologia. . . ."[41]

In opposition to those critics who find Swift ingenuously vain, others affirm that the vanity is contrived and therefore exemplary.[42] This common preoccupation with Swift's "vanity" fails to yield up the poem's ultimate meaning, to which the concluding eulogy contributes only a part. Rather than the vanity attributed to the final, idealized portrait, "Verses" as a whole reveals egotism, the more generalized concern for self that is responsible for the poem's proliferation of self-images, both good and bad.[43] By refracting diverse views through his own shaping consciousness, Swift creates a multifaceted vision of self for his poem to perpetuate after his death.

Both "Verses" and "The Life and Genuine Character" use the La Rochefoucauld maxim and its exemplification as evidence that egotism makes the individual the best and perhaps the only person who can give himself justice. But this egotism further insures that he will inflate his own merits—hence the idealized portrait found in both poems. The unflattering portraits can equally be attributed to the impulse of egotism, for by playing all roles Swift exercises control over the negative as well as the positive versions of self. Such multiplicity has a universal application that transcends the depiction of Swift: it dramatizes the complexity of character and the difficulties of evaluating it in order to explore the power of reputation (the distanced view) and the nature of friendship (the close perspective).

Although the latter part of "Verses" has received the most extensive criticism, the poem's design can be apprehended only by an examination of the entire work, beginning once more with the prefatory maxim. Swift's free translation intensifies the cynicism by introducing an idea not found in the original, the attribution of this betrayal of friendship to nature:

> "In all Distresses of our Friends
> "We first consult our private Ends,
> "While Nature kindly bent to ease us,
> "Points out some Circumstance to please us."
>
> (7–10)

Swift's version also states, as the original did not, that our selfish impulse is the *first* response to a friend's misfortune. At the same time it is a gentler version of the maxim than the one Swift used for "The Life and Genuine Character."

In the first exemplifications of the maxim the reality of complacency and even self-congratulation in the face of a friend's misfortune contrasts unfavorably with an implied

ideal of friendship. With line 47 the *mea culpa* of the
speaker becomes specifically Swiftian. The poet's friends
are referred to by name and praised gracefully for their
literary accomplishments.

The shock value inherent in the maxim is extended in
the next section of the poem (11. 73–298) by the poet's use
of his own death as illustration. In the proem the speaker
had exposed his own ignoble feelings as one more example
of a general propensity that he shares with all men. In this
section he describes similar responses in friends and acquaintances. With the maxim as his guide the Dean is able
to foreknow the unflattering remarks his "special Friends"
will make about him. On the surface their comments
appear to be disinterested observations; their attitude—"I
wish he may hold out till Spring"—is solicitous. But the
climax of the passage reveals their underlying selfish concern: "THEN hug themselves, and reason thus; / 'It is not
yet so bad with us' " (115–16). The ironic exposition of the
friends' reactions continues to exhibit the contrast between their superficial feelings and outward behavior and
their real motives and attitudes. The tone is still light; the
sharply defined contrast between conventional piety and
the underlying real feeling provokes humor rather than
outrage at the perfidy of friends.

This humorous irony is maintained in the dialogue between a country squire and the London bookseller Lintot
that concludes the middle section of the poem. The subject is the death of Swift's writings, ludicrously following
his own demise by only a year. Lintot adopts a patronizing
manner toward the squire, who has naively inquired for
some of Swift's works, but the bookseller's speech shows
his own taste to be purely commercial, responsive only to
the latest popular novelty. Lintot lists a number of mediocrities whose works have replaced Swift's in the public
favor, such satiric targets of Pope and Swift as Colley
Cibber and Stephen Duck. In the bookseller's obtuse
praise of the renegade clergyman Woolston, the light irony
directed against Lintot is overlaid with indignation di-

rected against Woolston's blasphemous but widely read writings.

Given this duality of tone we may be undecided whether to laugh at Lintot or bemoan Woolston until we perceive a third perspective in the passage: the missing Dean is in evidence behind the mask of Woolston. An inspection of Woolston's virtues according to Lintot or sins according to the ironic undercutting of Lintot's words shows them to be ones often attributed to Swift himself: the popularity of his writings, his reward by the government, his "bravely running Priest-craft down." In the guise of the foolish bookseller Swift has just finished abusing several fellow priests of literature; he was often accused by his enemies of attacking religion and not believing in God. By the conclusion of Lintot's speech it is surely obvious that Swift is the subject as well as Woolston: " 'The Church had never such a Writer: / 'A Shame, he hath not got a Mitre!' " (297–98).[44] The underlying reference to Swift and the overt discussion of Woolston ironically conflate the two into one figure and thus voice the epistemological concern of so much of Swift's poetry of fictive self-portraiture. Once dead and unable to defend himself from libel, misinformation, and ill will, Swift may be remembered as just another Woolston.

The complexity of technique in the treatment of Woolston foreshadows the difficulties of the famous concluding section or eulogy (11. 299–484). Critics have generally scanted the first two parts of the poem, regarding the deflation of Swift as less in need of explanation and apology than the self-praise of the last portrait. But as the critical remarks cited earlier show, not all commentators perceive that the same spirit of irony and technique of exaggeration are operative in the last portion of the poem. The cause of critical perturbation lies not only in the uncomfortable fact that the poet is now praising rather than deprecating himself, but in the ambiguity of tone.

Like "The Life and Genuine Character," the third section of "Verses" interposes a speaker between the author and his portrait, "one quite indiff'rent in the Cause," who will report impartially. This ostensibly objective speaker is the perfect example of what Irvin Ehrenpreis calls the "ironical persona," a "mask that the reader at first supposes to be genuine, but at last sees removed."[45] In light of the humor of the first two-thirds of the poem, there is no reason to think that the claim of objectivity for the eulogy, delivered in the dubious setting of the Rose tavern,[46] is to be taken seriously. What follows is certainly a portrait of the best of all possible Swifts, a Swift as he would like to be remembered in contrast to the cynical exemplifications of the maxim that he has produced in the first part of the poem. This idealized version of Swift is supported by directly stated but highly partisan notes throughout the poem. The note to line 168, for example—"To *curse* the *Dean,* or *bless* the *Drapier*"— is typical in making clear which alternative is preferable:

> The Author imagines, that the Scriblers of the prevailing Party, which he always opposed, will libel him after his Death; but that others will remember him with Gratitude, who consider the Service he had done to *Ireland,* under the Name of *M. B.* Drapier, by utterly defeating the destructive Project of *Wood*'s Halfpence, in five Letters to the People of *Ireland,* at that Time read universally, and convincing every Reader. (*Poems,* 2: 558; emphasis removed)

Although the portrait constructed by the "objective viewer" is clearly ideal, there is always biographical resonance when Swift writes about Swift. The departures from the reality of Swift's history are so flagrant at times that it is scarcely believable that Swift thought the portrait would be accepted as true to life. Following his usual practice he teases the reader with a playful mixture of fact and fiction, plausible conjecture and half-truth:

> "HAD he but spar'd his Tongue and Pen,
> "He might have rose like other Men:
> "But, Power was never in his Thought;
> "And, Wealth he valu'd not a Groat:

"Ingratitude he often found,
"And pity'd those who meant the Wound.

(355–60)

The portrait is generalized enough to serve for the archetypal man of ability and integrity who attempts a political
career and fails as much through his own virtue as through
the vagaries of politics, but the picture can also be taken, as
it is offered, as a description of Swift's own political
career—a reading whose biographical ambiguity counter-
points the simplicity of the archetypal figure. Measured
against what was commonly known of Swift's career,[47] the
idea of the first couplet is suppositional but certainly highly
plausible. We need only recall Queen Anne's steadfast
opposition to the author of *A Tale of a Tub* to find it
persuasive, particularly in the speculative form it takes
here. The two assertions that follow (357–58), however,
are suspect by virtue of their absolute claims, and more
suspect yet in relation to the poet. "Ingratitude he often
found" is more like the first statement of the passage; that
is, it sounds likely enough, but there is no way of determining precisely how true it is, or how important, if true. To
penetrate this banal generalization biographically, we
would need to know if Swift encountered more ingratitude
than gratitude or more ingratitude than most people experience—or if he simply thought that he did. The next claim is
more readily evaluated, for there is sufficient evidence in
writing of Swift's irritation, rather than pity, toward those
"who meant the Wound." As a writer who acknowledged
his rage at the world's misdeeds both privately and pub-
licly, Swift knew that many would find the picture of
forbearance inaccurate as a view of himself. Here and
throughout Swift's poetry of fictive self-portraiture it is
clear that biographical data are not used to lead us to Swift
the man, but to borrow authority from the real Swift for a
fictive version.

This mixing of the recognizably true and false is one of
Swift's ways of indicating irony;[48] another is the relation of

the portrait to the governing maxim. According to the maxim, no such person as the one described in the third section of the poem could exist. After all of the perfidy and selfishness already chronicled, this ideal of disinterested benevolence is bound to be redolent with irony:

> "Without regarding private Ends,
> "Spent all his Credit for his Friends:
> . . . .
>
> ". . . succour'd Virtue in Distress,
> "And seldom fail'd of good Success.
>
> (331–32; 335–36)

The language is reminiscent of the maxim, which, however, made the opposite point: " 'In all Distresses of our Friends / 'We first consult our private Ends' " (7–8).[49] The reminder of the maxim recalls the first discussion of it, in which the Swiftian "I" admitted that he shared the weakness described by La Rochefoucauld. Evidently the speaker of the eulogy, who seems to have such intimate knowledge of his subject, is unaware of Swift's confession.

The exclamatory " 'And oh!" of line 371, followed by the general statement "how short are human Schemes!," marks a shift from Swift's personal crisis to that of society as a whole. The pronoun *our* reveals that the speaker shares Swift's Tory views, a further discrediting of his objectivity. Speaker and subject merge indistinguishably at this point; the mask of the impartial observer is dropped. What follows, an account of Swift's years in Ireland, directs against his enemies the *saeva indignatio* for which he is so well-known.

Having given an excellent demonstration of Swiftian satiric power, the speaker steps back behind the now transparent mask and returns to the subject of Swift. After the violent vituperation of the preceding passage, the summing up of Swift that concludes the poem is restrained and measured. Once again we find statements that proclaim an ideal but are questionable when applied to Swift:

> "Yet, Malice never was his Aim;
> "He lash'd the Vice but spar'd the Name.
> "No individual could resent,
> "Where Thousands equally were meant.
>
> (459–62)

Herbert Davis believes that Swift *"tries to think* that he has set down naught in malice and that no one will carry resentment against him" (emphasis added),[50] an interpretation that has the disadvantage of finding Swift guilty of the self-deception satirized in the remainder of the passage, and—even less likely—guilty of forgetting what he wrote only a few lines before. There he pointedly excoriated the judge who presided over the trial of the Drapier's printer and identified him by name in a note.[51]

The difficulty in this concluding section of "Verses," and throughout Swift's poetry of fictive self-portraiture, is in accurately assessing how the real functions to create the fictive self. As Edward Rosenheim writes: "Swift rarely sustains a single ironic posture for long, and there are certainly observations and sentiments within even the final section of the poem which . . . must be taken almost literally."[52] I would rephrase this to say that at times the real is incorporated into the fiction. The tension between real and fictive—always changing, often ambiguous—accounts for more interest than does the portrayal of the ideal politician/man/writer.

The meaning of "Verses on the Death of Dr. Swift," like that of "The Life and Genuine Character of Dr. Swift," is not the unadulterated self-laudation that Pope and others feared, or the true judgment on historical events that Edward W. Said finds.[53] Swift and the reader share the knowledge that he does not, indeed cannot, live up to what is claimed for him by the eulogist, but the poet has created such a spokesman because, like all men, he would prefer to be remembered at his best rather than his worst. Whatever Swift conceived the reality of his character to be, we must not expect to find it directly expressed in his poetry. What the poems of fictive self-portraiture reveal is an attempt to counter what Henry James called "clumsy life" with art: fictive Swift is a foil for the man who is prey to time and death; to the distortions of himself promulgated by others, both friends and enemies; to his own weaknesses; and—through his exposure in poetic self-portraiture—to the reader's laughter.[54] Nevertheless, in Swift's view he is less vulnerable when he can exorcise these destructive phenomena, including his own egotism, by creating a poetic world to order and contain them.

2

The Vulnerable Self

IN one sense all of Swift's poetry of fictive self-portraiture reveals vulnerability: the aesthetic constructs created and shaped by the poet show the self confronting those forces that elude control in the world outside his poem. This world both occasions and intrudes into the poetic universe, but through the resources of his art Swift generally controls and thereby exorcises threats to the self. In the group of poems considered here, a different situation obtains. Instead of being threatened by a powerful individual or group, the self is assailed by forces too strong to be completely mastered; consequently, exorcism is not achieved.

Physical and emotional vulnerability account for the portrayal of a more helpless Swift figure than elsewhere in the poetry of fictive self-portraiture. The two short poems of physical affliction, "In Sickness" and "On his own Deafness," are unique in taking physical debility as their subject, but this susceptibility to ailments contributes to the poet's emotional dependence on Stella, the theme of an important group of poems. Taken as a whole the poems for Stella's birthday describe a relationship whose very perfection makes it vulnerable to time and death, but this vulnerability is not starkly exposed until the final poem acknowledges Stella's imminent death. In this admission it serves as a companion piece to "Holyhead," Swift's most passionate confession of impotence and despair. "Cadenus and Vanessa" demonstrates another kind of emotional vulnerability. All of Swift's skill as poet creating the poem, and as teacher arguing within it, fails to convince or to achieve the intended resolution because the underlying difficulty is Cadenus's psyche.

1

For the most part, Swift's frequent illness is known from other sources than his poetry. Except for the mandatory birthday tribute to Stella, "Written . . . when I was sick in bed," it seems unlikely that Swift forced himself to compose poems when he was ill, and when he was well other topics were understandably more attractive. "In Sickness" and "On his own Deafness" are thus exceptional, but they seem to be inspired not by physical affliction alone, but by the powerful conjunction of illness and isolation. There is wit, but no laughter: what palliation of bleakness exists is bitter rather than genuinely compensatory.

"In Sickness," significantly subtitled "*Written soon after the Author's coming to live in Ireland, upon the Queen's Death,* October, 1714," combines two circumstances apt to be depressing to Swift: his enforced residence in Ireland and his various bodily sufferings. Like the two great poems based upon a maxim of La Rochefoucauld, "In Sickness" envisions Swift's death. Unlike them, it presents a single sharply defined self-portrait. The opening " 'Tis true" is all the more effective for having no antecedent. What is true? The grim reality evoked by the bare particulars of the title—Swift's illness, the catastrophe of the Queen's death, his enforced stay in Ireland. Given this situation, the poet may well wish for a speedy end to misery: "Then why should I repine / To see my Life so fast decline?" (1–2). The rhetorical question conveys as much, but it is followed by another, real question: "But why obscurely here alone? / Where I am neither lov'd nor known" (3–4). Those abiding concerns of so much of Swift's poetry of fictive self-portraiture—reputation and friendship—are united in this complaint. In contrast to his present friendless condition, Swift thinks of Arbuthnot, a man who lives up to the Swiftian ideal of friendship by placing it above selfish or

material concerns. Others, instead, are content with superficial protestations made not out of feeling for the individual
Swift but in the interest of "meer Humanity." Swift portrays himself as receiving only what is accorded in charity
to any anonymous sufferer; his anguish stems in part from a
denial of his selfhood by others. For a man whose friend-
lessness has stripped him of individuality in the eyes of the
world, a quick death is best: "Expir'd Today, entomb'd
To-morrow, / When known, will save a double Sorrow"
(27–28). The tidy parallelism of the first line and the ironic
thrift of the second appropriately cut short the mood of
self-pity. By refraining from railing and by transforming
self-pity into consideration for friends, Swift creates a
convincing portrait of desolation confronted yet not entirely mastered.

The poem needs nothing outside itself to work perfectly,
but the use of recognizable biographical facts functions as it
does everywhere in Swift's fictive self-portraiture to inten-
sify the effect. Swift was neither friendless nor obscure at
this time, and he could hardly have expected "more" from
Stella, for instance, but the truth of the large verifiable
particulars extends credibility to the rest. Rather than
creating a playful counterpoint to the fiction, or complicat-
ing the portraits as they do in the more ambitious poems,
the biographical facts reinforce the air of sincere feeling of
the whole.

Defeat through isolation of the self also informs Swift's
other poem on physical incapacitation, "On his own Deafness":

> DEAF, giddy, helpless, left alone,
> To all my Friends a Burthen grown,
> No more I hear my Church's Bell,
> Than if it rang out for my Knell.
>
> (1–4)

To complete the opening image of impotence only the
further particular of burdening friends is needed. Being cut

off from the Church bell, thunder, and passing carts sepa-
rates Swift in some measure from vocation, nature, and
man. These sounds are completely excluded, loud though
they are, whereas a "Woman's Clack" can still be faintly
heard although its exclusion would be more of a blessing
than a deprivation.[1] At best the joke is weak enough, and it
suffers all the more in contrast to the strength of the first
four lines. The attempt at humor does not reassure us that
the poet has his world of deafness under control; it simply
shows us that he is making an attempt to exorcise a threat
in a way that has worked in other situations but falls short
here. The strength of the poem is in the opening collocation
of adjectives and the image of isolation and helplessness
that no commonplace joke can banish.

2

In writing to James Stopford about Stella's approaching
death, Swift insisted that "violent friendship is much more
lasting, and as much engaging, as violent love."[2] This
refusal to call his feelings by the usual name did not spare
Swift from the emotional vulnerability associated with
love, but his peculiar term for the relationship to Stella has
an obvious rationale. Defining his feelings as other than
love allowed Swift to remain free of the kind of official
recognition and commitment he was unwilling to offer.
Nevertheless, like any Renaissance sonneteer, Swift presents himself in the poetry addressed to Stella in a dual
role. Vulnerably human, he depends upon his mistress to
allay his suffering, but he is also artistically powerful, the
poet who preserves her merit in art. The tension between
the two aspects dominates the poems, either overtly in the
fiction of the poet overcoming his own inadequacy or
implicitly in the defense of Stella against the malevolent
effects of time.

What is chiefly dramatized and made memorable in the
poems for Stella's birthday is her unfailing devotion to

Swift and her absolute powers of transforming reality for him:

> . . . when indecently I rave,
> When out my brutish passions break,
> With gall in ev'ry word I speak,
> She, with soft speech, my anguish chears.
>
> ("To Stella," 1724, 10–13)

Stella is a counter-Circe whose exemplary humanity reclaims Swift from the destructive loss of control induced by illness. Here the effect is a positive metamorphosis, a change back to self-control and to more restrained behavior. Such power as Stella has over Swift has a dangerous side as well, for just as her presence can create his happiness, her absence can destroy it. Swift's apprehensions of such an eventuality are revealed in a letter to John Worrall, written when he thought Stella to be dying: "The Remaind[r] of my Life will be a very melancholy Scene. . . . I am of Opinion that there is not a greater Folly than to contract too great and intimate a Friendship, which must always leave the Survivor miserable."[3]

This aspect of their relationship is not directly expressed in the birthday poems, reasonably enough, but is revealed in "Holyhead, Sept. 25. 1727," a poem written about Swift's inability to cross from England to Ireland at a time when he believed Stella to be dying.[4] A number of images of coercion establish him as a victim of forces beyond his control, "fasnd both by wind and tide," and "forc't to stay," but this is only the apparent cause of the poet's frustration. "Holyhead" achieves its considerable power through an unexpected revelation of total despair, effected by a shift from a comic principle of unity to a tragic principle of expansion: the poem's concern with a journey delayed opens out into a concern with life and death, and the comic vulnerability of the first part of the poem is transformed into tragic dependence upon a dying friend. Swift deliberately avoids this shift in the prose journal that he kept at Holyhead. He writes there: "I shall say nothing upon the suspense I am in about my dearest friend; because that is a case extraordinary, and therefore by way of amusement, I will speak as if it were not in my thought, and only as a passenger who is in a scurvy unprovided comfortless place without one companion."[5] In reality, Swift's rage in the poem is provoked by his utter impotence in the face of an unthinkable misfortune, the loss of Stella:

> But now, the danger of a friend
> On whom my fears and hopes depend
> Absent from whom all Clymes are curst
> With whom I'm happy in the worst
> With rage impatient makes me wait
> A passage to the land I hate.

(23–28)

Now that Swift has named the real source of his anxiety, it infuses the comically depicted irritations of the first two-thirds of the poem with portentous meaning. In retrospect, the misleading aggravation seems to be a device to avoid naming the poet's fear as long as possible.

That Stella can so radically alter the poet's world dramatically renders the magnitude of his dependence on her and accounts for the despair with which he describes the absence prefiguring ultimate separation. The device of absolute statement prominent in the first part of the poem is now used to completely different effect. "All Christian vittals stink of fish" and "absent from whom all Clymes are curst" are both extravagant, but the first is comically banal, the second a passionate utterance that helps establish, in a poem with much comment on weather and geography, the depth of Swift's feeling. "The danger of a friend," Stella's mortal illness, is a vague and hurriedly passed over introduction to Swift's vividly depicted feelings. Most of the passage's length and energy are devoted to that picture of helplessness and frustration, of total and inescapable imprisonment, which characterizes the vulnerable self. Swift is seen to be at the mercy of a number of forces beyond his control: nature, sea captains, the danger of his dearest friend, and the hatefulness of the land he must travel to. Beyond these immediate causes, we can see a man in bondage to his own inner needs—for greater scope than an Irish deanery could furnish and for that dying friend who has become the repository of his hopes and fears.

Given the central paradox on which the poem is built—Swift's desperate yearning to go to the land he hates—there can be no completely positive outcome, no resolution that will salvage the situation through art. "Holyhead" is unique in Swift's poetry of fictive self-portraiture in making no attempt to invoke a strategy of self-defense. To reach the friend he loves is also to reach the land he hates; to remain on this "bleaky shore" is to have freedom from Ireland laced with the pain of separation from Stella.

Time brings decline and death, and the poems written for Stella's birthday, with their natural emphasis on the passing of time, inevitably take Swift and Stella along the road that ends in the unrelieved gloom of "Holyhead." But in contrast to "Holyhead," all but the final birthday poem successfully combat temporal change. Swift intends to demonstrate the exemplary uniqueness of his view that "time takes off from the lustre of virgins in all other eyes but mine."[6] While the poems insist upon squarely facing the effects of time, they also transcend them through the unconventional celebration of Stella's nonphysical attributes, qualities that are proof against the passing of time. The harmonious Swift-Stella relationship is celebrated just as emphatically as Stella herself. It, too, must contend with time, and in each instance but the last it triumphantly adapts to changing conditions. The givens of the poetry—Stella's worth and the perfection of their relationship—create the principle of unity challenged by the external forces of time and death. In an ongoing dynamic the poetic order expands to contain and exorcise the threats against it.

These exorcisms are only partially successful. Existing in the world of time, Stella and her relationship with the poet are perishable achievements. The birthday poems that praise and preserve them are at the same time a moving record of vulnerability to forces that eventually overwhelm them, even within the world of poetry.

"To Stella" (1719) advances a view that Swift would always adhere to in his treatment of Stella: the faithful chronicling of her increasingly less attractive physical appearance in order to expatiate upon its lack of importance. As he notes in "To Stella, Visiting me in my Sickness," when Swift first addressed Stella in poetry she was "no longer young." Although she was not yet old, Swift could nevertheless look back to a vanished time of Stella's youthful physical perfection. At the same time that he asserts the preeminence and permanent value of Stella's mind, so too does he perversely remind us of her physical decline, a train of thought further encouraged in the first birthday poem by the gratuitous phrase "before it grew too late." The doubling of Stella's size and years suggests the curious conceit developed in the remainder of the poem:

> Oh, would it please the Gods to split
> Thy Beauty, Size, and Years, and Wit,
> No Age could furnish out a Pair
> Of Nymphs so gracefull, Wise and fair.
>
> (9–12)

Doubling leads to thoughts of halving—perhaps an indication that, however much Swift may protest, he cherishes some nostalgia for the vanished form of the sixteen-year-old Stella. The poem's conclusion shifts the elaborate conceit to the poet with the first expression of his and Stella's compatibility: if Stella has virtue enough for two women, the poet equally has admiration enough for two.[7]

While Stella's mind and body are treated together to emphasize their disparity, paired references to Stella and the poet establish their ideal rapport. Just as the birthday poems celebrate the triumph of mind over body, permanent over transient charms, they exalt the right relation of Swift to Stella, which contravenes the Petrarchan tradition of suffering poets and cruel mistresses.

In the second birthday poem Swift meticulously notes that Stella's face is "a little crack't," but as is always the case in these poems, the physical loss is coupled with the growing attractiveness of Stella's nonphysical attributes. Stella's present condition, in fact, is lost sight of in the poem's conclusion, where Swift hastens on to describe a Stella at fourscore:

> When Stella's Locks must all be grey
> When Age must print a furrow'd Trace
> On ev'ry Feature of her Face.
> ("Stella's Birth-Day," 1720, 48–50)

It is as if Swift wants to disarm time by anticipating the ravages of old age before they arrive and deprecating their importance. His way of doing this is a variation on the splitting found in the first poem; he opposes the elderly Stella of his invention to a feminine rival who is Stella's real age.[8] A dual compliment results: Stella can rejoice in the idea that her virtues will continue to make her attractive in old age; at the same time she can take pleasure in her present age through the poet's use of it as a physical ideal. This imposition of control within the poetic world over the unwelcome circumstances of age and physical decay is a charm against an inevitable future, now ironically distanced but brought nearer by every birthday.

From the third birthday poem on, the poet demands as much or more attention than Stella, who is seen and valued primarily in response to Swift. The adaptation

required by time weighs more heavily on him than it does
on Stella:

> You, every Year the Debt enlarge,
> I grow less equall to the Charge:
> In you, each Virtue brighter shines,
> But my Poetick Vein declines.
> ("To Stella on her Birth-day," 1721, 7–10)

Rather than Stella herself, Swift's subject has become the
making of poetry about Stella, *his* contribution to their
relationship. Stella's mind and virtues compensate for her
declining physical state, but from the poet's point of view
this gain is his loss. Almost every line of the poem records
the mock-frustration of a supposed disparity between
Stella's virtue and Swift's ability to praise it, while at the
same time the poem illustrates the reverse, the enduring
harmony of their relationship. The polished verse and easy
flow of witty compliment, united with an avowal of pain
and difficulty, set up an ironic tension between form and
content whose effect is one of control and distance. It
seems unlikely that Swift felt any of the decline and decay
of which he writes: this fictive portrait functions as an
inversion of reality but, in addition, as a legitimate fear of
what the future will ultimately bring. Beyond the rhetorical strategy, Swift's act of containment in this poem is an
attempt to neutralize an inevitable future of physical decline and death.

"Stella's Birth-Day" (1723) is a similarly witty and polished performance about how difficult it is to write a
poem. Although Apollo's speech praises Stella in passing,
the poem is not the usual birthday tribute to her so much
as an account of Swift's efforts to produce it. The poem of
1722 described the predicament in general terms; this
poem dramatizes, with fanciful episode and concrete detail, the pains of Swift's annual task:

> I bit my Nails, and scratch'd my Head,
> But found my Wit and Fancy fled:

Or, if with more than usual Pain,
A Thought came slowly from my Brain,
It cost me Lord knows how much Time
To shape it into Sense and Rhyme;
And, what was yet a greater Curse,
Long-thinking made my Fancy worse.

(5–12)

All of the energy goes into the prelude to composition, and the praises of Stella never do get sung.

By Stella's next birthday (1724) the situation previously treated with wit and detachment is offered as reality. The poem is bluntly prefaced with the words "Written on the Day of her Birth, but not on the Subject, when I was sick in bed." Not writing on the subject was part of the joke the previous year; now it is presented seriously: "Tormented with incessant pains, / Can I devise poetic strains?" (1–2). The implication of the question and the assertion of the prefatory statement is that Swift is "unable grown to write." The 1722 poem constructed a stylized image of the writer courting a recalcitrant muse; this time we believe the pains are real, yet Swift transcends his suffering by making a poem out of it. Because of the circumstances and tone, the effect is of hard-won rather than easy skill. The poet is now more dependent on Stella's care than she is on his panegyric; time thus seems more inimical to him than to her.

The ideal rapport that the poet and his lady enjoy is menaced and temporarily disrupted, but their ability to adapt to new conditions restores equilibrium. Just as Swift's praise must match Stella's growing virtues, so her resources must increase to meet his needs. In spite of physical infirmities on both sides, the relationship tenuously maintains its harmonious balance: "So may we long continue thus, / Admiring you, you pitying us" (37–38).

The conventions of the Petrarchan sonnet, always a pervasive presence in the Stella poems, appear both straightforwardly and ironically here. The poetic structure

is a standard strategy of the love sonnet, which works
rhetorically in Swift's poem just as it does in that genre;
that is, the poet does what he says cannot be done, and we
admire his art the more because it triumphs over obstacles—time, pain, rejection, separation. Suggesting that he
is too sick to praise Stella, Swift nevertheless praises her
most effectively. But while this conventional structure is
the poem's principle of unity, the expansion is vigorously
anti-Petrarchan. The poet suffers the prosaic ills of the
flesh, not the pains of romantic love. His lady is not the
usual unkind or indifferent mistress; on the contrary, her
ministrations during his illness, and especially her exemplary patience toward his brutish behavior, are what the
poem praises. Thus, within the Petrarchan fiction, Swift
introduces a reality that by implication is worthier than the
passion celebrated by conventional love sonnets.

   "Stella's Birthday" (1725) brings together a number of
themes treated in previous years—Stella's aging combined
with the poet's insistence on her nonphysical qualities, the
difficulty of making the poem because of Swift's own
decline, and above all, the harmony of their relationship
that manages to triumph over all threats:

> No Poet ever sweetly sung,
> Unless he were like *Phoebus,* young;
> Nor ever Nymph inspir'd to Rhyme,
> Unless, like *Venus,* in her Prime.
> At Fifty six, if this be true,
> Am I a Poet fit for you?
> Or at the Age of Forty three,
> Are you a Subject fit for me?
>
> (19–26)

What appears as assertion and rhetorical question establishing that Swift and Stella are too old to be poet and lady
in the conventional terms of love poetry is actually an
intimate joke, dependent upon the private knowledge poet
and subject share that both are fit for their respective roles

and that the poet will produce the expected poem. In the next lines the surface statement is not to be categorically dismissed but accepted in several ways at once:

> Adieu bright Wit, and radiant Eyes;
> You must be grave, and I be wise
> Our Fate in vain we would oppose,
> But I'll be still your Friend in Prose.
>
> (27–30)

Time's bad effects are a reality that must be confronted, but the blow is softened, for gravity and wisdom are not disaster, and friendship continues. If time cuts off Swift's poetic voice, as he anticipates, he will circumvent its intention by extolling Stella in prose. Indeed, the reality of decline turns out to be bearable. What is salvageable, "Esteem and Friendship," is more valuable than what is lost—the ephemera of "bright Wit and radiant Eyes." Since opposition to fate must necessarily be in vain, it is desirable to give in gracefully.

With this introduction Swift goes on to develop the intertwined themes of his and Stella's decline more specifically. Having intimated above that he is no fit poet, Stella no proper subject, Swift wittily establishes their actual compatibility: "For Nature, always in the Right, / To your Decays adapts my Sight" (43–44). Here, too, time's effects are not ominous and uncontrollable, but are perfectly assimilated by the relationship. The poet both accepts an unpalatable reality and disarms it; Stella is decayed, but because of his failing eyesight he cannot see her wrinkles and gray hair. The description of physical decay leads naturally into Swift's customary praise of the nonphysical attributes for which he has always celebrated Stella. And just as Swift's defective sight is nicely suited to Stella's appearance, so his good hearing is suited to her virtues. This balance could be disturbed—the Stella poems never lose sight of the essential hostility of time—but the concluding couplet imagines an eventuality distanced by witty antithesis: "Oh, ne'er may Fortune shew her Spight, / To make me *deaf,* and mend my *Sight*" (53–54). This has a poignant irony for the reader who knows of Swift's later deafness, but in context loss of hearing must be thought to be as likely as restoration of sight, that is, unlikely.[9] Certainly, fortune may be spiteful in the future, but the dominant tone of this poem is one of harmonious adaptation and control.

Because it must acknowledge an immediate future worse than the gray hair and wrinkles of old age—death itself— the poem for Stella's last birthday ("*Stella's* Birth-Day." 1727.) fails to master vulnerability. In poems like "A Beautiful Young Nymph Going to Bed" and "The Progress of Beauty," vice could absorb some of the animus Swift actually felt toward bodily existence, but here he is forced to confront the issue of physical decline and death not as the merited punishment of flagrant sinfulness but as the inescapable end of an admirable life. In the first six poems Swift's strategy was to strip the metamorphosis of aging of its real and potentially tragic nature by denying its significance and shifting value to another area. Stella's transformation from a youth as "the brightest Virgin of the Green" to an age of gray hair and wrinkles is emphasized as the negative given that Swift could defeat with the resources of poetry.

Only when faced with Stella's imminent death—that is, with the dependence of the spirit on the body's impermanence—do Swift's strategies fail. Although the 1727 poem begins lightly with the determination to ignore unpleasant realities of age and illness, the customary conversion of the effects of time into compliments for Stella is notably absent. Indeed, since Stella is dying, there is no way to order the present or future except by converting it into the past. This, too, is a way of substituting mental for physical, the pleasure of the mind's remembrance for the virtuous act itself:

> For Virtue in her daily Race,
> Like *Janus,* bears a double Face;

Looks back with Joy where she has gone,
And therefore goes with Courage on.
She at your sickly Couch will wait,
And guide you to a better State.

                                        (73–78)

When the intellectual argument Swift has developed so
elaborately suddenly gives way to a moving emotional
appeal, the fragile nature of this mental triumph is exposed.
Swift admits the possibility that Stella's mind may be
subverted by physical ills to create a distorted negative
version of reality rather than accurately remembering past
achievements.

   The poem ends as it began, with the conjunction of Swift
and Stella's mutual decline and interdependence, but the
tone has altered from a controlled exposition to outcry and
plea:

Me, surely me, you ought to spare,
Who gladly would your Suff'rings share;
Or give my Scrap of Life to you,
And think it far beneath your Due;
You, to whose Care so oft I owe,
That I'm alive to tell you so.

                                        (83–88)

These concluding lines are an expression of impotence, an
admission that Stella's condition is beyond transformation, even in poetry. Swift cannot give his life to Stella or
share her suffering, however much he might want to do
so, and he has already revealed his last philosophical
consolation to be itself assailable by her illness. The
passage embodies a bald plea that the dying Stella spare
the poet, based not upon what she owes him, but on his
helplessness to aid her and to bear his own anguish.[10] In
this final crisis Swift is imprisoned within his own suffering and dependence, an egotism that furnishes a last test
of the understanding and patience that Stella customarily

opposed to his weakness.[11] Nevertheless, the conclusion reminds us of the more pleasing form of reciprocity that has informed the previous birthday poems: her contribution of care, his of poetry.

Here and in "Holyhead" the thought of Stella's approaching death engenders a despair that is articulated but not exorcised through art. As he wrote to Thomas Sheridan, "I look upon this [Stella's death] to be the greatest Event that can ever happen to me, but all my Preparations will not suffice to make me bear it like a Philosopher, nor altogether like a Christian."[12] Swift made witty poetry out of a number of threats to the self, including the potentially painful prospect of his own death and posthumous loss of reputation, but the plea of his last lines to Stella and the prison of impotent rage in "Holyhead" reveal the vulnerable self in its most extreme form.

3

The speaker of the Stella poems, an elderly poet offering friendship rather than love to a younger woman, is essentially the third-person Cadenus of the earlier poem "Cadenus and Vanessa." The anti-Petrarchan approach is found in both; Vanessa is praised for some of the same "masculine" qualities attributed to Stella, and the elaborately developed mythological framework is like similar strategies of the Stella poems. Nevertheless, "Cadenus and Vanessa" is significantly different from the Stella poems, for if the admiration of certain qualities is common to both, only the Stella poems reveal dependence and intimacy. For the speaker of the poems addressed to her, Stella is the creator and sustainer of his world and his very self. His last words to Stella in poetry were addressed to "you, to whose Care so oft I owe, / That I'm alive to tell you so." Measured against that acknowledgment, "Cadenus and Vanessa" appears less complimentary—a witty poem about an older man's problem of politely turning aside the affections of an eager young woman.

Unlike the Stella poems, which describe a mutually satisfactory relationship threatened by the external forces of time and death, "Cadenus and Vanessa" shows Swift's vulnerability to the limitations of his own nature, an inability to love that is as much beyond his control as Stella's decline and death. Stella and the Dean enjoy a harmony that the birthday poems define and extol; "Cadenus and Vanessa" expresses the tension of disequilibrium inherent within the relationship, a situation whose ambiguities and uncertainties are mirrored in the poem's inconclusive ending. This failure to achieve resolution is, once more, a mark of the vulnerable self.

Unlike the more direct *Dean* of the Stella poems, the title "Cadenus" creates a certain amount of distance, which is increased by the speaker's separation of himself from Cadenus. This same distance and separation occur in Swift's use of the abbreviation *Cad.* in his letters to Vanessa: "Cad—assures me he continues to esteem and love and value you above all things . . . but at the same time entreats that you would not make your self or him unhappy by Imaginations."[13]

In the first description of Cadenus commonly known biographical facts reverberate within the poetic statement to create a character recognizable as Swift, but one whose admirable attributes are qualified by humorous exaggeration:

> *Cadenus* is a Subject fit,
> Grown old in Politics and Wit;
> Caress'd by Ministers of State,
> Of half Mankind the Dread and Hate.
> . . . .
>
> *Cadenus* many things had writ;
> *Vanessa* much esteem'd his Wit,
> And call'd for his Poetick Works.
> (502–5; 510–12)

A curious mixture of praise and disparagement informs the

portrait, as if the poet wants to make certain that his tone of gentle ridicule, marked by hyperbole, is not missed. Line 510 is merely a general fact, but line 512 has the characteristic complexity of Swift's use of biographical data. Although he certainly had a manuscript collection of poems at the time, to refer seriously to what he had produced by 1713 as "Poetick Works" would have been laughably pompous. Swift delights in such interplays of true and fictive and in jokes upon himself, as when, continuing, he refers to Cadenus's poetry as a "feeble Volume."

As if to balance what was in the main a too-favorable picture, Swift describes Cadenus again, this time exaggerated to the opposite extreme:

> *Vanessa,* not in Years a Score,
> Dreams of a Gown of forty-four;
> Imaginary Charms can find,
> In eyes with Reading almost blind;
> *Cadenus* now no more appears
> Declin'd in Health, advanc'd in Years.
>
> (524–29)

One notable difference between the two portraits—which are not, after all, contradictory—is that the second is presented with the overlay of Vanessa's illusions. Because the tone is light, we read the disparity as comic rather than tragic. It is functional in the argument that Cadenus is no fit match for Vanessa, but appears to be one only to her love-struck gaze.

What remains constant in the portraiture, the poem's principle of unity, is the strategy of self-justification, which often contains a strong measure of defensiveness:

> Or grant her Passion be sincere,
> How shall his Innocence be clear?
> Appearances were all so strong,
> The World must think him in the Wrong.
>
> (640–43)

Against such accusations Swift asserts that Cadenus has always behaved appropriately: "His Conduct might have made him styl'd / A Father, and the Nymph his Child" (548–49). The father-child relationship suggests the idea of responsibility, which will be contrasted to a series of betrayals unworthy of Cadenus and open to ridicule by the world. A number of unattractive roles, all demonstrating a violation of trust on the part of an adult or surrogate father figure toward a young girl, are posited for the misunder-stood Cadenus:

> When Miss delights in her Spinnet,
> A Fidler may a Fortune get;
> A Blockhead with melodious Voice
> In Boarding-Schools can have his Choice;
> And oft' the Dancing-Master's Art
> Climbs from the Toe to touch the Heart.
> In Learning let a Nymph delight,
> The Pedant gets a Mistress by't.
>
> (736–43)

Each instance juxtaposes a young girl and an older man: she is described in the vocabulary of innocence—*Miss, Heart, Nymph*—and he is characterized with pejorative terms. All involve a transferral of enthusiasm from a legitimate to an illegitimate sphere, from activity to teacher. In all cases the pupil is obviously deluded rather than the teacher worthy. These unsavory fancies of mali-cious gossip loom as reductive versions of the Cadenus-Vanessa relationship, from which the self must be disso-ciated.

But the need for self-justification in "Cadenus and Vanessa" is twofold, and Swift's success in defending Cadenus against the imputations of dishonorable behavior is coupled with his failure to refute Vanessa's argument adequately. Cadenus's inability to respond to Vanessa is cursorily explained by references to propriety and age, but these are not insurmountable obstacles to love and marriage when weighed against mutual respect and intellectual compatibility. Elsewhere Swift always approved such qualities as the proper foundation for marriage. As he wrote in *A Letter to a Young Lady, on her Marriage:* "The grand Affair of your Life will be to gain and preserve the Friendship and Esteem of your Husband."[14] In "Strephon and Chloe" he counsels marriage partners:

> On Sense and Wit your Passion found,
> By Decency cemented round;
> Let Prudence with Good Nature strive,
> To Keep Esteem and Love alive.
>
> (307–10)

Clearly, by the standards Swift himself advocated, Cadenus and Vanessa are well matched. Cadenus seizes upon inadequate excuses because the real reason, the underlying psychological reality of his "Want of Passion," can be neither analyzed nor altered. Just as Vanessa's efforts are doomed to failure because of this genuine difficulty, so is the poet's attempt to make a persuasive case for Cadenus similarly doomed. The self created here is vulnerable not only to the problem of dealing with a persistent woman, but also to its own inability to make the usual kind of commitment to any woman. As Swift restated the problem in "Verses to Vanessa," there is no satisfactory answer to the questions raised:

> For who could such a Nymph forsake
> Except a Blockhead or a Rake
> Or how could she her heart bestow
> Except where Wit and Virtue grew.
>
> (19–22)

On its public level "Cadenus and Vanessa" succeeds in vindicating the fictive self from slander by expanding to present those situations in which young women fall in love with male teachers and then by effectively dissociating

Cadenus from this paradigm. On the private level, whose structure is assimilated to and magnified by the frame of mythological narrative, the poem fails to convince, and the dominant impression is irresolution. What happens within the poetic world of "Cadenus and Vanessa" is generally applicable to the body of poems of fictive self-portraiture; that is, public images of Swift created by other men are more successfully opposed than those versions of self which involve external and internal forces beyond human control.

PART II

Ordering the World:
The Satiric Poetry

3
The Verbal Universe

THE distinctive quality of Swift's plain and conversational style is a striking degree of verisimilitude which, like Mark Twain's vernacular, seems to transfer the cadences and language of common speech into literature. Swift uses this style for the ordinary purposes of speech within his poetry—for dialogue exchanges, narrative, and instruction:

> Say, *Stella,* feel you no Content,
> Reflecting on a Life well spent?
> Your skilful Hand employ'd to save
> Despairing Wretches from the Grave;
> And then supporting with your Store,
> Those whom you dragg'd from Death before.
> ("*Stella*'s Birth-Day," 1727, 35–40)

This verse moves purposefully and directly from point to point without calling attention to itself, catching the reader up in the argument Swift is developing. Undoubtedly, Dr. Johnson was thinking of this style when he remarked of Swift's poetry that "the diction is correct, the numbers are smooth, and the rhymes exact" and concluded that "there is not much upon which the critick can exercise his powers."[1]

Swift's other style is characterized by excess in all respects—outrageous makeshift rhymes, farfetched analogies and juxtapositions, absolutes of praise or blame, torrents of particulars.[2] When this style dominates, technique is foregrounded. The hapless astrologer Partridge, for example, is only an excuse to allow Swift to make a number of ingenious comparisons between two logically dissimilar trades:

> The *Horned Moon* which heretofore
> Upon their Shoes the *Romans* wore,
> Whose Wideness kept their Toes from Corns,
> And whence we claim our *shoeing horns,*
> Shews how the Art of *Cobling* bears
> A near Resemblance to the *Spheres.*
> ("An Elegy on Mr. *PATRIGE,* the Almanack-maker,"
> 35–40)

Dick, the putative subject of Swift's parody of Cowley, "Clad all in Brown," is not actually a presence in the poem.[3] The real subject is Swift's transforming wit, which turns "So Lillies in a glass enclose, / The *Glass* will seem as white as those" into "So Turds within a *Glass* inclose, / The Glass will seem as brown as those" (11–12).[4] A poem like "PETHOX the Great" is no more a satiric treatment of venereal disease than "Clad all in Brown" is an attack on Dick. It offers, instead, the pleasures of a verbal game, an extended riddle structured by the number of unexpected ways the poet can describe *syphilis* without giving away the answer. As for rhyme, here is Apollo addressing the Dean, a rare occurrence of feminine rhyme in the Stella poems:

> Though you should live like old *Methusalem,*
> I furnish Hints, and you should use all 'em.
> ("Stella's Birth-Day," 1723, 37–38)

This ramshackle yet somehow workable pairing simply overwhelms its context. It is this sort of engaging inventiveness that caused Byron to exclaim to Trelawney, "Swift beats us all hollow, his rhymes are wonderful."[5]

As William Gass has written, "It's not the word made flesh we want in writing, in poetry and fiction, but the flesh made word."[6] The conspicuous virtuosity of Swift's extravagant style is the mark of the verbal universe Gass refers to, where the play of mind in language preempts attention above all else, and the circular pattern of satire is incomplete: the poems do not lead back to the world that has occasioned them, but remain within the world of language. Their chief concerns and effects are metalinguistic. In this poetry the principle of unity is often furnished by a familiar literary form—pastoral, Ovidian metamorphosis, elegy—which the poet reshapes through a process of satiric expansion into its mock or counter-form. The pastoral thus becomes an urban genre, the elegy a poem disvaluing the dead, and the *ars poetica* a set of instructions on making a career as a bad poet.

It should be noted that there is no absolute correlation between the poetic attitude or intention and the two stylistic extremes I have isolated: technical extravagance neither reflects nor precludes emotional excess. Generally, however, the foregrounding of technique in an entire poem is coupled with distance, control, and a predominantly literary or linguistic focus. Only in the quintessential poem of the verbal universe, "On Poetry: A Rapsody," is so much technical extravagance combined with the serious satirizing of the experiential world.

"Saying the Thing which is not"

Gulliver's Houyhnhnm Master, on being told that men use language deceptively, says that speech exists for truth and understanding: "If anyone *said the Thing which was not,* these ends were defeated."[7] A number of Swift's satiric poems are not primarily concerned with the vicious or foolish actions that are typically grist for the satirist's mill, but instead focus upon a spectrum of linguistic offenses ranging from artificial metaphors and affected diction to the language of calculated deception. Although an action may be the official topic, this real event is displaced by a linguistic event, an abuse of language that preempts the poem's center. Where there is such an occasioning event, it is not only satirized by language but also transformed into a verbal occasion for satire.

As always in Swift's satire, the informing principle of the attack is a commitment to reality. Those completely rational creatures the Houyhnhnms had no words in their language to express lying or false representation. When Gulliver attempts to explain these concepts, his Master remarks that such linguistic practice would result in a state worse than ignorance, "for I am led to believe a Thing *Black* when it is *White,* and *Short* when it is *Long.*"[8] A great deal of Swift's satiric poetry focuses upon such deceptive linguistic practices.

Swift's simplest technique for satirizing reprehensible language is to exploit its own possibilities. He may carry a metaphor to an extreme in order to expose its inherent foolishness, hence the single-minded development of the moon / woman analogy in "The Progress of Beauty":

> Yet as she [the moon] wasts, she grows discreet,
> Till Midnight never shows her Head;
> So rotting Celia stroles the Street
> When sober Folks are all a-bed.
>
> (101–4)

A literary commonplace is defamiliarized by its reformulation in unsavory terms and by the reversal of the traditional tenor and vehicle. When idealistic language is Swift's target, he often mixes it with a vulgar idiom to emphasize its inappropriateness to the world of actuality. "Can *Chloe,* heav'nly *Chloe* piss" is oxymoronic in its combination of the romantically inflated idea of the beloved with the rudest word available to describe her function—one that would never be alluded to in a typical idealized portrait of a woman. In "A PASTORAL Dialogue" Swift's *nymph* and *swain* are Irish peasants whose matter-of-fact exchange of romantic vows in earthy metaphors points up the incompatibility of high-flown language

with their reality:"My Spud these Nettles from the Stones
can part, / No Knife so keen to weed thee from my Heart"
(11–12). In all of these instances Swift foregrounds the
verbal clash so that we are more conscious of linguistic
than material anomalies.

The same techniques are used in Swift's response to
Dean Smedley's *"EPISTLE to his Grace the Duke of
GRAFTON,"* addressed to the Lord Lieutenant of Ireland
in the hope of obtaining a more comfortable living. Smedley's fawning petition is quaintly phrased in an artificial
pastoral diction:

> But where shall *SMEDLEY* make his Nest,
> And lay his wandring Head to rest?
> Where shall he find a decent House,
> To treat his Friends, and chear his Spouse?
> Oh! *Tack,* my Lord, some pretty Cure,
> In wholesome Soil, and AEther pure.
>
> (27–32)[9]

Swift's exasperation with this cloying language is emphasized by the "Answer's" pointed italicizing of the offending words found in Smedley's poem:

> Talk not of *making of thy Nest,*
> *Ah never lay thy Head to Rest!*
> . . . .
> Down to your *Deanery* repair
> And build *a Castle in the Air.*
> I'm sure a Man of your fine Sense
> Can do it with a Small Expence.
> There your *Dear Spouse* and you together
> May breathe your Bellies full of *AEther.*
> ("His Grace's Answer to Jonathan," 13–14, 19–24)

Bellies crudely obtrudes the body into the pastoral world
of Smedley's prettified and artificial diction. In addition to
puncturing the overrefinement of such language, Swift's
poem extravagantly expands Smedley's suggestions, both

to expose their underlying presumptuousness and to emphasize their linguistic affectation. The abstract *AEther
pure* is transformed into the ludicrous specific image of
Smedley and spouse breathing deeply in unison to fill
themselves up with "AEther." If Smedley wants "AEther,"
Swift will give it to him in abundance—a castle in the air,
stars surrounding him, and finally, a mock-heroic transformation of himself and spouse into a new sun and moon.
Swift thereby implies that Smedley's overblown language is
suited only to a verbal fantasy that makes no claim to being
a picture of the real world.

When Patrick Delany made an appeal similar to Smedley's, Swift's censure was blunt: "Be Modest: nor Address
your Betters / With Begging, Vain, Familiar Letters" ("An
Epistle upon an Epistle," 117–18). Such a comment could
be applied to Smedley's epistle equally well if Swift were
more interested in bad manners than bad diction, but he is
clearly more exercised by the absurdity of Smedley's
idiom.[10] This tends to be the case in those poems whose real
subject is metalinguistic. There is an instance of culpable
action that provides the poetic occasion—Smedley did
write a fawning plea for preferment—but the satiric energy
is directed against a perceived violation of language.

Another poem in which a real event is not so much
described in language as eclipsed by it is the "Quibbling
Elegy on the Worshipful Judge *Boat.*" Although the poem
is one of Swift's satirical elegies, it is predicated as much
upon the linguistic fact of the judge's name as the event of
his death. For forty-four lines Swift's "quibbling"[11] explores
the possibilities of meaning in the conjunction of two labels
identifying the deceased, *judge* and *boat*. Swift nowhere
abandons the metaphor of the judge's name; rather, he
abolishes it. In a number of ingenious ways the man is fitted
to the thing so completely that Boat is reduced from proper
to common noun. First treated as having the usual accou-
trements and characteristics of boats—anchor, canvas,
ballast, lading—the judge is disassembled in the poem's
climactic image: the planks of the defunct boat are salvaged

to construct a gallows. Transformed from the human agent to the mechanical means, he can continue to expedite souls to hell. When the metaphor doesn't work exactly, Swift calls attention to it and then uses it anyway; this is part of the posture of insouciant extravagance: "A Post so fill'd, on Nature's Laws entrenches; / *Benches* on *Boats* are plac't, not *Boats* on *Benches*" (11–12). By developing name and profession into a linguistic offense, Swift introduces his theme of the disparity between the concept of judge and this particular judge. The semantic anomaly in the coupling of *boat* and *judge* is made more emphatic by Swift's assertion that it is an accurate reflection of reality: "*A* Boat *a Judge! yes, where's the Blunder? / A* wooden *Judge is no such Wonder*" (39–40). This might be called depersonification—the poet insists that there is actually no metaphor and no anomaly; the woodenness of the judge obliterates the distinction between animate and inanimate, and the state of the judiciary transforms a wonder into a commonplace.

Language is both technique and subject in the "Quibbling Elegy." Underlying the witty extended metaphor is a probing of the gulf between labels and the realities they supposedly point to. *Boat* and boat should be separate and unmistakable entities, but Swift is able to suit the description of boat-as-thing to the person named Boat and nullify the difference between them. In the process some ordinary connotations of the noun *judge*, judicial expertise and general humanness, are contravened by the properties of wood attributed to Judge Boat.

The persistent literalization of a metaphor also structures "The Description of a Salamander," but the issue of naming is overtly raised rather than implied. The poem opens with a disarming preamble on the practice of using human names for pet animals and animal names for humans. Much like *A Modest Proposal*, the poem claims a stance of dispassionate exposition: the matter-of-fact tone of the prologue suggests that the poet is a neutral observer, only telling us what we already know and accept without question. Although the common practice of naming dogs after heroes may beguile us into overlooking the differences between mastiffs and Caesars, such violations of order should always be suspect in Swift. The next example is a shade more pointed: tame birds given "Christian Nick-names like a Child" is an offense to religion as well as a failure to distinguish between what is due a jackdaw and a child.

The light expository prologue and the invocation of Pliny as a scientific authority are intended to disarm: in contrast to the pretended stance of uninvolved objectivity the venom of the satiric comparison between man and salamander comes as a shock. According to its controlling fiction that the metaphoric application is equally scientific, the poem methodically works through the points of Pliny's account: pseudo-naturalistic description of the reptile alternates with a similarly mock-scientific invective whose dispassionate voice is at variance with the harshness of the satire. Here, as in other metalinguistic poems, Swift exploits verbal incongruities: the neutral terminology of scientific description takes on some of the coloring of the satiric attack, which in turn is advanced under the aegis of impartial description. In the transmutation of "loathsom Spots his Body stain" into "All stain'd with Infamy and Vice," the word the two lines share conflates their sense into "his Body all stain'd with loathsom Spots of Infamy and Vice." This process is devastatingly effective in the ultimate point of comparison:

> And should some Nymph who ne'er was cruel,
> Like *Carleton* cheap, or fam'd *Duruel*
> Receive the Filth which he ejects,
> She soon would find, the same Effects,
> Her tainted Carcase to pursue,
> As from the *Salamander's* Spue.
>
> (61–66)

The clinically restrained description of the salamander's poisonous discharge expands through the repetition of *filth* and *spue* to participate in the image of venereal disease.[12]

In the final line Pliny's description is expanded to include the maximum of physical horror: *leprosy* is reiterated and then surpassed by *Pox,* which also caps Swift's portrait of moral degeneracy as well.

With the mocking refrain the poem circles back to its beginning, where Swift had invoked an audience of by-standers to judge his application of Pliny:

> *Then I'll appeal to each By-stander,*
> *Whether this ben't a* Salamander.

> (69–70)

The speaker's voice retreats behind the mask of scientific objectivity with its triumphant rhetorical question, but through its very success, Swift's powerful act of definition tends to obscure the issue that the technique raises, the abuse of language that allows *salamander* to become a heroic epithet for a man. Swift shows us that it can be similarly manipulated to become an epithet of satire.[13]

Another example of ironic disjunction between word and meaning is Swift's parodic translation, *"Whitshed's* Motto on his Coach,"* a demonstration of the Orwellian thesis that language can be corrupted by politics.[14] Although dialogue form is not observed, the poem is an exchange between two speakers, the second of whom is Judge Whitshed. The first speaker refuses to believe that the "Fine Words" *Libertas* & *natale Solum* could serve as the motto for an evil judge. Whitshed then justifies their use by translating the motto in such a way that the high-sounding abstractions are transformed into truths a self-serving man can live by: "native country" shrinks to "my estate" and liberty expands to license. From the opening statement of the motto to the concluding repetition of it, the words have been so radically redefined that the first speaker can now agree that the motto suits the man. At the same time he continues to maintain that the words were stolen, that is, perverted from their true meaning. Thus, in addition to the offenses enumerated in the "translation," Whitshed is guilty of a crime against language itself.

As is so often the case in Swift's poetry, the juxtapositions created by rhyme in "Whitshed's Motto" are pointedly satiric. Most of the rhyming pairs clash ironically:

> They swear I am so kind and good,
> I hug them till I squeeze their Blood.

> And, secondly, to shew my Fury
> Against an uncomplying Jury.

> Now, since your Motto thus you construe,
> I must confess you've spoken once true.
> (9–10, 13–14, 23–24)

Whitshed's proof of his goodness is one of Swift's ironically literalized metaphors: figuratively squeezing the tenants' blood becomes the physical hugging of affection. *Fury/jury* is another ironic pair, but is of less significance than the last example, the first speaker's acknowledgment that Whitshed is right. For *true* to be coupled with *construe* is a climactic irony; the construction Whitshed has given the motto is true only within the private verbal universe he has brought into being to justify the enormities of his conduct.

This same kind of linguistic deception, the Humpty-Dumpty logic that words mean whatever the speaker chooses them to mean, is treated as a political strategy in *"On the Words—Brother Protestants, and Fellow Christians, so familiarly used by the Advocates for the Repeal of the* Test Act *in Ireland, 1733."* The poem's opening scene, a barnyard inundation, expresses Swift's vision of the body politic as a space where "Things of heterogeneous Kind / Together float . . ." (4–5). Where there is physical contiguity, as in all of the subsequently offered examples, language must preserve distinctions. The poem argues against the obliteration of such distinctions, a process Swift attributes to inferior groups who seek to identify themselves with their superiors by appropriating desirable labels. In the initial series of simple examples the false relation of the label to what it designates is directly apparent: "Thus all the Footmen, Shoe-boys, Porters, / About *St. James*'s, cry, *We Courtiers*" (21–22). More complicated relations between signified and signifier follow. Swift's enemy of long standing, Richard Bettesworth, knows nothing of his profession, but nevertheless addresses Singleton as "Brother Serjeant." Since both men are sergeants, the linguistic fault is more subtle than the outright lie of a footman calling himself a courtier. In this case the umbrella of the rubric *sergeant* extends over individual instances of varying worth; the label fails to indicate differences in quality. While Bettesworth may rightfully call himself a sergeant, the title assumes a competence that he—like Judge Boat—does not have. This same discrepancy between an ideal of definition and the actuality also applies to Swift's central example, the labeling of religious dissenters:

> And thus Fanatic Saints, tho' neither in
> Doctrine, or Discipline our Brethren,
> Are *Brother Protestants and Christians,*
> As much as *Hebrews* and *Philistines.*
>
> (29–32)

Here, too, there is a possible basis for calling these sects Protestant and Christian, but Swift asserts the greater importance of their differences. Because of their beliefs, Swift maintains, they are not ideal Protestants and Christians (any more than Bettesworth is an ideal sergeant). Lice suck our blood and maggots invade our bodies, the poem continues, without our confounding their identity with our own. Clearly, the line of demarcation between species is more easily drawn than between kinds of men, but it is to the advantage of Swift's argument to insist that both are valid discriminations: linguistic precision should reflect meaningful differences.

"On Dreams" explores the opposite process at work in language, the false separation of men and their actions by labels that enforce a spurious differentiation. Just as *"On the Words* Brother Protestants" questions the validity of the labeling process in terms of blurring valid distinctions, "On Dreams" questions it in terms of setting up misleading categories. By yoking together labels that are widely separated in meaning, the poem exposes a basic identity underlying artificial distinctions of language:

> Orphans around his Bed the Lawyer sees,
> And takes the Plaintiff's and Defendant's Fees.
> His Fellow Pick-Purse, watching for a Job,
> Fancies his Fingers in the Cully's Fob.
>
> (23–26)

Both the lawyer and the pickpurse are thieves, but one has a criminal, the other a respectable label. Just as the lawyer's actions blur the distinction between plaintiff and defendant, so the poet assimilates the lawyer to a common pickpocket; similar pairings reveal that the tyrant is a murderer, the soldier a butcher, the divine a mountebank.

In this satiric emphasis Swift's imitation differs strikingly from the original. Swift follows Petronius in presenting the self as inescapable in dreams, but Petronius simply shows a seemingly random cross-section of society, whose dreams range from routine activities to catastrophe: "The hunter flushes the woodland with his hounds. / The sailor dreams he is doomed."[15] Swift's examples are arranged according to a pattern: the first couplet in a quatrain describes a professional figure while the second shows his lower class counterpart. The process of coupling brings down the socially higher figures to the level of the lower—soldier/butcher, senator/scavenger—and conversely, makes the lowly appear relatively innocuous in comparison with their grander equivalents:

> The Statesman rakes the Town to find a Plot,
> And dreams of Forfeitures by Treason got.
> Nor less Tom-Turd-Man of true Statesman mold,
> Collects the City Filth in search of Gold.
>
> (19–22)

Treason can be turned to profit for the Statesman; Tom-Turd-Man's scavenging for discarded valuables is equally self-interested but lacks the harmful potential of the plots the statesman hopes to discover. The poem probes conventional definitions in two ways: revealing the statesman's selfish interest in treason undermines the positive connotations of the word from one direction, while pairing it with "Tom-Turd-Man" diminishes the positive image of the statesman from another. The syntax and vocabulary make the comparison emphatic: "Nor less Tom-Turd-Man of true Statesman mold." "On Dreams" invites us to contemplate once again an abyss of deception between words and the realities they stand for.

In keeping with Swift's satiric bent for discovering widening circles of corruption, "The Place of the Damned" shows a dishonest split between language and reality to be characteristic of the language we all use. This time Swift has not taken his occasion from a particular practitioner like Whitshed or a specific example of language abuse such as he found in the movement to identify Dissenters as "brother Protestants." Instead, he focuses upon general usage. The poem's announced purpose is to define the location of hell "by *Logical* Rule." Since, by the poet's definition, hell is wherever the damned are, the body of the poem is an incantatory naming of those who qualify:

> Damn'd *Lawyers* and *Judges,* Damn'd *Lords* and Damn'd
>   *Squires,*
> Damn'd *Spies* and *Informers,* Damn'd *Friends* and
>   Damn'd *Lyars.*
>
> (9–10)

These abstract categories indict flesh-and-blood realities less than the language used to establish such categories. To couple *Friends* with *Spies, Informers,* and *Lyars* is to strip it of positive connotations and provoke a reassessment of the word itself. This proximity suggests that the ordinary meaning of friends can be a hypocritical cloak for the same kinds of evil plainly indicated by the other terms, while the blanket condemnation of lawyers, judges, lords, and squires implies that every positive or neutral label potentially masks corruption. More compelling than the use of language to effect a satiric purpose is the satiric questioning of language itself: going beyond the pointing out of certain kinds of malefactors, the poem reveals a serious breakdown of the labeling process.

In spite of the widespread misuse of language Swift discovers and satirizes, he remains convinced of a primal linguistic integrity. His precepts about usage, his *Proposal for Correcting, Improving, and Ascertaining the English Tongue,* and his definition of style as "proper words in proper places" all bespeak a confidence in the ability of language to be a precise instrument of communication. Swift also expresses a faith in the importance of individual effort similar to that of George Orwell, who ends his essay "Politics and the English Language" with the supposition that some improvement will result if "you simplify your English."[16] In the same vein Swift writes to the Vice-Provost of Trinity College:

> I quarrell . . . with all writers and many of your Preachers, for their careless incorrect and improper Style, which they contract by reading the Scribblers from England, where an abominable Tast is every day prevayling. It is your business who are coming into the World to put a stop to these Corruptions; and recovr that simplicity which in every thing of value ought chiefly to be followed."[17]

Literary Disorder

Swift's satirizing of literary genres and conventions is based upon the same principle that informs his attacks on linguistic abuses—not a total abjuration of poetry but a disavowal of what is inaccurate and deceptive.[18] That certain literary forms intentionally portray an ideal world is not germane; regardless of rationale, Swift dislikes all gilding of the lily. It is not so much that he delighted "to go through the whole realm of poetry, turning everything upside down,"[19] although the element of delight is there. What Swift intends is to set things right side up that have been traditionally accepted upside down. He thus explodes romantic conventions, fills noble forms with vulgar contents, and fashions dazzling heroines whose bodies, dramatically presented as filthy and disease-ridden or merely subject to natural functions, expose the fraudulence of their representation in poetry as nymphs and goddesses.

Swift's mockeries of poetic genres bring together a form and a content that depend upon different assumptions about the nature of reality. One way in which satiric humor is generated is by the clash of an elevated, idealistic form with a banal and down-to-earth subject. Although Swift could praise eloquently, he mistrusted the conventional forms of praise in poetry. As he wrote to Thomas Beach, an aspiring writer, "I have seen fewer good panegyrics than any other sort of writing, especially in verse."[20] Swift's own panegyrics are libels, his elegies witty celebrations of the passing of unadmirable men. Both the obvious staleness of the vocabulary of grief brought into the elegy on Marlborough, and the repeated abandonment of the panegyric intention in the early odes, reflect Swift's feeling that panegyric and elegy are inherently excessive, demanding unrealistic perfection and immoderate, potentially insincere sentiments. His own strong preference for restraint in the public expression of feelings of any sort and his equation of extravagant emotional display with affectation made Swift uncomfortable with the poetry of praise or grief.[21]

If the failure of the early odes indirectly suggests that panegyric is a difficult and unappealing genre for Swift, the successful satirical elegies on deceased unworthies provide a more overt criticism. Behind the attack on a literary form whose conventions foster insincerity and exaggeration is an assertion that even in death the unadmirable should be truthfully confronted and unsparingly judged. When the propriety of his attack on Whitshed was questioned, Swift defended the principle vigorously: "If an ill Man be alive, and in Power, we dare not attack him; and if he be weary of the World and of his own Villainies, he has nothing to do but die, and then his Reputation is safe. For, these excellent Casuists know just *Latin* enough, to have heard a most foolish Precept, that *de mortuis nil nisi bonum.*"[22] Truth demands holding the dead accountable for their evils. As Swift further insisted: "Yet, although their Memories will *rot,* there may be some Benefit for their Survivers, to smell it while it is *rotting.*"[23]

This principle could produce harshly critical portraits, but the dominant literary motive of Swift's anti-elegies turns the satiric energy against the genre more than the subject. Of the five satirical elegies Swift wrote,[24] all are "quibbling," as the poem on Judge Boat is styled: all ring changes on a central metaphor or body of conventional poetic language. Two of Swift's victims, Partridge the astrologer and Dicky, are ridiculed but not sharply satirized. The poet obviously regards two others, Demar and Boat, with disfavor, but the verbal games played with the ruling passion of the one and the name of the other envelop and eclipse the men who furnish the poetic occasion. They exist for us as unindividualized types, the miser and the hanging judge. In all of these poems the element of verbal play overshadows the satiric castigation of the subject.

In the "Satirical Elegy on the Death of a Late Famous General" the satire is instead divided equally between subject and genre. Unlike the other elegies, it contains no fun; even the irreverence (" 'Twas time in conscience he should die") is made part of the solemn criticism of the man and of the elegiac clichés Swift methodically negates. Rather than a single unifying idea or image, the "Satirical Elegy" draws a general picture of unworthiness by constantly questioning its subject's ability to live up to the honors conferred upon him.[25] A context of positive values is explicitly invoked by such terms as "his grace," "mighty Warrior," "Honours," "widow's sighs," and "orphan's tears." These elegiac clichés function ironically, but they also stand as a measure of Marlborough's failure. In each case the idea embodied in the language is seen to be inapplicable to the general; the trappings of power and prestige conceal an inner emptiness. "His Grace" in the first line is countered by "how very mean a thing's a Duke" in line 30; the "honours" of line 22 become the "ill got honours" of line 31. The "mighty Warrior" dies ingloriously in his bed of unromantic old age, and the lamentations of widow and child that might normally follow his hearse have already been unnaturally evoked by his conquests. In the face of this void, the satirist inverts the conventional sentiment of the elegist: "This world he cumber'd long enough"(13). The lesson to be drawn from Marlborough's death is not the general message of human impotence in the face of death or the vanity of all things, but a warning to those who have risen by favor rather than by merit:

> Let pride be taught by this rebuke,
> How very mean a thing's a Duke;
> From all his ill-got honours flung,
> Turn'd to that dirt from whence he sprung.
>
> (29–32)

Each line undercuts some positive quality: pride is rebuked, a Duke exposed as a mean thing, the man sharply separated from his unearned emoluments by the violence of "flung." Finally, the culminating blow in this process is the reduction of the great man, stripped of the badges of rank enumerated above, to the meanness of dirt. Swift's last line changes the gentle biblical phrase into an ugly and more vivid image. Rather than the universal human cycle of "dust unto dust," the return to dirt is the specific case of the king's favorite, whose undeserved elevation from obscurity is a violation of order—a great man should not spring from the lowliness and uncleanliness of dirt.

Like the satirical elegies Swift's best known anti-pastorals, "A Description of the Morning" and "A Description of a City Shower," probe the weakness of conventional ways of ordering experience. In both cases the word *description* in the title calls attention to a purpose of naturalistic observation at variance with the unreality of the pastoral vision,[26] and in fact the density and specificity of the particulars of each description are what provoke interest.

The title "A Description of the Morning" sets up pastoral expectations that are immediately rebuked by the first-line revelation of the urban setting. After the announcement of the "Ruddy Morns Approach," the description is carefully restricted to human activities. All strata of the urban population find their way into the poem, often paired symbiotically: Betty and her master, the apprentice and his, a lord and his duns, the turnkey and his flock (of prisoners rather than sheep). Two of the relationships are immoral, but the impression of the whole is one of routine—the ordinary, trivial, repetitious rituals of morning in the city.

The presentation is conspicuously low-keyed and restrained: Moll does not whirl a filthy mop; Betty, unlike other loose ladies in Swift's poetry, is not gummy-eyed and stinking. The Prentice, Moll, the youth, the Small-coal man, the Chimney-Sweep, are ordinary members of the working class who hardly exemplify Marius Bewley's severe contention that the poem "cleverly presents us with Swift's prejudice that man is a very mean creature."[27] F. W. Bateson's is an even more excessive response to what Swift gives us: "The amoral urban automata once seen in their true light, *must* become objects of contempt."[28] We may assume that menial and routinized work is mechanical and devoid of human contact or personal satisfaction, but the poem does not say so or even hint at it. The one flagrant example of public disorder and wrongdoing, the connivance of a representative of the law with thieves, is positioned so as to constitute simply another item on a list that enumerates without classifying. After the motion and noise of the workers beginning the day, the poem winds down anticlimactically: the activity of the thieves presumably ends with the coming of morning, the bailiffs stand silently, the schoolboys lag.

Swift's refusal to arrange the examples in some way that we could recognize as meaningful order emphasizes the importance of straightforward description to the poem, but it also obliquely conveys a judgment. Not the strong condemnation of disorder that Bewley and Bateson find or an attack on London, but instead the poem shows a smooth-running mechanism in which corrupt elements, indicative of societal disorder, contribute to the same superficial order of the morning routine that the honest and harmless are caught up in. The very commonplaceness of the turnkey/thief relationship—inserted among examples of people performing in legitimate roles reveals the city's failure to make effective moral judgments (it has, of course, made an ineffective one by putting the thieves in prison) and its ability not merely to tolerate disorder but to routinize it into a "mock order."[29] By strictly adhering to neutral description the poem stresses the assimilation of all activities into a pragmatic pattern devoid of any meaning beyond its capacity to function efficiently. If this machinery is at variance with the promise of "Ruddy Morns Approach," it nevertheless ironically achieves the pastoral ideal of harmony between man and milieu.

The longer "Description of a City Shower" does utilize the unsavory and displeasing. Where the coming of morning in the first poem provides the principle of order for the human activities described, the rainstorm disrupts the life of the city and turns its order into confusion. Rather than serving as a focal point for a routine, it enforces departures from routine and hierarchy that in turn create a temporary new order:

Here various Kinds by various Fortunes led,
Commence Acquaintance underneath a Shed.
Triumphant Tories, and desponding Whigs,
Forget their Fewds, and join to save their Wigs.

(39–42)

The difference between streets and neighborhoods, the
order that man has imposed upon the land, is also overrid-
den by the storm. Driven from all parts to merge in one
huge stream, the garbage of the city is memorably item-
ized:

Sweepings from Butchers Stalls, Dung, Guts, and Blood,
Drown'd Puppies, stinking Sprats, all drench'd in Mud,
Dead Cats and Turnip-Tops come tumbling down the
Flood.

(61–63)

Swift's note calls attention to his purpose of parodying the
triplet and alexandrine, but the parody of form is itself
swept before the flood of particulars that Swift has arranged so effectively. Instead of ridiculous, the devices
seem entirely appropriate to express this irresistible del-
uge. Here, too, pastoral expectations are ironically ful-
filled by what Ralph Cohen has felicitously called "a
harmony of garbage."[30]
   Brendan O Hehir, who explores the affinities between
Swift's cloudburst and a number of other literary storms,
sees the shower as a pronouncement of "cathartic doom
upon the corruption of the city."[31] When applied to the
data Swift gives us, the judgment seems overly harsh. The
city depicted in the poem is banal and dirty rather than
corrupt; "brisk Susan," the "needy Poet," the "dagled
Females," and Swift's other city denizens are innocuous
little people;[32] the refuse of the city is unpleasant but not
evil, and not even markedly urban—butcher's sweepings,

dead animals, turnip-tops would be just as suited to a rural setting. What notably differentiates Swift's milieu from the pastoral predecessors he draws upon is the typically urban profusion of things and activities, illustrative of triviality rather than simplicity, and—O Hehir notwithstanding—the complete absence of catharsis. The sense of rain as life-giving, revitalizing, or cleansing is completely absent; on the contrary, the shower drowns puppies and cats, spoils the poet's only coat, and distributes over everything a dirty mixture of water and dust. The parody of form is ultimately controlling, so that we are made vividly aware of how unsuited the pastoral design is to the realities of urban experience. The city can ill accommodate a cloudburst.

Metamorphosis

As Denis Donoghue describes Swift, "No writer in English literature is less exhilarated by the possibilities of growth, expansion, enlargement or range."[33] All of the phenomena cited by Donoghue are kinds of change, and the philosophically conservative Swift resisted change in most areas. He upheld the position of the Church of England as a state religion and favored the Test Act and other laws directed against Dissenters; he defended the ancients against the moderns; and he earnestly addressed the prime minister with a proposal for fixating the English language. Not surprisingly, Swift's poetry also reflects this concern: poems on a variety of subjects represent the process of metamorphosis as consistently negative, a way of reducing the greater to the lesser and blurring important distinctions between true and false, value and disvalue, appearance and reality.

Like the elegy and the pastoral, in Swift's hands the Ovidian metamorphosis becomes an inappropriate container for a mundane reality whose lack of transcendent significance makes the supernatural paraphernalia ludicrous and mechanical. Swift's version of "Baucis and Philemon" thus keeps the basic narrative of Ovid but comically alters everything else. As an extravagant verbal fantasy causes the classical form to recede into irrelevance and foolishness, attention shifts to the immediacy and vivid particularization of ordinary rural scenes and characters.

Swift replaces the serious and dignified tone and diction of the original, preserved by Golding and Dryden in their versions of the myth, with the informal and colloquial. As part of the process of stripping away the moral, the couple's much-admired piety and conjugal affection disappear almost entirely. Philemon's wish to become a churchman, for example, springs from worldly motives rather than a desire to serve God: "I'm Old, and fain wou'd live at Ease,/Make me the *Parson,* if you please" (115–16).[34] While Swift completely omits Philemon's speech on his and Baucis's mutual devotion and greatly reduces the ritual of hospitality, so much so that the meal is comically hurried, he expands other portions of the episode. Following Ovid, Golding and Dryden perfunctorily report that the gods tried a thousand homes and found a thousand doors closed against them. In Swift's manuscript version the rejection becomes a full-blown scene, detailed with relish and wonderfully excessive. Swift provides physical infirmities and a drenching rain to discomfort his saints, who make bathetic appeals suggestive of Chaucerian religious con men. In response, the churlish villagers threaten them with piss pot and stick and a good deal of indignant invective. Addison's influence eliminated all of this fun and changed the poem's beginning to the same kind of brief general report found in Ovid.[35] The essential Swiftian flavor happily survives, but Addison's alterations move the poem back in the direction of Dryden—hardly what Swift originally intended or where his own talents lay.

The other major expansion serves to ridicule Ovidian metamorphosis by applying it everywhere. Creating witty correspondences between past and present identities, Swift transforms the house, part by part, into a church:

> A Bedstead of the Antique Mode,
> Compact of Timber many a Load,
> Such as our Ancestors did use,
> Was Metamorphos'd into Pews;
> Which still their antient Nature keep;
> By lodging Folks dispos'd to Sleep.
>
> (101–6)

The muted satiric note is characteristic of Swift's treatment of the church throughout the poem. For the transformation of Baucis and Philemon into parson and dame, another instance of gratuitous metamorphosis on Swift's part, the same meticulous degree of detail is supplied. Here the process is laughably ordinary rather than supernatural—a change of clothing serves to transform the poor cottager into a churchman.

Once changed into trees, Baucis and Philemon do not survive to become garlanded moral exempla as they do in the classical fable and its faithful imitators. They come to a prosaic end like the trees they are:

> Here *Baucis*, there *Philemon* grew.
> Till once, a Parson of our Town,
> To mend his Barn, cut *Baucis* down;
> At which, 'tis hard to be believ'd,
> How much the other Tree was griev'd,
> Grew Scrubby, dy'd a-top, was stunted:
> So, the next Parson stub'd and burnt it.
>
> (172–78)

The yews are first referred to as "Baucis" and "Philemon," then it is "Baucis" who is cut down, but the final reference is to "the other Tree," a pointed reminder that calling trees Baucis and Philemon is silliness.[36] There is an abruptness in "stub'd and burnt it,"[37] but this is a comic rather than a serious denouement; the terse realistic description, coupled with the sly insinuation " 'tis hard to be believ'd," works to discredit the heroic myth and its supernatural machinery. In reality these are trees, and the poet insists upon treating them as such.

This same mockery of supernatural metamorphosis also figures in "His Grace's Answer to Jonathan," where Swift imagines Jonathan Smedley and wife translated to the firmament as a new sun and moon, and "An ELEGY on Mr. *PATRIGE,*" which places the astrologer among the stars. In both poems Swift uses supernatural metamorphosis as an occasion for witty invention. Smedley's fanciful language in his *"EPISTLE to his Grace, the Duke of* Grafton"—his calling for "AEther pure"—provokes Swift to be equally extravagant, to apotheosize Smedley. The anomalous pair of trades practiced by Partridge, cobbling and astrology, is similarly provocative:

> Thou, high-exalted in thy Sphere,
> May'st follow still thy Calling there.
> To thee the *Bull* will lend his *Hide,*
> By *Phoebus* newly Tann'd and Dry'd.
> For thee they Argo's Hulk will Tax,
> And scrape her Pitchy Sides for *Wax.*
>
> (73–78)

This is Swift at his most playful, creating an autonomous world of words that makes no claim to be an image of reality. The fantasy of supernatural metamorphosis can be treated gently because it exists only in the world of literature. Unlike Wood's Patent and the Irish Senate, it has no substance in reality and thus poses no threat.

Swift finds an arresting image of real metamorphosis in the ruins of Whitehall made into a private house by the playwright John Vanbrugh. The excessive interest he takes in this event—the subject of two poems, one of which exists in two distinct versions[38]—suggests that the transformation of noble ruins into an inferior structure strikes Swift as an emblematic violation of order. Ronald

Paulson writes that "the metaphor of a house or building of some kind is common in the poems that deal with permanence and transience."[39] This is true, but the image of the transformed palace in the Vanbrugh poems is a special case. Unlike the other examples Paulson cites, Whitehall is a real building with established associations of value that acquire further meaning in Swift's poetic context. Specifically, in these poems this event becomes a symbol of modern presumption and a metaphor for literary disorder, the palace of art pulled down and made into modern rhymes. Swift is disturbed not only by change, which he invariably regards as decline,[40] but by the temerity and self-delusion that misappropriate the noble artifacts of the past. While things of value are wrongly diminished or destroyed, the unworthy is inflated. Vanbrugh is an anti-Renaissance man who can do nothing well, but makes grandiose attempts that are heralded as achievements by other mediocrities.[41]

The two versions of "Vanbrug's House," both with the explicit subtitle statement that it was built from the ruins of the burnt Whitehall, exploit different aspects of the metamorphosis. Although in both treatments Vanbrugh represents modern mediocrity, the shorter manuscript poem directs most of its attention to a general group of "modern Rhymers," while the revised poem focuses on Vanbrugh himself. Each poem begins by setting forth a former correspondence, suggested by the myth of Amphion, between the classical hierarchy of poetic genre and kinds or parts of buildings:[42]

> Each Number had it's diff'rent Power;
> Heroick Strains could build a Tower;
> Sonnets and Elegyes to Chloris
> Would raise a House about two Storyes;
> A Lyrick Ode would Slate; a Catch
> Would Tile; an Epigram would Thatch.
>
> (manuscript poem, 7–12)

Beneath the tongue-in-cheek literalism that renders the idea ludicrous, much as it does in "Baucis and Philemon," the latent content of the myth asserts that poetry was once a source of power and a respected calling, one that could be gainful, that is, translated into material sustenance. Now the two have become separated; the poet is cut off from genuine inspiration and from tangible recompense.

In the manuscript poem the myth is linked to an insect metaphor by the motif of undesirable proliferation and consequent mediocrity invading the realm of art. The "numerous Race" of poets is reductively transformed into "Broods of Insect Poets," reminiscent of the "swarms of gnats" in Swift's early "Ode to Congreve" and presaging later equations of scribblers to vermin in his poetry.[43] The worm that "consumes it self to weave a Cell" is also kin to the bragging spider in *The Battle of the Books:* "This large Castle . . . is all built with my own Hands, and the Materials extracted altogether out of my own Person."[44] Self-delusion, which mistakes false art for true, unites the poet's insubstantial castles of air with the worm's awkward wings, the scribbler's ill-spun play, the spider's flimsy web, and ultimately with Vanbrugh's house. The bee in *The Battle of the Books,* whose wings and voice are genuine gifts from heaven, is the antithesis of the insect playwright who, "bourne on fancy's Pinions, thinks / He soars sublimest when he Sinks" (51–52).

The house itself, when Swift finally turns to it halfway through the poem, is ridiculously small, the culminating illustration of the downward spiral of metamorphosis.[45] Whitehall, the Phoenix, "Animals of largest Size," and "the Poetry of Ages past" still stand for worth and grandeur, but they themselves have been debased or destroyed. In one metamorphosis after another order becomes disorder, the greater becomes the lesser, the valuable becomes the worthless. And in each case an accompanying delusion has engendered a pride that conceals from the agent the reality of nonachievement. So chemists "boast" of their power to produce some faint resemblance of a flower from its ashes, modern poets "wisely" overthrow the poetry of the past, and Vanbrugh rejoices in his equal skill as poet and builder.[46]

The second and published version of "Vanbrug's House" proceeds from the same general introduction of the manuscript poem directly to the illustration of poetic building furnished by Vanbrugh.[47] Having eliminated the middle term of insect imagery, Swift vividly develops his representative instance rather than creating a large background of analogous follies. The second poem's emphasis on Vanbrugh, the agent of change, provides more particulars than the manuscript version (such as the pertinent information that the playwright plagiarized from a French play) and also heightens effects that were realized only obliquely in the earlier treatment. Where Vanbrugh's hubris had to be inferred before, it now takes the form of a presumptuous speech that conflates the prayer to the gods and the hero's boast of epic poetry. Vanbrugh intends that his edifice will equal Whitehall, but insincerity and lack of talent can produce nothing admirable.

The duplication of Vanbrugh's self-delusion in the poets who gather to admire his "palace" (undoubtedly the same "insect Poets" of the manuscript poem) balances the opening picture of true poets and valid achievement—or, typical of the satiric perspective, overbalances it. Right relation existed only in the past, like the symbols of value held up by the poem: Whitehall is burnt, the Phoenix is mythically remote, large animals are corrupted to vermin, and ancient poetry is a looted rubbish heap. The present, on the other hand, is characterized by the process of reductive metamorphosis in all areas: architecture, chemistry, nature, and—above all—poetry.

"The History of Vanbrug's House" focuses on a single aspect of the more complex "Vanbrug's House" poems, the arrogance of the unskilled poet/builder in undertaking a work of magnitude: "Van's Genius without Thought or Lecture / Is hugely turnd to Architecture" (7–8). "Hugely" reverberates throughout the poem as an accurate ironic measure of Vanbrugh's self-delusion. Everything is appropriately miniaturized: his aspiration is based not on real buildings, but on play structures made by children out of cards and clay. When Vanbrugh does construct his house, it is not an imposing edifice but a "monstrous Pile," an embodiment of the negative meanings of the words: "monstrous" because it has no proper form and thus no place in the hierarchy of things, "pile" in the less usual sense of a heap or jumble.[48] By modern standards Vanbrugh is assimilated to Vitruvius, a man of pretensions equated with a genius.

Although the tone of "The History of Vanbrug's House" is consistently playful, the implications of the conclusion are ominous: "We might expect to find next Year / A Mousetrap-man chief Engineer" (47–48). The "Mousetrap-man" is the only example of the reductive animal imagery so noticeable in the two versions of the other poem, but here it stresses the inconsequentiality of vermin rather than their loathsomeness. The transformation of things of value into the small and insignificant (Whitehall shrunk into Vanbrugh's house) is paralleled by the elevation of the trivial. More fearful than the simple eclipse or disappearance of value is its metamorphosis into its opposite, with an ensuing confusion of true and false. For Swift, the Ovidian metamorphosis is merely a foolish example of literary disorder, deserving of burlesque, while the real metamorphosis of palace ruins into monstrous pile is a powerful emblem of the pervasive modern attitude that threatens value in every sphere. Vanbrugh himself is a curiously familiar figure—the realistically inept protagonist of so much recent literature, a representative of the uninspired average who, in Swift's view, stood ready to overwhelm the few men of genius produced by any age.

Concluding his poem "To Stella, Visiting me in my Sickness," Swift returns to the image of the transformed palace to warn Stella that she should not endanger her own life by ministering to his:

> Best Pattern of true Friends, beware;
> You pay too dearly for your Care;
> If, while your Tenderness secures

> My Life, it must endanger yours.
> For such a Fool was never found,
> Who pull'd a Palace to the Ground,
> Only to have the Ruins made
> Materials for an House decay'd.
>
> (117–24)

As object of the action, Stella undergoes several changes from palace to ruins to materials for a house decayed. Each stage of the transformation is a further descent and more of a loss of identity: from an imposing edifice to ruins, which may still evoke admiration and recall the original splendor, to mere building materials, now no longer identifiable with the palace but anonymously incorporated into a structure far inferior to either the palace or its ruins. Stella's identity has thus been swallowed by Swift's, her life placed in the service of and perhaps sacrificed to his decline. The putative agent of metamorphosis may well be the speaker, who has demanded and depended upon Stella's ministrations in spite of his concern for her well-being, or, since Stella is addressed, she may be the instigator of her own destruction. With the word *never,* Swift avoids the issue of responsibility by making the process contrary to fact, a warning rather than a reality.

Politics and Poetry

One of Swift's greatest satiric poems, "On Poetry: A Rapsody,"[49] marries the verbal universe of poetry to the political world. The poem is a definitive statement on a number of Swiftian concerns: the proliferation of bad poetry, the relationship of poetry to politics, and most significant, the connection between political corruption and a pervasive misuse of language.

In spite of the poem's wealth of detail and range of observation, it is tightly structured around a sequence of episodes in a representative poetic career and unified by recurrent chain-of-being imagery. Panoramic expansiveness coupled with a relentless downward spiral links "On Poetry" most forcibly with Book 1 of *Paradise Lost* and secondarily with the *Dunciad*. Most often presented in static tableau, Pope's Dulness is a reifying weight spreading inexorably over the values of Augustan civilization, while the frenetic energy of Swift's scribblers produces a headlong rush into the "infinite below," infernal regions reminiscent of Milton's hell. This here-and-now world of false poetry is unworthy of serious epic treatment, but perfectly suited to Swift's satiric exuberance. The momentum is maintained until *caetera desiderantur,* the Latin phrase to indicate that the rest of the work is missing, abruptly calls a halt. Whatever might be supplied in its place, and the literal meaning of *desiderantur,* longed for or needed, is relevant here, Swift has demonstrated that there can be no release in reality from the literary disorder symbiotically fostered by corrupt politics.[50]

The poem falls into three major sections: a prologue on the general difficulties of a poetic career (1–70), the body of the poem, presented as instruction given by an "experienc'd Sinner" to a "new Attempter" (71–410), and a concluding illustration of false poetry—the insincere but profitable flattery of the powerful (411–95). From the prologue's overall view of the poet's lot the poem proceeds to a detailed examination supposedly governed by the purpose of differentiating between the "poet's Vein and scribbling Itch." But both explication and prologue lead irresistibly to a politically motivated abandonment of true poetry:

> Lay now aside all Thoughts of Fame,
> To spring more profitable Game.
> From Party-Merit seek Support;
> The vilest Verse thrives best at Court.
>
> (183–86)

The concluding section translates precept into practice with a fulsome panegyric that makes the ideal of true poetry seem increasingly remote.

The prologue is a series of witty variations on the central theme of the obstacles to becoming a true poet set forth in mock logical order. Swift's antitheses establish a perverse formulation of Augustan harmony and balance; whatever is least rational is most predictable: "But *Man* we find the only *Creature,* / Who, led by *Folly,* fights with *Nature*" (19–20). Moreover, the degree of ability required by poetry is greater than that demanded by other exalted professions. Assuming that these hurdles are surmounted, that the aspiring poet truly has genius, external obstacles must be faced. In a beautifully crafted version of the closed couplet—alliterative, balanced, climactically ordered— Swift confines the comprehensive disorder of corruption spreading both geographically and morally: *"Court, City, Country* want you not; / You cannot bribe, betray, or plot" (47–48).

Should the poet be proof against worldly neglect, he must still encounter one final deterrent, the critics. Swift had treated this same theme in a similar passage in the earlier poem "To Doctor Delany on the Libels Writ against him" (1730):

> How oft' am I for Rime to seek?
> To dress a Thought, may toyl a Week;
> And then, how thankful to the Town,
> If all my Pains will earn a Crown.
> Whilst, ev'ry Critick can devour
> My Work and me in half an Hour.
> Would Men of Genius cease to write,
> The Rogues must die for Want and Spight,
> Must dye for Want of Food and Rayment.
>
> (65–77)

Instead of building climactically, Swift's first version drops the potential metaphor of devouring and trails off in weak general statement. More significantly, in presenting critics as parasites utterly dependent upon poets' works for sustenance, Swift accords size and dignity to poets,

who are "Men of Genius" plagued by "Rogues." As a
whole, "To Doctor Delany" conveys a more positive view
of the true poet as beset upon, but capable of rising above
the aggravations of the world.

"On Poetry" retains the essentials of the Delany version
but more vividly rendered and significantly changed in
emphasis:

> And here a *Simile* comes Pat in:
> Tho' *Chickens* take a Month to fatten,
> The Guests in less than half an Hour
> Will more than half a Score devour.
> So, after toiling twenty Days,
> To earn a Stock of Pence and Praise,
> Thy Labours, grown the Critick's Prey,
> Are swallow'd o'er a Dish of Tea;
> Gone, to be never heard of more,
> Gone, where the *Chickens* went before.
>
> (61–70)

In contrast to the Delany poem, "On Poetry" gives size
and dignity to the critics, whose relationship to poets is
predatory rather than parasitic. Poems, and by extension
poets, are equated with humble chickens, a diminution
supported by changes Swift made in several details. The
period of poetic gestation is lengthened from a week to
twenty days and the monetary reward reduced from a
crown to "a stock of pence"; longer labor and less remu-
neration thus conjoin with the poet's powerlessness
against the critic. Swift transforms the metaphoric hint of
eating in the Delany poem into the central thesis of the
later passage, announced as a simile, but then developed
as literal process. The verb *swallow'd,* and the particular-
izing of an accompanying beverage, make the business of
ingestion real rather than metaphoric, even before the
otherwise gratuitous last line specifically assimilates
poems to chickens in the oblivion of digestion. Seen as the
culmination not only of the poet's encounter with the

critic, but of the entire discussion of poetry, "gone, where the *Chickens* went before" is devastatingly reductive.

Although the next section of the poem begins with the announced intention of distinguishing between true and false, the true has already been buried under the diverse obstacles energetically marshaled by the prologue; poetry from now on will be false or politicized poetry:

> A Pamphlet in Sir *Rob's* Defence
> Will never fail to bring in Pence;
> Nor be concern'd about the Sale,
> He pays his Workmen on the Nail.
>
> (187–90)

This representation of the reality of practical poetry is far different from Swift's advice to Patrick Delany:

> By Party-steps no Grandeur climb at,
> Tho' it would make you *England's* Primate.
>
> ("To Doctor Delany," 109–10)

Swift's description of the conventions of politicized poetry calls to mind Hugh Kenner's observation on *A Tale of a Tub:* "Its method is to emphasize to the point of grotesqueness exactly those features which distinguish the printed book *per se,* the printed book as a technological artifact, from a human document."[51] Swift's satire is directed against the poem as a printed artifact, whose effects are achieved mechanically by capitals, dashes, and italics, and in addition, the poem as a marketable product, launched anonymously, conveyed to a well-known printer, advertised, and circulated among critics. Swift also catalogues the various banalities and unnecessary embellishments a bad poem exhibits. On foolish epithets alone he offers a wonderfully diverse group of images whose vitality almost causes us to forget that they are all representations of a void:

Or oft when Epithets you link,
In gaping Lines to fill a Chink;
Like stepping Stones to save a Stride,
In Streets where Kennels are too wide:
Or like a Heel-piece to support
A Cripple with one Foot too short:
Or like a Bridge that joins a Marish
To Moorlands of a diff'rent Parish.
So have I seen ill-coupled Hounds,
Drag diff'rent Ways in miry Grounds.
So Geographers in *Afric*-Maps
With Savage-Pictures fill their Gaps;
And o'er unhabitable Downs
Place Elephants for want of Towns.

(167–80)

Like the other brilliant catalogues that flesh out the somber description of careerism in poetry, this random profusion resists classification: "The sequence of images takes on a life of its own and makes the question of relationship to a subject seem irrelevant."[52]

What undermines genuine order is not this sort of disorderly collection but the meticulous ordering of the inconsequential and unworthy. When the aspiring poet is unable to eschew his follies, he has the alternative of a career within the politicized literary establishment. From the setting up as a critic and the acquiring of disciples to perpetuate the manipulative merchandising of poetry, Swift moves to the endless gradations and degrees of the proliferating false poets. The hierarchies minutely set forth constitute an unnatural anti-order comparable to the fallen angels' parodic heaven in hell or the kingdom of the dunces.

From description, the instructing voice suddenly and briefly shifts to condemnation:

O, what Indignity and Shame
To prostitute the Muse's Name,
By flatt'ring Kings whom Heaven design'd
The Plagues and Scourges of Mankind.
Bred up in Ignorance and Sloth,
And ev'ry Vice that nurses both.

(405–10)

By omitting a long diatribe against kings following line 410, Swift made his point more dramatically effective. The brief statement of proper values is immediately followed by a saccharine and verbose exemplification of prostituting the muse. Such gross flattery is all too typical of the sincere panegyric of court poets, but Virgil's praise of Augustus in the *Aeneid* resonates to provide a positive standard of what monarchs and poets should be. The patently ridiculous circumstances Swift adduces—"From him the *Tartar,* and *Chinese,* / Short by the Knees intreat for Peace" (423–24)—only emphasize the gulf between Augustus and George. Toward the end the panegyric becomes more frenzied and extravagant until even Christ must take second place to George. Atheism is heralded as the logical consequence of worshiping secular rulers, a situation in which false poetry is clearly implicated.[53]

From its early declaration that true poetry is useless to the state on to its expatiation on the principle that "the vilest Verse thrives best at Court," "On Poetry" exposes the relationship between poetry and politics. The world of politics creates a world of poetry in its own image, reflected in the poem's persistent political idiom. While waiting for a verdict on his anonymously launched work, the fledgling poet is advised to be "silent as a Politician." The critic also operates in a political fashion in controlling the poem's reception: "(Like *Courtiers,* when they send a Note, / Instructing *Members* how to Vote.)" (271–72). And the network of hack poets is a replica of a political organization: "In ev'ry Street a City-bard / Rules, like an Alderman his Ward" (285–86). The connection between political sins and a pervasive misuse of language is causal; the politicized microcosm of "Jobbers in the Poets Art" serves the political macrocosm with the insincere language of flattery, a relationship that reflects the debased condition of both establishments. As Swift wrote in his *Proposal for Correcting, Improving, and Ascertaining the English Tongue,* Latin declined because of "the slavish Disposition of the Senate and People; by which the Wit and Eloquence of the Age were wholly turned into Panegyrick, the most barren of all Subjects."[54] This poetry of political expedience is best served by the stale and formulaic: "Your Garland in the following Reign, / Change but the Names will do again" (231–32).

For Swift, as for George Orwell, "the great enemy of clear language is insincerity."[55] Swift writes in "A Letter to the Writer of the Occasional Paper" that bad politicians can find men of wit to serve them, "but the misfortune is, that the heads of such writers rebel against their hearts; their genius forsakes them, when they would offer to prostitute it to the service of injustice, corruption, party-rage, and false representations of things and persons."[56] "To Doctor Delany" makes the same connection between expression and value:

> What Pamphlets in a Court's Defence
> Shew Reason, Grammer, Truth, or Sense?
> For, though the Muse delights in Fiction,
> She ne'er inspires against Conviction.
>
> (103–6)

The language of politicized poetry is not only insincere and deceptive, but it also suffers distortion through typographical attention-getting devices—unnecessary capitalization, italics, and dashes—which further remove it from an accurate relation to reality:

> When Letters are in vulgar Shapes,
> 'Tis ten to one the Wit escapes;

But when in *Capitals* exprest,
The dullest Reader smoaks the Jest:
Or else perhaps he may invent
A better than the Poet meant.

(97–102)

"On Poetry" asserts an *ars poetica* structure as its principle of unity, but its principle of expansion is the corruption of the poet and the merchandising of the word. In the encounter between true and false poetry, the poem concludes that only the deceptive and opportunistic can thrive. Proving Swift's point, Queen Caroline took the gross flattery of the ironic panegyric at face value until enlightened by Lord Hervey.[57]

Turning art into political jobbery entails the perversion of language from fidelity to experience to an automatic reiteration of political orthodoxy in all aspects of poetry: the content of extravagant panegyric, the form of typographical gimmickry, and the manipulative strategies of selling poetic wares. Placed in the service of vested interests, language is unable to function as the instrument of truthful communication it should ideally be in order to "make us understand one another, and to receive Information of Facts."[58]

Within the verbal universe Swift moves from literary to political satire, from the playful treatment of overblown diction and traditional genres, all of which he regards as inaccurate representations of reality, to political abuses of the word. Although the satiric treatment of literary forms continues as a tendency throughout Swift's poetry, not surprisingly, the more strictly literary and metalinguistic poems are early. In such witty fantasies as "An Elegy on Mr. PATRIGE" and "Baucis and Philemon" Swift foregrounds his extravagant wit. There are no real culprits or dangerous malefactors; while certain literary practices strike Swift as foolish, they are not harmful. By the end of his poetic career Swift finds the verbal universe overwhelmed by the world of men and events, the muse coopted by a corrupt political establishment. The imagination that playfully transformed Baucis's kettle into a church bell in such ingenious detail persists in the inventive abundance of "On Poetry's" catalogues, but it is now subordinated to an issue of primary importance—the political corruption of poetry.

4
"Foppery, Affectation, Vanity, Folly, or Vice": The Disordered World of the Gentlewoman

A noticeable division in Swift's poetry exists between poems devoted to the frivolous and superficial in women and poems about feminine physicality. The women adjudged frivolous, often referred to as "ladies," are gentlewomen, whose mental selves and social behavior are Swift's satiric targets. The faults of mind of these women of his own class and frequent association were well-known to Swift, but he seldom particularizes or satirizes their physical appearance. The few details of physical description for Stella and Daphne—Stella's gray hair and wrinkles, Daphne's leanness—suggest affectionate intimacy rather than serious criticism. Although they are unflattering, they serve as evidence in support of Swift's thesis that women should cultivate nonphysical charms. The question of decorum may also be involved. Women without social status would be fair game for harsh satiric treatment, but Swift might have felt that gentlewomen required more restraint on his part. Those women depicted in the poetry as unclean, decaying, or merely excreting are perceived as sexual beings who in some way connected with the body either deceive men actively or passively feed masculine illusions. Feminine sexuality in any form is punished by the evils of the body, excretory filthiness or venereal ravagement. Not all of the women thus portrayed are prostitutes, but their social status is almost always rendered dubious by some action—Phillis's running off with a servant in "The

Progress of Love," Chloe's descent into vulgarity and shamelessness in "Strephon and Chloe," Celia's tainted petticoats in "The Lady's Dressing Room."

Delving into Swift's psyche might suggest reasons for this dichotomized approach, but explanations can readily be found in some aspects of the poet's world. Swift might well have preferred to deal with excretory and erotic themes in terms that would remain safely distanced from his women friends. Moreover, the most obvious examples of the kind of physicality Swift portrays would not be found among women of his own social class and acquaintance. The poor are apt to be dirtier that the rich in any age, prostitutes more flamboyantly made up than genteel ladies and more likely to exhibit the effects of syphilis.

1

A helpful preface to Swift's poems about gentlewomen is his *Letter to a Young Lady, on her Marriage,* addressed to a newly married young woman Swift professes to value highly. If the bride followed Swift's instructions to reread the letter often, she must have been disheartened by the anatomy of feminine failings Swift invokes to justify his lack of respect for most women. "I am afraid," he writes, "it will be hard for you to pick out one Female Acquaintance in this Town, from whom you may not be in manifest Danger of contracting some Foppery, Affectation, Vanity, Folly, or Vice."[1] More disturbingly, the calm tone of rational discourse is broken by rage on several occasions. A startling eruption of satiric spleen occurs when Swift dilates on a favorite theme, the feminine preoccupation with dress: "When I reflect on this, I cannot conceive you to be human Creatures, but a Sort of Species hardly a Degree above a Monkey; who hath more diverting Tricks than any of you; is an Animal less mischievous and expensive; might, in Time, be a tolerable Critick in Velvet and Brocade; and, for ought I know, would equally become them" (p. 91).

In two instances images of physical violence to women also intrude upon the decorum of the *Letter*. To corroborate his advice on cleanliness, Swift relates what "a pleasant Gentleman said concerning a silly Woman of Quality; that nothing could make her supportable but cutting off her Head; for his Ears were offended by her Tongue, and his Nose by her Hair and Teeth" (p. 87). Similarly, Swift's thoughts on women who use bold language and gossip irresponsibly are harshly vengeful: "I have often thought that no Man is obliged to suppose such Creatures to be Women; but to treat them like insolent Rascals, disguised in Female Habits, who ought to be stripped, and kicked down Stairs" (p. 93).

These outbursts, all of which violate the tone and purpose of the *Letter,* reveal rage channeled into punitive fantasy, in short, a satiric process. Like Swift's description of even the best women as "beasts in petticoats,"[2] these images strip away an assumed innocence to expose and punish a culpable reality, either by radically transforming women into a lesser species or—in the case of the "silly Woman of Quality"—by decapitation. In context the images are both indecorous and extreme; as C. J. Rawson describes the flayed woman and dissected beau in *A Tale of a Tub,* they are "momentary intensities which do not merely *serve* the argument they are meant to illustrate, but actually *spill over* it."[3]

While such intrusions suggest the impatient satirist, and are startlingly inappropriate, the *Letter* as a whole reveals a thoughtful observer of the customs and prejudices that limit the scope of women and consequently make them susceptible to vanities and idle pastimes. Much as Swift commends the young lady's parents, he tells her that "they failed, as it is generally the Case, in too much neglecting to cultivate your Mind" (p. 85). From this common error a great deal to the disadvantage of women must follow, as Swift realized: "It hath sometimes moved me with Pity, to see the Lady of the House forced to withdraw, immediately after Dinner . . . as if it were an established Maxim, that Women are incapable of all Conversation" (p. 90). Swift recommends that a woman prefer the company of men and acquire the knowledge, though not the experience, usually reserved for men. He counsels against the predilections and pastimes commonly indulged in by women.

None of this exemplifies a Swiftian animus against women so much as a dispassionate assessment of the enforced differentiation of the sexes, which Swift consistently regarded as detrimental to women and unnecessary to society. His desire for equality in terms of character traits is remarkably liberal: "I am ignorant of any one Quality that is amiable in Man, which is not equally so in a Woman. . . . Nor do I know one Vice or Folly, which is not equally detestable in both" (pp. 92–93). But where admirable qualities may exist in men simply because they are admirable, in women—Swift always insists—they have the important practical value of attracting men more firmly than beauty and youth. As he instructs the young lady, "the grand Affair of your Life will be to gain and preserve the Friendship and Esteem of your Husband. . . . You will, in Time, grow a Thing indifferent, and perhaps contemptible, unless you can supply the Loss of Youth and Beauty with more durable Qualities" (p. 89). Here too Swift voices a legitimate interest of women based upon the reality of their position; their only approved role—first as marriageable girls, then as wives and mothers—made them subordinate to and dependent upon men, and thus greatly concerned with attracting and pleasing them.

The combination of satiric spleen and thoughtful instruction in the *Letter* accurately reflects Swift's views. His sympathetic awareness that social forces beyond the control of women make them what they are does not check his exasperation with the resultant feminine follies. The vivid satiric images that break the measured instructions of the *Letter* bear witness to Swift's exasperation, but their harshness can be duplicated in his treatment of kings, critics, and politicians.

Like the *Letter to a Young Lady,* the poems that satirize women can be read most fruitfully as the satirist's response to a society with rigidly defined roles for men and women and, in addition, as an effective literary strategy for ridiculing the idealization of women in poetry. Swift satirizes men in a number of different categories, most of which are occupational. Women, who could participate in none of the activities considered important in the world of public affairs, are therefore satirized as a sex. When Swift looked at a man, he saw a person filling a particular public role—lawyer, churchman, writer, country squire. When he looked at a woman, he saw a person without occupational identity, confined to the private sphere of the home, lacking education and serious interests while cultivating frivolous pastimes and transient charms.

2

In the poems about gentlewomen, women of the class he encountered socially, Swift is primarily concerned with manifestations of disorder rather than with their underlying causes. "Satire, as Ronald Paulson writes, "characteristically judges by consequences rather than by causes and motives, which are too slippery; the final standard is an objective one like success or failure."[4] To observe as acutely as Swift does implies some understanding of motivation, but he is not interested in relating motives to patterns of acculturation and social behavior. In "The Furniture of a Woman's Mind" he observes that women affect illness and that this gives them attention and power. This behavior is satirized as an illegitimate means to an end, but the poetic statement goes no further. Only in "Cadenus and Vanessa" does a sense of society's coercion and men's complicity receive more than passing attention, but here too Swift does not probe the forces at work in order to discover why women have no legitimate roads to power. The satirist's role is to record and condemn—not analyze and explain—the errors of the times.

Swift's earliest poem in his mature poetic voice, "Verses wrote on a Lady's *Ivory Table-Book*" (1698), belongs among those poems primarily concerned with disorder in the world of respectable women. An examination of the lady's table-book reveals a confusion of values similar to what Pope would later discern in Belinda's life. Items of feminine decoration—perfume, paint, lace—mingle incongruously with snatches of love letters, but Swift buries his trenchant examples in explicit commentary. Instead of the indirections of dramatic presentation he would later master, a heavy-handed railing dominates the poem:

> Peruse my Leaves thro' ev'ry Part,
> And think thou seest my owners Heart,
> Scrawl'd o'er with Trifles thus, and quite
> As hard, as sensless, and as light.
>
> (1–4)

The items assembled document the poet's accusation of frivolity not only in substance but in form. The impossible spelling indicates ignorance, the jumble of unrelated things a lack of order and seriousness. Unlike the perfume and lace, the letters at least have the potential of significance, but the extravagance of the expressions—*Dear Charming Saint, lovely Nymph*—reduces them to trite nonsense. The woman whose life is reflected in the pages of the table-book oscillates between two interests: self-adornment and love. As seen here, love is a series of foolish letters that are interspersed with down-to-earth notations of money spent. Because frivolity is expensive and empty-headed, the most welcome lover is both wealthy and foolish.

In a more elaborate treatment of the phenomenology of ignorance and frivolity, "The Furniture of a Woman's Mind" gives the familiar failing—ignorance, sham, frivolity—new exemplifications. More important, its strategy of presenting its data is more effective. By a calculatedly random ordering of particulars, "Verses" mirrored the lady's mental chaos. "Furniture" instead makes its points methodically, to illustrate the woman's mechanical responses: the expansion of this principle of unity uncovers the bankruptcy of the ordering process, its lack of foundation in thought or will. The first piece of furniture—"a Set of Phrases learn't by Rote"—is typical of the whole. Whether it involves responding to a man or a mouse, all of the woman's behavior is learned by rote, and behind each automatic response is a void:

> When at a Play to laugh, or cry,
> Yet cannot tell the Reason why:
> Never to hold her Tongue a Minute;
> While all she prates has nothing in it.
> ....
> Has ev'ry Repartee in Store,
> She spoke ten Thousand Times before.
>
> (3–6; 11–12)

The lines themselves follow a monotonous pattern of naming an activity and then revealing its lack of meaningful substance. A spurious order is thus apparent in both form and content; the orderly development of the description and the mechanical order of the woman's behavior add up to an anti-order—a confusion of values in which wit is first defined as nonsense and then as rudeness.

Having no other road to power and attention than the maintenance of an image of fragility and helplessness, a woman reserves her greatest efforts for artifice and subterfuge designed to enhance this image: "If chance a Mouse creeps in her Sight, / Can finely counterfeit a Fright" (33–34). Part of this behavior is based upon the extreme differentiation of men and women: if men are "robustious" and unfrightened, women must be delicate and readily frightened. Swift argues vigorously against feminine cowardice in his *Letter to a Young Lady:*

There is, indeed, one Infirmity which is generally allowed you, I mean that of Cowardice. Yet there should seem to be something very capricious, that when Women profess their Admiration for a Colonel or a Captain, on Account of his Valour; they should fancy it a very graceful becoming Quality in themselves, to be afraid of their own Shadows. . . . At least, if Cowardice be a Sign of Cruelty, (as it is generally granted) I can hardly think it an Accomplishment so desireable, as to be thought worthy of improving by Affectation.[5] (p. 93)

Culturally induced necessity causes women to become mechanical and insincere in areas of life that should be governed by nature and spontaneity rather than by art. One should not be sick according to policy. What is more lamentable, the sham hardens into a routinized response that can no longer be distinguished from a natural one:[6]

> If *Molly* happens to be careless,
> And but neglects to warm her Hair-Lace,
> She gets a Cold as sure as Death;
> And vows she scarce can fetch her Breath.
>
> (43–46)

Is the cold real, psychosomatic, or merely feigned? The extravagance of *vows* certainly suggests an element of calculation or exaggeration, while *sure as Death* indicates the automatic nature of the process. Expected to be delicate and sickly, women become delicate and sickly.

Although Swift has considered his topics one by one in parodic order, his point is that the order that seems to exist has no rational basis. Women are ardent political partisans, for example, but underneath this seeming manifestation of order their choice is completely misguided: "Her Arguments directly tend / Against the Side she would defend" (51–52). Like the mistaking of nonsense for wit, the mistaking of Tory for Whig is an absolute kind of confusion. This same device is used in the poem's conclusion when the poet refers to the faults he has just finished enumerating as virtues. In the accepted view of women such manifestations of ignorance, intolerable in men, are considered to be virtues.

"The Journal of a Modern Lady" is more successful than either "The Furniture of a Woman's Mind" or "A Lady's Ivory Table-Book" because the organizing device of a woman's day provides structure without sacrificing naturalness. In the lady's monologue replaying her card game of the night before, order is inverted everywhere: serious matters enter only tangentially—the goldsmith carrying off household articles to be pawned, the money for coal going to pay a gambling debt. The poet's voice concludes the scene: "Through ev'ry Game pursues her Tale, / Like Hunters o'er their Evening Ale" (78–79). Although the lady's card game is a tame drawing-room pastime, it is exciting, hazardous (to the purse), and memorable to the player—the masculine world of adventure writ small. The commercial world similarly enters the lady's day in the form of bargaining over fabrics and ornaments. Swift dubs this the "Business of Importance," a twofold irony in that these trivial dealings are called important business and actually function as such in the lady's world.

In keeping with the greater seriousness of the faults that now become its theme, the satire takes on a sharper note. When Swift turns from frivolity and stupidity to malice, scurrility, and hypocrisy, his use of physically disgusting details seems shockingly intrusive in the upper-middle-class world of the modern lady:

> *Mopsa,* who stinks her Spouse to Death,
> Accuses *Chloe*'s tainted Breath;
> *Hircina* rank with sweat, presumes
> To censure *Phillis* for Perfumes;
> While crooked *Cynthia* swearing says,
> That *Florimel* wears Iron Stays.
>
> (156–61)

Under the veneer of respectability, the description intimates, these women are indeed sisters of those light ladies whose physical selves are presented in gross and revolting detail in other Swift poems. Characteristically, the examples draw their energy from the extreme nature of the physical images they present while purporting to function in another area altogether, that of hypocrisy and lack of self-awareness.

All things reflect the disorder of this world: the condemnation of another for one's own fault, the preference for scandal in conversation and frivolity in pastimes, and the deafening babble of tongues. After first protesting his inability to convey such a torrent of meaningless verbiage, Swift proceeds to find apt comparisons everywhere. Rather than imposing order on a number of particulars, his catalogue implicates them in a common disorder:

> Their Chattering makes a louder Din
> Than Fish-Wives o'er a Cup of Gin:
> Not School-boys at a Barring-out,
> Rais'd ever such incessant Rout:
> The Jumbling Particles of Matter
> In Chaos made not such a Clatter:
> Far less the Rabble roar and rail,
> When drunk with sour Election Ale.
>
> (180–87)

In all the examples a violation of order produces an uncontrolled and senseless racket. Swift makes both a social and a moral judgment: the quarreling of the card players violates the rituals of good manners; at the same time, the accusations of cheating are true, and its practice is accepted by the players. Juxtaposing the game to art, Swift reminds us of the difference between the real order of art and the trivial order of the game, here ironically referred to as art:

> How can the Muse her Aid impart,
> Unskill'd in all the Terms of Art?
> Or in harmonious Numbers put
> The Deal, the Shuffle, and the Cut?
>
> (220–23)

The final action of the day is hurriedly telescoped, but since the last games only repeat what Swift has already treated in detail, there is no need to describe them. Time dominates the last movement, from the opening reference "too precious now to waste," through the gobbled supper and feverish return to play, to the reminder of the hour in the watchman's knock. In spite of the haste to get home, the ladies make arrangements to play the next night. With real reasons for tears now, Madam "steals" to bed like a thief, forswearing the game she will play again tomorrow:

> Unlucky Madam left in Tears,
> (Who now again *Quadrill* forswears,)
> With empty Purse, and aching Head,
> Steals to her sleeping Spouse to Bed.
>
>   (290–93)

This final image brings together the main components of the lady's life and shows the disorder of misvaluation. While the tears are genuine, they are shed in an unworthy cause, the same one that has emptied her purse and made her head ache. We know from the morning's experience that the renunciation of quadrille is insincere; there will be no enduring alleviation of purse and head. The husband is seen in a passive and uninterfering position, but his presence, along with the empty purse, is a reminder of the domestic order and conjugal obligation that the lady violates.

The poem has come full circle, for the end of this day presages another like it. The logical unit of the day, the principle of unity that structures the narrative, is actually bankrupt, for the poetic expansion of this order reveals that the container contains nothing; there is no real progress from morning to night, no meaningful sequence. Superficial order conceals a vacuity that is exposed whenever the lady is thrown upon her own resources for a moment. Like Pope's insects preserved in amber, the modern lady is enclosed in an aesthetic structure that can only throw her unworthiness into sharper relief.

3

The same sort of picture of feminine frivolity serves as a foil to the sensible, intelligent woman in "Cadenus and Vanessa," Swift's most comprehensive poetic treatment of the position of women. By means of the trial mechanism that frames the narrative, women are accused of an inversion of values brought about by lightness of mind. In opposition to this stereotype of fashionable society Swift creates an ideal woman. The standards set for this paragon are high, but in spite of the mythological machinery surrounding her, Vanessa is offered as a possible specimen of womankind. After all, her much-lauded exceptional qualities consist of the union of beauty and intelligence and the rejection of fripperies and nonsense. Added to this is the excellent education Vanessa receives, a circumstance that would distinguish her from most women of her time. Although she can be viewed as comically inept in her attempts to deal with the unruly and unreasonable world, Vanessa is not a satiric victim but herself the instrument of satire, the familiar naive figure whose innocence points up the world's defects.[7] Vanessa is not, as James L. Tyne maintains, "somewhat deficient as a human being,"[8] for her rationality is not proof against falling in love in a quite ordinary way. She then uses her reason not to extricate herself from folly, but to pursue it—a not very Houyhnhnm-like, but recognizably human course of action.

Before Vanessa is endowed with "masculine" intelligence, however, she is described as exemplary of more traditional feminine virtues. These turn out to be cleanliness, beauty, and—above all—decency of mind:

> Where not one careless Thought intrudes,
> Less modest than the Speech of Prudes;
> Where never Blush was call'd in Aid,

That spurious Virtue in a Maid,
A Virtue but at second-hand;
They blush because they understand.

(166–71)

Although the major irony of the poem is the unsuitability of the perfect woman to the imperfect society of actuality, Swift shows no awareness of the incongruity between the extreme purity of mind he insists upon for Vanessa and the whole province of masculine knowledge he wants to make available to her. Through the stratagem of pretending that she is a boy, Vanessa is given qualities "for manly Bosoms chiefly fit" (204). These constitute an imposing array of traits generally regarded as admirable: knowledge, judgment, wit, justice, truth, fortitude, honor, generosity. The paucity of feminine virtues in contrast to the number and scope of those usually reserved for men is striking, but what is equally noteworthy about Swift's portrait of Vanessa is the desire to divorce admirable qualities from gender and unite the best of both sexes in one person. Vanessa is not an unattainable ideal, but one that could be realized if artificial distinctions between the sexes were obliterated.

In the poem's depiction of the beau monde, men are as frivolous and ignorant as women, although the poetic fiction causes the faults of women to receive more attention. I cannot agree with Irvin Ehrenpreis that because Vanessa is an exception to the rule of her sex and Cadenus simply a rare specimen of his that "ultimately . . . it is man's and not woman's nature that triumphs."[9] Vanessa is described as seeing some superior people of "either sex," but given the central situation of the poem—that she is a test case on the subject of love—it is understandable that there is no place for other worthy women characters. The issue, moreover, is a matter of culture rather than nature. Swift always writes as if social convention alone is responsible for the difference in masculine and feminine norms of behavior.

When the trial is concluded at the poem's end, Venus unexpectedly finds the accusing sex to be guilty:

> "She saw her Favour was misplac'd;
> "The Fellows had a wretched Taste;
> "She needs must tell them to their Face,
> "They were a senseless, stupid Race:
> "And were she to begin agen,
> "She'd study to reform the *Men*.

(868–73)

The narrative frame thus illustrates certain general principles of relationship between men and women. A paragon among women cannot find a lover because men expect women to be foolish and empty-headed, and the one man who can appreciate her extraordinary merits is crippled perhaps by too much of the very faculty that makes the appreciation possible. Without changing both sexes, the poem concludes, there is little chance of improvement. As Swift wrote in an unfinished essay, "Of the Education of Ladies," "Considering the modern way of training up both sexes in ignorance, idleness, and vice, it is of little consequence how they are coupled together."[10]

What makes the poem disturbing is a sensed incongruity between the principle of unity created by the narrative frame and the story of Cadenus and Vanessa that expands upon it. The investigation of love produces an explicit statement: both men and women are guilty of foolishness, which is primarily a compound of ignorance and affectation, and both must be reformed or neither. If Venus throws up her hands at the sorry situation, the poet-moralist does not: he advocates the correctives of reason and sense, embodied in the perfection of Vanessa. Having established Vanessa as a serious model—to be emulated, if not equaled—the poem then depicts her failure in love. Vanessa's choice is *not* made through an over-reliance on reason, but in the prudent manner Swift consistently recommended whenever he wrote about love or marriage in both poetry and prose. His remark in *Thoughts on Religion* that "no wise man ever married from the dictates of reason"[11] suggests to me that perfect wisdom counsels celibacy, not that Swift approves or advocates the abandonment of reason in choosing a marriage partner. As he wrote in the indisputably serious *Letter to a Young Lady, on her Marriage:* "Yours was a Match of Prudence, and common Good-liking, without any Mixture of that ridiculous Passion which hath no Being, but in Play-Books and Romances" (p. 89).

Vanessa has wisely selected someone intellectually compatible and admirable in character. Even at forty-four, Cadenus should be an excellent choice, as he knows himself—hence his vacillation and seizing upon flimsy excuses, and the poem's final irresolution about the outcome.[12] If all of this is designed to show the limitation of human reason—Vanessa's reason leading her to the wrong suitor, Cadenus's prohibiting any passion whatsoever—then such a theme ill accords with the framing satire of foolish amatory behavior resulting from lack of reason. The silly belles and beaux might feel themselves fortunate indeed to avoid the debacle of Cadenus and Vanessa.

Certainly the need for more rationality and the limitations of reason are both possible themes for Swift, but only the first is characteristic of his poetry, and both in the same poem would seem to be at cross-purposes.

4

In the two poems praising Stella—"To Stella, Visiting Me in my Sickness" and "To Stella, Who Collected and Transcribed his Poems"—the difficulties of "Cadenus and Vanessa" are avoided because there is no satiric fiction. "To Stella, Visiting Me in my Sickness" is reminiscent of the standard Dryden panegyric in which a figure is set up as a paradigm of virtue for a particular role—king, consort, whatever—and discussed according to the qualities that constitute worth in that particular sphere. Dryden tends to view these qualities as givens, to see his poetic job not as justifying or defining criteria, but as fitting his subject to the accepted criteria in such a way that the individual merges with the abstract, the specific person becomes the ideal. Honor in Swift's poem is comparable to the givens of Dryden's panegyrics, but it is not treated as a given. It must be dissected and defined, faulty conceptions of it must be vigorously rejected, and a large segment of humanity, perhaps all but Stella, must be condemned in the process. The logic of relationship suggests a progression from order to disorder, the ideal of Stella linked with the heroic and mythic past in contrast to the generality of eighteenth-century mankind.

This is only one thrust of the poem, however. Another, equally emphatic, is a redefinition of masculine and feminine behavior that demonstrates that the order existing in this realm is spurious. Here too the pattern figure of Stella provides an ideal, this time in contrast to foolish affectation. But while the blending of subject and pattern on the level of abstract qualities in analogous to Dryden's practice, Swift concludes his poem with a vivid personal involvement far removed from Dryden's distanced idealizing. Although the method is different, Stella is praised to the extravagant extent that a Dryden subject is typically praised—to a greater extent, one might say, since the speaker makes an emotional plea to Stella of the sort that Dryden never permits himself.

The first two-thirds of "To Stella, Visiting Me in my Sickness" also recalls the redefinition of the feminine ideal undertaken earlier in "Cadenus and Vanessa." This should be differentiated from the literary romantic ideal Swift often satirizes in his poetry, for the ideal embodied in Stella and Vanessa is attainable, if rare; it depends more on rejecting acculturated traits such as vanity and affectation than on implausible natural endowments. The romantic ideal, in contrast, depicts women as goddesses and is thus totally removed from actuality. Both poems credit the gods with combining the best qualities of both sexes to create an ideal woman. In "Cadenus and Vanessa" this is achieved by an elaborate framing device, a cumbersome apparatus that qualifies the seriousness and distances the issue while somehow communicating that Swift is *not* coming to terms with it. Here the device is less redolent of evasion, more suggestive of a purely graceful compliment without special resonance. The union of masculine and feminine qualities in Stella is not surrounded by the paraphernalia of trickery and ambiguity as it is in Vanessa, but offered simply and forthrightly as the human ideal. In both poems Swift characterizes stereotypical feminine behavior as an artificial and affected set of responses, neither natural nor desirable. While an exclusively feminine folly is attacked through the character of Stella, the more serious charges are leveled against an undifferentiated human nature.

Dramatically involving both himself and the reader, the speaker sinks the particular characteristics of each sex in this general human nature, a quotidian standard that reveals Stella's virtue even more emphatically. The identification of Stella with "Heroes and Heroins of old," the explanation that both Pallas and Prometheus contributed to her creation, and the assertion that there is "a Lesson she alone can teach" combine to isolate Stella from the defects of universal human nature as much as from the special defects of her sex.

After the philosophical and abstract discussion of honor and then of Stella's honor in particular, the poem suddenly becomes vividly personal. The poet has listed the affected kinds of behavior not to be observed in Stella; now he describes her virtue in action in the context most significant to himself—their relationship. Traditional roles are reversed here: the male poet is weak and helpless, lamenting "in unmanly Strains," while Stella, infused with manly courage, has the strength to master her own severe suffering in order to sustain him. Swift depends on Stella to preserve his life, which in turn makes it possible for him to celebrate her in poetry. The poet's sense of unworthiness and even guilt, implicit in the description of his illness and her ministrations, is overtly expressed in the poem's climax, first by an assertion that Stella's attention to him may jeopardize her own fragile health and then by the image of the ruined palace made into an inferior structure.

"To Stella, who Collected and Transcribed his Poems" seems to take up where the preceding poem leaves off,[13] with the threatening idea of Stella's loss of identity partially distanced by its expression in another building metaphor. Instead of beginning with the general and abstract and ending with the anxiety-provoking personal situation, this poem begins with a direct statement of the problem and then proceeds to rectify the announced wrong of Stella's neglect by giving her her due. But once again the energy and emphasis are divided between a macrocosm of false value, bad poets and their apostrophized ladies, and a microcosmic ideal, Swift and Stella.

Although Swift makes passing references to other women in some of the birthday odes, this poem is his only extended juxtaposition of the two categories of women he perceived in poetry as radically different: those whose minds are satirized, usually gentlewomen seen in frivolous and empty-headed activities; and those women identified as sexual beings, whose bodies are the focus of the satire. As usual in his treatment of the latter, Swift's aggressively anti-Petrarchan assertions and examples seem to be unnecessarily harsh and sweeping, as if any mere mention of physical attractiveness in a poem proves the lady a whore and the poet an untruthful wretch. A fair appearance inevitably masks repulsiveness of one sort or another in Swift's poetry; beauty goes before the pox and a number of other misfortunes: "Before he could his Poem close, / The lovely Nymph had lost her Nose" (77–78). This image goes well beyond the ironic incongruity of idealized feminine portraits created by false poets in prettified diction and the vulgar reality of flesh-and-blood women. The lack of a nose is, after all, a common indicator of syphilis, which can hardly coexist with the romantic ideal of femininity. Moreover, compared to a number of less striking deformities, the absence of the central feature of the face is especially shocking and irremediable. As C. J. Rawson has noted about the flayed woman in *A Tale of a Tub,* "A haze of *extra* hostility hangs in the air, unaccounted for, dissolving the satire's clean logic into murkier and more unpredictable precisions, spreading uneasiness into areas of feeling difficult to rationalize and difficult for the reader to escape."[14] In making his point with a vengeance, Swift elicits the peculiar *frisson* that grotesque deformity inspires.

The actual panegyric to Stella, ostensibly the theme of the poem, is overshadowed by the discussion of true and false art with their attendant examples. Direct compliments are notably few, but it is their abstract quality that makes them less memorable than other parts of the poem:

> If it both pleases and endures,
> The Merit and the Praise are yours.
>
> (7–8)

> But his Pursuits are at an End,
> Whom *Stella* chuses for a *Friend*.
>
> (23–24)

> Your Virtues safely I commend,
> They on no Accidents depend.
>
> (79–80)

In reality, Stella's virtues have not been commended so much as insinuated. We can assume from lines 79–80 that they are nonphysical and thus not subject to the permutations of time; we can further assume that because she is worthy of friendship and esteem and praise, Stella has qualities that are admirable and attractive, but the speaker is more interested in developing other subjects than in a specific enumeration of Stella's virtues. The description of Stella's one fault and false poets celebrating the deceptive and impermanent realm of externality both receive more attention. The praise of Stella is the rather standard stuff of panegyric; when Swift turns to an exposure of Stella's "weaker side," he proceeds with notably greater energy and enthusiasm for fifty-eight lines. This does not shift the poetic statement from praise to blame, however, for the examination of Stella's fault occurs within the clearly established context of the poet's affection, concern, and high regard for her.

Stella's one fault is that her passionate nature, a positive endowment, can be perverted by anger into unworthy speech: "One Passion, with a diff'rent Turn, / Makes Wit inflame, or Anger burn" (117–18). The same point is made in "An Epistle to a Lady" when the poet declares: "In a jest I spend my rage"; a basic impulse can be constructively or destructively channeled.[15] Through the dominant image of fermentation Swift emphasizes the importance of art controlling nature to achieve the proper state, a process that must be distinguished from the feminine cosmetic artifice Swift so often satirizes. The Celias and Corinnas use artifice to deceive the beholder by replacing and disguising an unsavory reality rather than enhancing nature. In addition, cosmetics are for the body and always to some degree associated with sexual attractiveness, whereas Swift always deprecates the value of the body in his poetic address to Stella. What Swift urges on his friend is the harmonious completion of nature by art, not a deceitful masking but the ordering and developing of a quality already possessed.

The poet's confidence that Stella can frankly face up to her fault, be willing to overcome it, and bring about the desired improvement is the new order that emerges from the poetic confrontation of Stella's almost-perfection with her one fault. The compliment Swift pays Stella shows his deep feelings for her value and his faith in her commitment, like his own, to truth. Beyond this, it is the illustration of the true poet's method that balances, or more accurately, overbalances the false poet's depiction of a suburb trull as a lovely nymph. Because he is truthful, Swift includes Stella's defects in his portrait. And because the qualities that concern him are of character rather than of physical appearance, they cannot be destroyed by time, but may be altered—unlike the depredations of the pox— by intention.

5
Poetry of Excess: The Body and the Body Politic

The Scatological Poems

AMONG the numerous charities Swift systematically practiced throughout his life, one seems especially striking. As Thomas Sheridan writes, Swift was in the habit of frequenting a number of mutilated, old-women street-vendors: "One of these mistresses wanted an eye; another, a nose; a third, an arm; a fourth, a foot."[1] Swift playfully referred to these women by names invented to suit their physical conditions, such as "Cancerina" and "Stumpa-nympha." The interest that led Swift to "seek out objects in all quarters of the town from which the bulk of mankind turn with loathing"[2] is part of a larger concern with physicality: its impermanence, its limitations, its constant enmity to man's rational and spiritual life. This preoccupation with the body, which down through the centuries has attracted opprobrium to Swift's name, is a key to his worst fears about the human condition. Both the writings and the numerous references in letters to his own history of constant bodily ills make it clear that Swift was humbled and depressed by fleshly frailty. Patronizing these afflicted women was a direct confrontation with physical vulnerability in an extreme form, yet beauty could also provoke thoughts of bodily corruption inasmuch as all physical existence must ineluctably partake, as he wrote in "Strephon and Chloe," of the "gross and filthy."

171

Although from a satiric perspective Swift mocks the cosmetic arts that seek to disguise the deterioration and imperfections of the body, and the romantic imagination that also turns away from real physicality, his concern is tragic as well: the processes of physical change and decay are universal and inescapable, dreadfully inherent in the very fabric of existence. It is this twofold vision—satiric and tragic—that accounts for the tonal complexity and troubling ambiguities of so much of Swift's poetry of the body. Swift's streetwalking nymphs and slovenly coquettes attempt to create a false self by cosmetic artifice, an illusory transformation that obscures the true condition of the body. What draws Swift to the unpleasant revelations of the boudoir, however, is not only its deceptive practices but the nature of physical existence itself, the body's vulnerability to old age, disease, and even ordinary physical functions. The principle of unity in the scatological poems is a justifiable satiric condemnation of vice, deception, and romantic illusion, but the expansion that occurs produces an unacknowledged subtext, the satirizing of bodily existence per se. Instead of this dialectic's creating a new order, the failure to make the necessary distinction between the given of bodily nature and those human errors which are legitimately the province of satire leads to thematic confusion. Where Swift wishes to condemn, the human condition pulls in the direction of acceptance. His scatological poems move uncertainly between these opposed and ultimately irreconcilable perspectives.[3]

This kind of failure is avoided by "The Progress of Beauty" because the inherent division between what can be condemned and what must be accepted is not brought to our attention by the poem's technique. The parallel metamorphoses of a woman and the moon are treated like the comic transformations of Baucis, Philemon, Smedley, and Partridge. Although not a comic figure, Celia is no more than an abstract counterpart of the moon; she never comes alive as an individual whose specific miseries might undercut the satiric perspective. It scarcely matters whether the

shifting narrative attention is directed toward the lady or
the moon; neither is real, and both are equally remote.
What particularization there is, and it is found only in the
first third of the poem, provokes neither sympathy nor
horror because it is restricted to fairly trifling matters
readily brought under control. When, for example, the
colors of Celia's complexion change their ground, she can
"with ease reduce . . . / Each colour to it's Place and Use"
(45, 47).

The poem remains safely distanced from its implied
reality of decaying flesh:

> Love with White Lead cements his Wings,
> White lead was sent us to repair
> Two brightest, brittlest earthly Things
> A Lady's Face, and China ware.
>
> (61–64)

Such generalizing epigrams, and the witty anti-Petrarchan
extravagance of the controlling analogy, keep the tone
light. The cavalier conclusion demands no sacrifice of
sensibility because the poem has created no real women to
be consigned to oblivion along with their vices:

> Ye Pow'rs who over Love preside,
> Since mortal Beautyes drop so soon,
> If you would have us well supply'd,
> Send us new Nymphs with each new Moon.
>
> (117–20)

To read "The Progress of Beauty" as "an impossible
choice between false art and monstrous nature"[4] is to miss
the central importance of the *jeu d'esprit*. False art and
monstrous nature are both condemned, and were a serious
point made of this we would surely be troubled by the
difficulty of condemning them in the same way. They are
so enveloped in generalities and wit, however, so distanced from reality, that the idea of an "impossible

choice" between them does not obtain. A poem that calls for new nymphs with each new moon is far too playful to be read as a naturalistic description of the world.[5]

Actually, the poem succeeds by keeping our attention away from an impossible choice, and it does this by maintaining distance; technique keeps Celia satirically remote. When Swift approaches his subject at close range in other scatological poems, he is likely to expose his conflicting attitudes. More accurately, a failure to see that there are two different kinds of metamorphosis, each requiring a different attitude, results in thematic confusion.

Such an instructive difference exists between "The Progress of Beauty" and "A Beautiful Young Nymph Going to Bed." Much the same story is told by both poems, but instead of taking a remote general view, "A Beautiful Young Nymph" methodically and explicitly follows the routine of one woman's transformation from an artificially created wholeness to the reality of dismemberment. Because we see Corinna at close range, accompanying her through this process step by detailed step, the gruesomeness of her situation is vividly realized. While the narrative voice condemns both real and contrived metamorphoses as the wages of sin, from which the speaker is appropriately distanced, the poetic technique—reflecting Swift's underlying concern with the general phenomenon of bodily decay—diminishes distance and establishes complicity with Corinna. C. J. Rawson's description of the flayed woman and dissected beau in *A Tale of a Tub* is applicable here, too: "The images, which begin as specific tokens of guilt aimed at certain human types, teasingly turn into general signs of the human condition."[6]

Both kinds of metamorphosis, real bodily decay and the illusory cosmetic artifice called upon to disguise it, are appalling to Swift, but for different reasons. Cosmetic transformation obscures the body's real condition and is thus blameworthy as deception; the deterioration of the body is attributable to vice, another standard target of satiric condemnation. Nevertheless, whether it is prema-

turely induced by vicious living or not, this change is a
universal experience that even the most virtuous must
inevitably undergo. What draws Swift to Corinna's boudoir
with such voyeuristic interest is not only vice, as the satiric
posture asserts, but the nature of physical existence itself.

Insofar as Swift is ridiculing vice, his comic technique is
the skillful reversal of conventional formulas. The poem's
first line bestows an approval that is comically turned into
disapprobation when the couplet is completed: "*Corinna,*
Pride of *Drury-Lane,* / For whom no Shepherd sighs in
vain" (1–2). After Corinna has removed the artificial aids
that produce an illusion of physical wholeness, she proceeds to patch up her real body:

> With gentlest Touch, she next explores
> Her Shankers, Issues, running Sores,
> Effects of many a sad Disaster;
> And then to each applies a Plaister.
>
> (29–32)

Here, too, the couplets turn expertly with the same kind
of comic incongruity observed in the opening lines. The
quiet beginning, with its sympathetic suggestion of skill
and care, introduces a repulsive specific list that is in turn
dissolved into a general and dignified statement. This line
is then deflated by the anticlimactic banality of the repair
job and the bouncing humor of the feminine rhymes of
lines 31–32.

The comedy of these much-studied lines is a vehicle for,
not a subversion of, the condemnation.[7] In these and
similar passages the problem is not Swift's proficiently
realized satiric comedy, but the image of a hapless human
being that emerges to counter the condemnatory thrust of
the comedy.[8] Designed to establish the reality of vice,
Swift's graphic particulars build a sympathetic portrait
contrary to the satiric purpose. Satire and sympathy pull
in different directions, and this precludes the kind of
reading a number of commentators give the poem,

namely, that Swift has a "grudging admiration" for Corinna's struggles or reveals "covert sympathy" for her.[9] It is
owing to Swift's *inadvertent* fascination with the body's
vulnerability that Corinna is not sufficiently distanced or
vicious to rule out sympathy. The avoidable evil of the
streetwalker's life may be the root cause of Corinna's
misery, but the poem focuses on the effects: the ravaged
body and "the Anguish, Toil, and Pain" of dealing with it.
Corinna's nightmare is satirically intended to depict vice,
just as the comic procession of animals who destroy her
mechanical aids is intended to dramatize the frailty of such
artifice. Yet in each case Corinna's unbearable life is also
rendered more vivid.

As the harsh closing image emphasizes, Swift's official
role in the poem is that of the stern moralist who unequivocally condemns the false appearance of order that conceals
the essential disorder of unworthy materials and deceptive
intentions: *"Corinna* in the Morning dizen'd, / Who sees,
will spew; who smells, be poison'd" (73–74). But what he
fears and knows is that all physical nature is subject to
decay and all measures are finally ineffective in arresting it.
How to cope with the body's impermanence is Swift's
problem as well as Corinna's, and it generates much of the
poem's energy and intensity. Unlike the predictable repudiation of vice, Swift's view of the inexorable metamorphosis
of the body admits of no comforting resolution.

The scatological poems about excretion are closely related to those of bodily decay, but the process of metamorphosis that structures them is a change of attitude rather
than an enduring physical transformation. Poetic intention
is obviously problematical in these poems— "Cassinus and
Peter," "The Lady's Dressing Room," and "Strephon and
Chloe"—because the women who are transformed from
goddesses to "filthy mates" exemplify neither vicious behavior, worthy of satiric condemnation, nor physical
decay, worthy of commiseration. Kenneth Burke has justified the treatment of excretion in literature as a subspecies
of purgation,[10] but Swift's excremental poetry is notable for

its failure to purge. In each poem a mask of deception that passes for truth is shattered to expose a presumably shocking reality, but this mechanism of satire functions within a larger satiric frame. Those who are shocked by the revelation that women excrete are themselves satirized as foolish extremists. Misleading cosmetic metamorphosis and the masculine illusions it provokes are reasonable satiric targets, yet the poetic statement is uncertain because these apparent concerns are not so charged with significance as the unacknowledged expansion upon them. All three poems are implicitly predicated upon an assumption that the fact of excretion, whether openly accepted or concealed, is a problem capable of wrecking human relationships. Here, as in the poems about bodily decay, the line between subjects deserving satiric treatment and those requiring some other attitude is unclear.

"Cassinus and Peter" exhibits the least uncertainty of the three because, like "The Progress of Beauty," it maintains the distanced perspective necessary to satiric censure. Neither revels in explicit scatological detail: the earlier poem overwhelms its subject with fanciful epigrammatic wit, while "Cassinus and Peter" applies its broad comedy to Cassinus rather than to his discovery. Caelia is not a real presence; the poem refers vaguely to the magnitude of her offense, but until the climactic revelation it specifies only what she has not done. The character focused upon throughout is the extravagant lover, a naif so deluded that he perceives his mistress to be tainted by the excretory function while he himself is physically filthy, and so morally misguided that he would be less offended if Caelia "play'd the Whore."

Cassinus's tragic posture is consistently and unequivocally subjected to a satiric ridicule so effective that we fail to go beyond his wrongheaded response to wonder what Swift is advising men to do with the knowledge that women excrete. The tone of "Cassinus and Peter," like that of "The Progress of Beauty," forestalls serious thought about its subject. In light of "The Lady's Dressing Room" and

"Strephon and Chloe," the success of "Cassinus and Peter" can be seen to depend upon its preservation of the comic tone. Poet and reader can unite in regarding Cassinus's view as a joke; there is no need to deal with it seriously Donald Greene's question, "Who, except neurotic egotists like Strephon and Cassinus, cares whether Caelia ——?",[11] might safely be considered rhetorical on the basis of "Cassinus and Peter" alone. Unfortunately, "The Lady's Dressing Room" and "Strephon and Chloe" suggest that although Swift is separable from his neurotic protagonists, he is implicated in their neurosis. Both poems insist that we seriously accord the excretory function a weight that it can bear only comically. Like "A Beautiful Young Nymph Going to Bed," these poems are pulled apart by conflicting attitudes.

"The Lady's Dressing Room" is a wealth of ugly particulars held in check by a controlling comic fiction. Like Cassinus, Strephon is a ridiculed naif who is both patronized ("poor Strephon") and playfully egged on by the speaker when he investigates Celia's boudoir: "Why Strephon will you tell the rest? / And must you needs describe the Chest? (69–70). In spite of the devastating trail she has left, Celia is never actually observed by the poem; for all of their unpleasant specificity, the details of the dressing room lack the direct connection with a character which diminishes the distance between the reader and Corinna. Clearly, the "grand Survey" of the dressing room satirizes both Strephon and Celia: one for foolish illusions, the other for filth and disorder.

It is Swift's effort to take the poem beyond the presentation of a satiric scene to a concluding statement that creates thematic uncertainty.[12] Most discussions have seriously misread the ending by identifying Swift's view with that of the speaker,[13] whereas the speaker's total acceptance is just as patently ludicrous as Strephon's total rejection; their views are complementary extremes. Perhaps the analogies offered by the speaker have a superficial rhetorical persuasiveness. Closely examined, one and all are untenable:

> Should I the Queen of Love refuse,
> Because she rose from stinking Ooze?
> To him that looks behind the Scene,
> *Satira*'s but some pocky Quean.
> When *Celia* in her Glory shows,
> If *Strephon* would but stop his Nose;
> . . . .
>
> He soon would learn to think like me,
> And bless his ravisht Sight to see
> Such Order from Confusion sprung,
> Such gaudy Tulips rais'd from Dung.
> $\qquad\qquad\qquad$ (131–36; 141–44)

The passage is filled with specious reasoning. If the queen of love *remained* covered with stinking ooze as the careless Celia is tainted by the "excremental Smell" clinging to her petticoats, it would indeed be sensible to refuse her. This example does not apply to the situation described by the poem. Nor is the analogy of the actress persuasive, for this is an admitted artifice; Satira [sic], the character created on stage, should not be confused with the private person playing the role.[14] Celia, of course, may be emulating an actress in radically altering herself, but this confusion of art and nature would hardly be approved of by Swift. To ask Strephon to stop his nose is literally absurd and metaphorically an offense against truth and experience, absolutes that Swift never repudiates in his own voice.

It would similarly be mistaken to argue that the poem's concluding lines (141–44) are Swift's moral. All of the rationales proffered by the speaker involve a dangerous blurring of distinctions. That the satirist who elsewhere expends so much energy on the exposure of illusion is arguing in favor of a "ravisht Sight" and the necessarily false order springing from confusion is unthinkable, yet it has been adduced because the poem fails to establish any other authoritative voice. An appeal to conventional values implicit within the satiric attack offers no firm guidance, for what is the value involved in the subject of excretion? To imagine that Swift's distance from all three characters implies an unstated middle way is simply to indulge the critic's desire to make meaning. "The Lady's Dressing Room" neither states nor implies the needed direction.

When Swift does construct a framework of values for his subject in "Strephon and Chloe," he fails most decisively. The poem introduces the familiar romantic naif, Strephon, who marries the goddesslike maiden Chloe—only to acquire on his wedding night the same knowledge of her bodily functions that so disillusioned Cassinus and the Strephon of "The Lady's Dressing Room." Swift considers another possible attitude with this protagonist, for unlike his predecessors, this Strephon reacts with complacency, a denouement that establishes his kinship with the speaker rather than with the Strephon of "The Lady's Dressing Room." This resolution is not approved by the speaker of "Strephon and Chloe," who characterizes the couple's mutual openness as "the beastly way of Thinking" (209). What is recommended instead seems to be no different from the earlier Strephon's "foul Imagination" that is mocked as another sort of foolish extremism in "The Lady's Dressing Room." The speaker laments that Strephon did not play the voyeur before his marriage in order to watch Chloe relieve herself:

> Your Fancy then had always dwelt
> On what you saw, and what you smelt;
> Would still the same Ideas give ye,
> As when you spy'd her on the Privy.
> And spight of *Chloe*'s Charms divine,
> Your Heart had been as whole as mine.

> (245–50)

"*Chloe*'s Charms divine" are presented as a deceptive metamorphosis obscuring the unpalatable reality of excretion, but this is obviously an unnecessary polarization. The idea that Strephon should persistently contemplate images of Chloe excreting in order to remain invulnerable to love is absurd.

The final section of the poem has been regarded as structurally inappropriate,[15] yet such an objection can be countered more easily than that of thematic inconsistency. What Swift has done is to divide the poem into an exemplum followed by a moral, with each part embodying a different aspect of the total lesson. The fiction offers an instance of blameworthy behavior while the moral both comments on the fiction and makes a positive pronouncement in opposition to it.

If "Strephon and Chloe" had ended at line 250, it might be read in the same way as "The Lady's Dressing Room," that is, as a presentation of two different but equally untenable views and unsatisfactory as a totality because of the absence of an authoritative voice. The serious concluding section brings to the forefront those issues submerged with greater or lesser success in the other scatological poems. How women can maintain that decency which Swift finds essential to marital well-being when men are urged to spy into the privy is not clear, and the complete concealment of feminine functions recommended by the speaker would surely foster an attitude removed from both sense and reality. The poem asserts, ultimately, that either man must be completely shielded from awareness of the excretory process in women, thus perpetuating a version of the romantic idealization previously castigated in both Strephons, or he will embrace the other extreme and find "society in stinking." The effect of this knowledge is so powerful that a moderate acceptance of it does not seem possible, or, Swift indicates, desirable.

The overt moralizing at the end of "Strephon and Chloe" reveals the underlying difficulty of all three poems about excretion, namely, Swift's oscillation between a distanced satiric view of certain legitimate targets and an attitude of concern with feminine excretion as a serious problem.

Unlike the bodily deterioration in "A Beautiful Young Nymph Going to Bed," the metamorphosis from goddess to filthy mate is not a potentially tragic reality but merely a foolish illusion, one that Swift seems to share to the extent that he allows himself to be drawn away from satire to the detriment of coherence.

Their Name Is Legion: Swift's Political Poetry

Like the scatological poems, Swift's political poems are flawed and excessive because some element is inappropriate to the aesthetic totality: a preoccupation with inescapable bodily deterioration and elimination in the first group, and in the second, a rage too powerful for the structure that attempts to contain it. As Swift wrote in "An Epistle to a Lady," the "Nation's Represeters" are the malefactors he would hang if he could. Rather than on literary ineptitude, self-delusion, or misplaced idealism, his political poetry focuses on the premeditated and coldly intellectual evils that Dante placed in the deepest circles of his inferno.[16] The combination of public power and corruption may have excited Swift's greatest animosity, but most of his political poems are either too static or are marred by too obvious sermonizing, as if Swift's own sense of the outrageous nature of these offenses caused him to rely on the mere naming of evil.

Where a political message is his paramount concern, Swift often fails to create a viable fiction to sustain it. In "The Character of SIR ROBERT WALPOLE," for example, the absence of narrative shape and point produces flat and unmemorable lines. The one vivid personal reference—"he's loud in his laugh & he's coarse in his Jest" (2)—is soon swallowed up by the monotonous mechanicality of the poem Swift is imitating, a lampoon on Cardinal Fleury. In French the balanced lines have an elegant grace, but this kind of structure is more suited to Pope than to Swift; his renditions are lackluster abstractions and predictable antitheses such as "oppressing true merit exalting the base" (7). In other political poems Swift willfully breaks the fiction with explicit moralizing. The majority that employ a fiction, most commonly suggested by classical mythology or the beast fable, are guilty of such awkward intrusions of political message.[17] After recounting the myth of Salmoneus, "On *Wood* the Ironmonger" concludes with its application to the Wood's Patent controversy: "The Moral of this Tale is proper, / Apply'd to *Wood's* adult'rate Copper" (31–32). In sermon fashion, moral automatically follows exemplum in poem after poem.

In Swift's most successful passages of *saeva indignatio* his satiric energy seems capable of raging indefinitely against the world's endless supply of folly and vice. "Dick, a Maggot" has only one point to make—evidently Richard Tighe, its subject, had a dark complexion—but it brings such relish to the task that the triviality of the accusation is overcome. Were the poem much longer than its fourteen anti-sonnet lines, it would seem both slight and monotonous in spite of the acidulous imagination that can describe a powdered dark skin as "a fresh Turd just dropt on Snow." When a tirade actually does go on at length, as it does in the second part of "Traulus," the effort is benumbing; fierce abuse is too single-minded and too intense to be sustained for very long. The torrent of denunciatory particulars that Swift can use so effectively within a controlling fiction to dramatize the disorder and shapelessness of the satiric target—witness "The Legion Club"—becomes counterproductive when a frame of reference is lacking. Complete chaos communicates nothing beyond itself.

The difference between the two Traulus poems illustrates what happens when Swift abandons a fictive framework for his invective. "Traulus Part I" is ostensibly a conventional satiric dialogue between Tom, the satirist as naif, and Robin, an adversary who patiently explains Traulus to Tom. Beneath the clash of perspectives that the mechanics of the dialogue form imposes is a common agreement that Traulus (Lord Allen) has acted despicably toward the

Dean. While Tom can find no justification for such aberrant
behavior, Robin insists repeatedly that Traulus is mad.
Apparently an investigation of Traulus's motives by an
unbiased observer, the poem is actually an excoriation of
Traulus and a vindication of the Dean, a satiric chain or
praise and blame that is typical of Swift's poetry of fictive
self-portraiture: Swift is the victim of Traulus, who is the
victim of Tom, a character created by Swift.

The poem's principle of unity is the question-and-answer
logic of the dialogue, which assumes that there must be
some explanation for Traulus's behavior. Within this order
the dialectical expansion that becomes its response is the
dramatic rendering of irrationality. The carefully deployed
praise of Swift that dominates Tom's opening speeches is in
fact an instrument of blame directed against the man who
has maligned him. Tom's questions establish that there is
no evidence to support Traulus's accusations, that the
Dean is a renowned patriot, and that Traulus had professed
great friendship for the Dean before capriciously slandering
him. Ironically, each of Robin's attempts to palliate Tom's
indignation with the defense of madness only brings
Traulus lower. Finally accepting that Traulus is mad
allows Tom to place him beneath the wretches of Bedlam,
who in throwing their excrement are at least able to
distinguish between friend and foe: "While *Traulus* all his
Ordure scatters / To foul the Man he chiefly flatters"
(31–32). The comparison with other lunatics is followed by
a rhetorical comparison of Traulus to a mad dog, illogical
but appropriate to the ingenuous character of Tom. Robin,
whose brief replies have up to this point emphasized how
little could be said in Traulus's defense, now has his single
long reply, which extenuates by proclaiming Traulus completely ineffectual. The very monstrousness of his lunacy
renders Traulus innocuous.

As Patricia Meyer Spacks has written, "the metaphor of
madness is particularly useful to convey simultaneously a
comic and a tragic understanding of life. . . . Madness was
in the eighteenth century still considered a comic spectacle,

but it was also felt to be a tragic reality.[18] Granting Robin's point, which seems to reduce Traulus to total impotence and thus dismiss him, Tom alters its implications and places Traulus within a larger context, the hierarchy of malice and evil:

> I own, his Madness is a Jest,
> If that were all. But he's possess't:
> Incarnate with a thousand Imps,
> To work whose Ends, his Madness pimps.
> Who o'er each String and Wire preside,
> Fill ev'ry Pipe, each Motion guide.
> Directing ev'ry Vice we find
> In Scripture, to the Dev'l assign'd:
> Sent from the Dark infernal Region
> In him they lodge, and make him *Legion*.
>
> (69–78)

Swift uses a combination of absolutes and specifics to good effect: *each String and Wire, ev'ry Pipe*, and *each Motion* establish the sweeping course of evil through the most minute channels. The concentration of verbs of movement and direction—*preside, fill, guide, directing, sent*—reinforces the sense of an energetic and comprehensive dominion. Paradoxically, Traulus is too mad to be taken seriously and yet is dangerous as a conduit for all the anarchic forces of evil in the universe. Like the archetypal repository of evil with whom he is identified, Traulus has tremendous negative power. Himself nothing, he can unleash those uncreative energies of darkness that mechanically parody the movements of life and order.

In the poem's final section Traulus is swallowed up in the numberless mass—packs of curs, nest of hornets, legion of devils—whose insignificant units possess power only in the aggregate. Against this horde stands the heroic individual, the satirist-Dean, who attempts to combat the transvaluation of values that has made madness reason, virtue a crime. Like "The Legion Club," this poem concludes with a suggestion that the satirist give over the

unequal and futile struggle and abandon the ungrateful world
to the devil's party: " 'Tis Time at last to spare his Ink, / And
let them rot, or hang, or stink" (101–2). Characteristically,
Swift finds a forceful image in the corruption of the body, an
appropriate symbol for a world whose allegiance has been
given to the materialism of the devil.

The first part of "Traulus" is effective satire. Beyond what
the poem contains we need know nothing of the historical
Lord Allen, the original of Traulus or, for that matter, of
Swift. They are significant as universal figures of evil and
good, whose contest takes place within the tension-building
dramatic structure of Tom and Robin's dialogue. Lacking
the framework of fiction, the second part of "Traulus" is
unalleviated invective—vigorous and skillful, but ultimately
tiresome. Traulus is not attacked as a representative figure,
but as an individual whose weightiest crime, if the satirist's
preoccupation is any indication, is to number a mason and a
butcher among his antecedents. The portion of the indict-
ment that does not expatiate on the evils of these two trades
is highly abstract and, consequently, unconvincing:

> Positive and over-bearing,
> Changing still, and still adhering,
> Spightful, peevish, rude, untoward;
> Fierce in Tongue, in Heart a Coward.
>
> (9–12)

Without the vivid picture of Traulus as a wicked man that
the first part of the poem affords, and without the structure of a satiric fiction, the catalogue lacks point and
forcefulness. The insults are witty and well crafted, and
carry some of Swift's usual exuberance in attacking an
enemy, but the poem as a whole has too slight a rationale
to sustain it. This Traulus is merely an unpleasant fellow;
Swift develops no larger implications.

The extreme topicality of so many of the political poems
is another difficulty related to the weakness of a controlling satiric fiction. When the fiction is well developed, an

understanding of topical references adds another but not essential layer of meaning. Certainly for a full savoring of a poem it is helpful to be able to expand contexts cryptically rendered by the poet, but a poem like "The Legion Club" is aesthetically viable without one's knowing the specific historical misdeeds of the members of the Irish parliament singled out for individual castigation. How the satirist manipulates his rage to make a powerful poem is more compelling than the reasons that produced the rage. At the other end of the spectrum are poems that depend almost entirely on the historical knowledge the reader can bring to them. *"Toland*'s Invitation to *Dismal,"* for example, is a mine field of alphabetical puzzles:

> Wine can give *P--rt--d* Wit, and *Cl--v--nd* Sense,
> *M--t--g--e* Learning, *B--lt--n* Eloquence:
> *Ch--ly,* when Drunk, can never lose his *Wand,*
> And *L--nc--n* then imagines he has Land.
>
> (23–26)

Supplying the names—Portland, Cleveland, Montague, Bolton, Cholmondeley, and Lincoln—does not notably improve the passage as poetry, but in either case the intention is clear enough: only the false transformation brought about by wine gives the characters positive qualities. The poem gives us no way of determining the importance of its assertions, nor, since the substance of the epistle imitated has been altered, does the Horatian original illuminate Swift's version; the names, unsupported by any characterization, must carry the weight of meaning. Historical and biographical evidence might supply a motive or confirm the suitability of the satiric thrusts, but it could do nothing to reclaim the passage as poetry.[19]

While it is important as a criterion for present-day intelligibility, topicality in and of itself need not reduce a poem to obscurity. *Absalom and Achitophel* is highly topical, but its topicality is accessible in a way that most of Swift's political poetry is not. Dryden focuses upon the major figures of a nationally significant drama, a political event of some magnitude. More important, *Absalom and Achitophel* does not depend entirely on topical references. The well-developed fiction is buttressed by analogy to a familiar biblical episode, and the poem also has many of the characteristics of epic. The topicality of Swift's political poetry is generally both unsupported and lacking in magnitude. In England Swift writes like a party infighter about the ephemera of Whig and Tory squabbling, and in Ireland, despite his more disinterested stance as a patriot, even such matters as the considerable threat posed by Wood's Patent suffer diminution in the perspective of Ireland's long history as an exploited colony. This perspective informs *A Modest Proposal* but not the poetry.

Swift's most successful poetic attacks on specific examples of public malfeasance are two late poems, "Helter Skelter" and "The Legion Club." Both exhibit the pleasing harmony of satiric denunciation: a wealth of damning particulars is matched by the satirist's energy and inventiveness in raging against them. While "Helter Skelter" preserves this equilibrium to the end, totally imprisoning the attorneys within the circle not only of their journey but of the satiric attack, "The Legion Club" ends with the satirist's withdrawal from the field.

Imitating the bumpy rhythms of the lawyers' journey on horseback, the relentless jog trot of "Helter Skelter" lashes the riders with an equally unremitting flood of satiric particulars. The sense of an overwhelming accumulation is emphasized by the poem's repetitive structure; anaphora marks the stages of the satiric movement from outward grandeur to the underlying reality of borrowed finery, but it also points up the abundance of material to satirize and the poet's virtuosity in turning it all to account. Every particular expands into a catalogue of offenses:

> Thorough Town and thorough Village,
> All to plunder, all to pillage;
> Thorow Mountains thorow Vallies;
> Thorow stinking Lanes and Allies.

(39–42)

Like the rushing verse, the rampaging army of attorneys
sweeps through the countryside in a frenzy of illicit activity. The pervasive military imagery is used both seriously
and ironically to describe the sham of their outward trappings and the reality of their destructiveness. On their
borrowed horses they look big as giants, but they are only
"little Mars's," who "draw their Swords and run away."
After the typically satiric stripping away of false appearances, Swift presents the lawyers' diminutive reality:

> And with very little Pence,
> And as very little Sence:
> With some Law but little Justice.
>
> (29–31)

The compatibility of "some Law" with "little Justice"
reflects the central theme of Swift's political satire—the
inherent disorder in the world's way of despising genuine
merit and elevating the mediocre and the unprincipled.
Nonentities in themselves, the attorneys are empowered
by the government to ride the circuit where, in their
borrowed authority and borrowed finery, they cheat and
cuckold the populace.

"A Character, Panegyric, and Description of The Legion Club" is similarly inspired by those who abuse the
public trust, again a collective entity rather than powerful
individuals. Swift's longest and most celebrated piece of
invective is directed against real men occupying a particular
office of government and carrying out their activities at a
specific location:

> Not a Bow-shot from the College,
> Half the Globe from Sense and Knowledge.
> By the prudent Architect
> Plac'd against the Church direct.
>
> (3–6)

All of these specifics indicate that there is to be no subterfuge here, no lashing the vice while sparing the name. Moreover, the physical location has great ironic potential: the building, situated between learning and faith where good government should be found, is "large and lofty," but the outwardly favorable appearance only emphasizes the inward lack.

For such a group of powerful adversaries the satirist proposes radical measures, either complete destruction by the devil or conversion of their building into a madhouse by "Swift." It was generally known that Dean Swift had made provision in his will for a charitable institution for lunatics; Swift the satirist does the same within his poem in order to provide a proper setting for a special group of dangerous lunatics. The transformation of parliament into a conflation of hell and bedlam alters the effect of the members' actions rather than the actions themselves. Because the legislators behave as if they were mad, Swift changes their milieu into a madhouse, where their performance is harmless.[20]

Invective, which offers the primitive satisfaction of straightforward name-calling and open insult, is Swift's chief weapon in the enumeration of mad legislators. As W. B. Carnochan has observed in discussing *A Tale of a Tub*, "one of the things satire typically tries to do is to obliterate its subjects,"[21] a response in kind to the obliterating nature of vice and folly. The genius of Swift's description of Sir Thomas Prendergast, for example, lies in the quality of overflow and shapelessness, its lack of logical coherence. Developing by accretion from the subject's infinite supply of knavery and the writer's corresponding ease in satirizing this knavery, the invective does not slacken or peak; it is simply cut off:

> LET Sir Tom, that rampant Ass,
> Stuff his Guts with Flax and Grass;
> But before the Priest he fleeces
> Tear the Bible all to Pieces.
> At the Parsons, *Tom*, Halloo Boy,
> Worthy Offspring of a Shoeboy,

Footman, Traytor, vile Seducer,
Perjur'd Rebel, brib'd Accuser;
Lay thy paltry Priviledge aside,
Sprung from Papists and a Regicide;
Fall a Working like a Mole,
Raise the Dirt about your Hole.

(63–74)

The quality of satiric overkill is primarily attributable to the rushing energy, which moves the victim from one contemptible act to another and equally propels the satirist from one term of abuse to another. From an ass Sir Tom proceeds in Swift's admirably thorough denunciation through a number of despicable human guises to end as a lowly creature burrowing in the dirt. The animal imagery is appropriately reductive; in Michel Foucault's words, "for classicism madness in its ultimate form is man in immediate relation to his animality."[22] These transformations also suggest the shape-shifting of black magicians, another sign of the all-encompassing nature of evil, and the forceful, idiomatic verbs—*stuff, fleeces, tear, fall a working*—demonstrate the ceaseless activity of evil and its manifold forms.

Swift characteristically pushes a metaphor to an uncomfortably literal point with vivid details; the banality of calling Sir Tom an ass is redeemed by the sharp particularity of "stuff his Guts with Flax and Grass." A similar principle is at work in lines 65–66, where the concrete image of tearing up the Bible gives substance to the vagueness of fleecing the priest. In both examples a knowledge of the political occasion enriches but is not essential. Swift's rage is specifically directed against parliament's attempt to strip the clergy of the agistment tithe on pasturage and the tithe on flax, a motive expressed by references to the actual products at issue. A legislator is turned into a domestic animal that literally consumes grass and flax, and fleecing the clergy is both the deprivation of real fleece and the metaphoric robbing of the word's colloquial meaning.

The satirist-observer's tour of the madhouse is reminiscent of the descent into the underworld in the *Aeneid* and the *Inferno,* although it makes ironic departures from both.[23] A key difference is in the role of the guide, divinely appointed and wise in the *Aeneid* and the *Inferno,* fearful and overcome by the stench in "The Legion Club." After one obvious allusion to the *Aeneid,* in which the muse reassures the satirist that some menacing apparitions are only phantoms, she quickly abdicates her instructive functions in a reversal of the guide-protagonist relationship found in Virgil and Dante. In a parody of the replacement of Beatrice with Virgil for Dante's passage through hell, or Anchises' for the Sibyl, the satirist abruptly passes from the guidance of Clio to a keeper, who for a tip will point out and name the madmen. This reductive transition from classical literature to eighteenth-century actuality is the first subtle indication that reality will intrude and ultimately overcome the fiction.

Like hell, Swift's madhouse is a closed universe of punishment for those permanently arrested in vice: "Though 'tis hopeless to reclaim them, / Scorpion Rods perhaps may tame them" (157–58). In Virgil and Dante, however, the encounter with the damned is a terrifying experience that nevertheless demonstrates that the unknown world beyond death can be ordered and comprehended. The vision is enlightening as well as traumatic. Swift's underworld yields no such understanding. It is not encompassed and progressed through, but abandoned in revulsion; its denizens can be named and castigated, but not ordered or explained.

The rage of impotence is evident in the poem's conclusion, for although the poet has invented an appropriate world to contain his satiric targets, they triumph through the weight of viciousness that sheer numbers impose:

> Keeper, I must now retire,
> You have done what I desire:
> But I feel my Spirits spent,
> With the Noise, the Sight, the Scent.

> Pray be patient, you shall find
> Half the best are still behind:
> You have hardly seen a Score,
> I can shew two hundred more.
> Keeper, I have seen enough.
> Taking then a Pinch of Snuff;
> I concluded, looking round 'em,
> May their God, the Devil confound 'em.
>
> (231–42)

With the urbane ritual of taking snuff, the satirist dismisses his madmen and withdraws from the poetic world he has created to imprison them. In reality they cannot be thus neutralized; the sane world to which he returns accords them honor and power, while even within his own design the satirist retreats gracefully but exhaustedly. "By concluding his poem with the hope that Satan may rise up against his own," John Irwin Fischer writes, "he prays for precisely that division of Satan's house which he cannot accomplish, but which he knows Christ has promised."[24] Just as the unalterable terms of physical existence frustrate Swift's satiric intention in the scatological poetry, so the great numbers of his human adversaries, their multiple avenues of attack, and their endless misdeeds ultimately force the satirist to acknowledge the power of the real world and the tenuous nature of his artistic triumph.

Conclusion

The perception of the world as adversary that structures Swift's poetry is also found in his interpretation of his own life. The autobiographical prose fragment, "Family of Swift," the correspondence, and Irvin Ehrenpreis's admirable biography all document Swift's repeated difficulties and ultimate failure to establish himself in the world, a history punctuated with bitter references on Swift's part to those whose action or inaction thwarted his hopes.[1] Late in life, Swift's letter to Pope introducing his cousin Deane Swift describes his family unfavorably: "I am utterly void of what the World calls natural Affection, and with good Reason, because they are a numerous Race, degenerating from their Ancestors. . . ."[2] Included in Swift's account of those relations who wronged him is his father, dead two months before Swift's birth: "His son . . . hath often been heard to say that he felt the consequences of that marriage [to a woman undistinguished in family and fortune] not onely through the whole course of his education, but during the greatest part of his life."[3] Whether the *often* is merely rhetorical emphasis, the cherishing of this prenatal misfortune is sufficiently striking.

Other early instances of neglect and bad treatment Swift recounts illustrate, as Louis A. Landa writes, "an emerging pattern of disappointment, frustration, and disillusionment."[4] As a university student he was so ill-used by his "nearest Relations" that his studies suffered; as a young man trying to make his way, he saw a bribe to Lord Berkeley's secretary procure a rich deanery for another claimant. Lord Romney failed to help Swift to preferment in spite of professing love for him, and even an opportunity

194

to impress King William at Moor Park turned out badly: although Swift explained an issue of foreign policy persuasively, it failed to influence the King. The few pages of family history Swift wrote take him no further, but the pattern of promise frustrated, as he wrote to Bolingbroke, continued to dominate his own perceptions of his life: "I remember when I was a little boy, I felt a great fish at the end of my line which I drew up almost on the ground, but it dropt in, and the disappointment vexeth me to this very day, and I believe it was the type of all my future disappointments."[5] The image is aptly emblematic, for Swift was tantalizingly close to power during much of his early life and inevitably thwarted in obtaining the career rewards he hoped for. Accounts of Swift written by those who knew him confirm the impression of lasting resentment connected with his youth and young manhood.[6]

Genius denied its rightful scope and scantily rewarded is Swift's own view of his years of ambitious struggle before the death of Queen Anne and Harley's fall permanently condemned him to his Irish deanery. In spite of Swift's zealous work under both Whig and Tory ministries to secure the First Fruits for the Irish clergy, a cause he had made his own, the considerable credit that he deserved and yearned for proved elusive.[7] In Ireland he became a celebrated figure, but never received the coveted mitre, nor, as he confessed to Archdeacon Walls, the expression of gratitude that he felt he merited: "Although I have done more service to *Ireland,* and particularly to the Church, than any man of my level, I have never been able to get a good word."[8] Later in life he wrote more generally to Lord Palmerston: "In the time when I had some little credit I did fifty times more for fifty people, from whom I never received the least service or assistance."[9]

What Swift experienced in his own life he also saw as the pattern of a world more comfortable with false appearance and mediocrity than with merit. He warns his fellow clergyman Patrick Delany: "A Genius in the Rev'rend Gown, / Must ever keep its Owner down" ("To Doctor

Delany," 79–80). The cynical "Advice to a Parson" offers complementary advice:

> Wou'd you rise in the *Church*, be *Stupid* and *Dull*,
> Be empty of *Learning*, of *Insolence* full:
> Tho' Lewd and Immoral, be Formal and Grave,
> In *Flatt'ry* an *Artist*, in *Fawning* a *Slave*,
> No Merit, no Science, no Virtue is wanting
> In him, that's accomplish'd in *Cringing* and *Canting*.
>
> (1–6)

Swift speaks as a churchman here, but elsewhere the same perspective embraces most of humankind: public figures betraying their trust, lovers idealizing their all-too-human mistresses, fools claiming to be wits, and friends failing to perform the duties of friendship. The indictments are sweeping. In "The Place of the Damn'd" and "The Day of Judgement," almost everyone belongs in hell:

> "Offending Race of Human Kind,
> By Nature, Reason, Learning, blind;
> You who thro' Frailty step'd aside,
> And you who never fell—*thro' Pride*;
> You who in different Sects have shamm'd,
> And come to see each other damn'd."
>
> ("The Day of Judgement," 11–16)

Altogether the poems reveal an impressive multitude of unworthies, from national heroes like the Duke of Marlborough and Lord Cutts to lowly functionaries like Swift's personal enemies, Richard Tighe and Richard Bettesworth; from men who represent a clear and present danger to the country like William Wood to laughable quacks like John Partridge.

Swift is usually equal to individual adversaries, but beyond the varieties of humankind that provoke his satiric response loom the ultimate enemies, those powerful forces which constantly resist man's attempts to impose order. As Alvin B. Kernan describes the myth of satire, it springs from an impulse that eludes rational control: "The fears which the myth images and the satirist exploits seem not to originate in our conscious minds so much as in our bones or . . . in the irrational darkness of our unconscious."[10] In Swift this impacts as a deep and ineradicable disorder in life itself, an urge toward entropy that invariably confounds the desire for order. Such awareness of the chaotic and random nature of the cosmos, as it appears to man, informs his outcry to Stella on the death of Lady Ashburnham: "I hate Life, when I think it exposed to such Accidents and to see so many thousand wretches burthening the Earth while such as her dye, makes me think God did never intend Life for a Blessing."[11] This perspective also engenders the scatological poems, where satiric rage is misdirected against the unalterable conditions of physical existence, and also the political poems— including "On Poetry: A Rapsody"—where disorder created by man becomes an all-encompassing force beyond the poet's power to order and control.

Swift nevertheless achieves some notable victories against the powers of darkness: he subdues devouring time in all but the last poem for Stella's birthday and makes triumphant poetry out of the world's distortions of his own reputation. For Swift the satirist, however, and for Swift the Christian and Augustan, success within poetry can only partially compensate for defeats suffered beyond its boundaries: the stance of the satirist is necessarily one of involvement in the world he recreates in paradigms of foolishness and knavery. The basic structure of Swift's poetry is thus a dynamic struggle between vulnerability to a powerful adversary and the formidable resources of art; his greatness as a poet lies in the wit and energy with which he articulates the pessimistic vision of satire.

Notes

Notes to Introduction

1. George P. Mayhew, "Recent Swift Scholarship," does not mention the poetry except to take notice of Harold Williams's edition of it. *Jonathan Swift 1667–1967: A Dublin Tercentenary Tribute,* ed. Roger McHugh and Philip Edwards (Dublin: Dufour Editions, 1968), pp. 187–97.

2. Maurice Johnson, *The Sin of Wit* (Syracuse, N.Y.: Syracuse University Press, 1950).

3. Irvin Ehrenpreis, "Swift's Letters," *Focus,* ed. C. J. Rawson (London: Sphere Books, 1971), p. 197.

4. Samuel Johnson, "Swift," *Lives of the English Poets,* ed. George Birkbeck Hill (Oxford: Clarendon Press, 1905), 3: 65.

5. Philip Roberts, "Swift's Poetry," *Swift,* ed. W. A. Speck (New York: Arco, 1970), p. 49.

6. Rachel Trickett, *The Honest Muse: A Study in Augustan Verse* (Oxford: Clarendon Press, 1967), p. 121. A similar omission occurs in Percy G. Adams, *Graces of Harmony: Alliteration, Assonance, and Consonance in Eighteenth-Century British Poetry* (Athens, Ga.: University of Georgia Press, 1977). Separate chapters are devoted to Dryden, Pope, and Thomson, while Swift has only a few scattered references.

7. Trickett, *Honest Muse,* p. 121.

8. Oswald Johnson, "Swift and the Common Reader," *In Defense of Reading,* ed. Reuben A. Brower and Richard Poirier (New York: E. P. Dutton, 1962), p. 189.

9. Herbert Davis, "Swift's View of Poetry," *Fair Liberty Was All His Cry,* ed. A. Norman Jeffares (London: Macmillan, 1967), p. 62.

10. W. R. Irwin, "Swift the Verse Man," *Philological Quarterly* 54 (1975): 222.

11. D. H. Lawrence, Introduction to *Pansies,* reprinted in *Phoenix: The Posthumous Papers of D. H. Lawrence,* ed. Edward D. McDonald (London: William Heinemann, 1936), pp. 281–82; Aldous Huxley, "Swift," *Do What You Will* (London: Chatto & Windus, 1929), pp. 93–106; F. R. Leavis, "The Irony of Swift," *Determinations* (London: Chatto & Windus, 1934), pp. 79–108. Milton Voigt, *Swift and the Twentieth Century* (Detroit, Mich.: Wayne State University Press, 1964), provides a good overview of both nineteenth- and twentieth-century attitudes toward Swift.

12. Lawrence, *Phoenix,* p. 282.

13. Leavis, "Irony of Swift," p. 106; Huxley, "Swift," p. 99.

14. O. Johnson, "Swift and the Common Reader," p. 177.

15. Bonamy Dobrée, *English Literature in the Early Eighteenth Century, 1700–1740* (Oxford: Clarendon Press, 1959), pp. 466, 465.

16. Edmund Wilson, *The Shores of Light* (New York: Farrar, Straus and Young, 1952), p. 700.

17. Nora Crowe Jaffe, *The Poet Swift* (Hanover, N.H.: University Press of New England, 1977); John Irwin Fischer, *On Swift's Poetry* (Gainesville: University Presses of Florida, 1978); Peter J. Schakel, *The Poetry of Jonathan Swift: Allusion and the Development of a Poetic Style* (Madison: University of Wisconsin Press, 1978). The paucity of references to these books in my discussion of Swift's poetry reflects the stage of my own work when they appeared rather than any judgment on their merit.

18. Claudio Guillén, *Literature as System* (Princeton, N.J.: Princeton University Press, 1971), p. 278.

19. Ibid., p. 279.

20. Maynard Mack, "The Muse of Satire," *The Yale Review* 41 (1951): 88.

21. Maurice Johnson, "Swift's Poetry Reconsidered," *English Writers of the Eighteenth Century*, ed. John H. Middendorf (New York: Columbia University Press, 1971), p. 248.

22. Michael Shinagel, *A Concordance to the Poems of Jonathan Swift* (Ithaca and London: Cornell University Press, 1972), p. 945. Other common nouns are used far less frequently: *place*, 126 times; *face*, 122; *day* and *man*, both 120; *time*, 117.

23. The criticism of "Verses on the Death of Dr. Swift" is an excellent illustration of this difference in attitude. While little attention has been paid to the first two-thirds of the poem, where Swift is a ridiculed or ignored figure, from Pope on, commentators have focused on the "eulogy" (11. 299–484) as the key to the poem's interpretation and the source of critical problems. See, among recent examples, John Irwin Fischer, "How to Die: *Verses on the Death of Dr. Swift*," *Review of English Studies* 21 (1970): 422–41; Arthur H. Scouten and Robert D. Hume, "Pope and Swift: Text and Interpretation of Swift's Verses on His Death," *Philological Quarterly* 52 (1973): 205–31; Hugo M. Reichard, "The Self-Praise Abounding in Swift's *Verses*," *Tennessee Studies in Literature* 18 (1973): 105–12; Peter J. Schakel, "The Politics of Opposition in 'Verses on the Death of Dr. Swift,'" *Modern Language Quarterly* 35 (1974): 246–56; and David M. Vieth, "The Mystery of Personal Identity: Swift's Verses on His Own Death," *The Author in His Work: Essays on a Problem in Criticism*, ed. Louis L. Martz and Aubrey Williams (New Haven, Conn.: Yale University Press, 1978), pp. 245–62.

24. Swift to Lord Bathurst, October 1730, *Corres.*, 3: 410: "For, having some months ago much & often offended the ruling party, and often worried by libellers I am at the pains of writing one in their style & manner, & sent it by an unknown hand to a Whig printer who very faithfully published it."

25. Letter of April 5, 1729, *Corres.*, 3: 330–31 (emphasis added).

26. Swift to Archbishop King, October 10, 1710, *Corres.*, 1: 185.

27. Faulkner's note from the original publication of the poem in the 1735 *Miscellanies* is reproduced in *Poems*, p. 889, n. 88. Emphasis removed.

28. "Thoughts on Various Subjects," *Prose Works*, 4: 243.

29. Geoffrey Hill, "Jonathan Swift, The Poetry of 'Reaction,'" *The World of Jonathan Swift*, p. 196.

30. Robert C. Elliott, *The Power of Satire: Magic, Ritual, Art* (Princeton, N.J.: Princeton University Press, 1968), p. 186.

31. Letter of May 31, 1737, *Corres.*, 5: 42; letter of March 21, 1729, *Corres.*, 3: 383.

32. Patricia Meyer Spacks, *An Argument of Images: The Poetry of Alexander Pope* (Cambridge, Mass.: Harvard University Press, 1971), p. 252.

33. "Marginalia," *Prose Works*, 5: 249; Cherbury, *Life and Raigne of Henry VIII*, p. 468.

34. Ibid., p. 251; Cherbury, p. 575.

35. No. 38, April 26, 1711, *Prose Works*, 3: 141.

36. Letter of April 5, 1733, *Corres.*, 4: 138. In spite of the satirist's assertion of the desire to reform in "An Epistle to a Lady," this comment suggests that Swift regarded satire primarily as a vehicle for exposure alone. Cf. Swift's annotation of Bishop Burnet's comment that satire "may awaken the world to just reflections on their own errors and follies." Swift wrote: "This I take to be nonsense" ("Marginalia," *Prose Works*, 5: 266).

37. Walpole issued a warrant for Swift's arrest, but when he was told that it would require an army of ten thousand men to remove Swift from Dublin, he changed his mind. Thomas Sheridan, *The Life of the Rev. Dr. Jonathan Swift, Dean of St. Patrick's, Dublin*, 2d ed. (London: J. F. & C. Rivington, 1787), p. 240.

38. See "An Epigram Inscribed to the Honorable Sergeant Kite" *(Poems,* 3: 817–18): "For who would not think it a much better choice, / By your knife to be mangled than rack'd with your voice" (3–4).

39. *Poems*, 3: 810.

40. Mack, "Muse of Satire," p. 89.

41. "Epilogue to the Satires: Dialogue II" (208–9), *Imitations of Horace*, ed. John Butt (London: Methuen, 1939), p. 324. See also Swift to Pope, June 1, 1728: "You despise the follies, and hate the vices of mankind, without the least ill effect on your temper; and with regard to particular men, you are inclined always rather to think the better, whereas with me it is always directly contrary. I hope however, this is not in you from a superior principle of virtue, but from your situation, which hath made all parties and interests indifferent to you, who can be under no concern about high and low-church, Whig and Tory, or who is first Minister" *(Corres.*, 3: 289).

42. "The First Satire of the Second Book of Horace Imitated" (151–53), *Imitations of Horace*, pp. 19, 21

43. Swift uses *jest* in this sense in "Traulus, Part I": "I own, his Madness is a Jest" (69).

44. Letter of November 26, 1725, *Corres.*, 3: 117.

45. C. J. Rawson, *Gulliver and the Gentle Reader* (London: Routledge & Kegan Paul, 1973), p. 12.

46. Cf. *The Intelligencer*, no. 3 (1728), *Prose Works*, 12: 33: "It [humor] is certainly the best Ingredient towards that Kind of Satyr, which is most useful, and gives the least Offence; which, instead of lashing, laughs Men out of their Follies, and Vices; and is the Character that gives *Horace* the Preference to *Juvenal*."

47. James Sutherland, *English Satire* (Cambridge: Cambridge University Press, 1958), p. 47, writes about the Juvenalian tradition: "The more *saeva* the *indignatio*, the more a satirist must bring to his work a fine control."

48. *Journal to Stella*, 1: 72. Swift's view is much like that of Nathanael West's Miss Lonelyhearts, who perceives a basic incompatibility between man and nature: "Man has a tropism for order. . . . The physical world has a tropism for disorder, entropy," *Miss Lonelyhearts* (New York: New Directions, 1962), p. 209.

49. *A Tale of a Tub,* ed. A. C. Guthkelch and D. Nichol Smith (Oxford: Clarendon Press, 1920), p. 172.

50. Ronald Paulson, *The Fictions of Satire* (Baltimore, Md.: Johns Hopkins University Press, 1967), p. 16.

51. *Le Rire* (Paris: Presses Universitaires de France, 1962). pp. 38–39; my translation.

52. C. J. Rawson, "The Nightmares of Strephon: Nymphs of the City in the Poems of Swift, Baudelaire, Eliot," *English Literature in the Age of Disguise,* ed. Maximillian E. Novak (Berkeley: University of California Press, 1977), p. 69.

53. As Swift wrote about Richard Bettesworth in "The Yahoo's Overthrow": "He kindled, as if the whole Satire had been / The oppression of Virtue, not wages of Sin" (41–42). Cf. Swift to Knightley Chetwode, June 2, 1723: "They that most deserve contempt are most angry at being contemned, I know it by experience" (*Corres.,* 2: 457).

54. "The Legion Club" also concludes with a withdrawal from the satiric task and a renunciatory malediction: "May their God, the Devil confound 'em" (242).

55. Letter of August 28, 1730, *Corres.,* 3: 405.

Notes to Chapter 1: Strategies of Self-defense

1. Letter of March 15, 1728–29, *Corres.,* 3: 317–18; Swift to Bishop Atterbury, July 18, 1717, *Corres.,* 2: 279.

2. Letter of January 10, 1720–21, *Corres.,* 2: 374. See also "On Censure": "The World, a willing Stander-by, / Inclines to aid a specious Lye" (13–14).

3. Robert C. Elliott, "Swift's 'I,' " *The Yale Review* 62 (1973): 380.

4. Several good discussions of the odes exist. See Kathleen Williams, *Jonathan Swift and the Age of Compromise* (Lawrence: University of Kansas Press, 1958), pp. 38–41, 146–48; Irvin Ehrenpreis, *Mr. Swift and His Contemporaries* (Cambridge, Mass.: Harvard University Press, 1962), pp. 109–41; Kathryn Montgomery Harris, " 'Occasions So Few,' Satire as a Strategy of Praise in Swift's Early Odes," *Modern Language Quarterly* 31 (1970): 22–37; Robert W. Uphaus, "From Panegyric to Satire: Swift's Early Odes and *A Tale of a Tub," Texas Studies in Literature and Language* 13 (1971): 55–70. A recent treatment that is especially comprehensive is John Irwin Fischer, *On Swift's Poetry* (Gainesville: University of Florida Press, 1978), pp. 7–54.

5. The inability to manage conflicting elements, which is an obvious surface phenomenon in the odes, also appears as a buried structure in a significant body of Swift's mature work—the scatological poems. Refusing to differentiate between a just condemnation of vice and an unjust censure of bodily existence, the later poems have the compensating virtues of technical brilliance and compelling subjects, which the odes markedly lack. In both cases, however, the poet's failure to clarify his attitude produces thematic confusion in the poetry.

6. Harris, "Occasions So Few," p. 22.

7. *The Poems and Fables of John Dryden,* ed. James Kinsley (London: Oxford University Press, 1958), p. 608.

8. As Swift wrote in his "Thoughts on Various Subjects": "All Panegyricks are mingled with an Infusion of Poppy" (*Prose Works,* 4: 252). Dryden's apocryphal remark to Swift might more accurately have been "Cousin Swift, you will never be a panegyrist."

9. Perhaps to increase their distastefulness, all of these occupations are described in terms of manual labor.

10. In his later poetry of fictive self-portraiture multiple and even conflicting versions of self are all labeled "Swift," but the poet's relationship to these created selves has the same ambiguity as his relationship to the muse in the odes.

11. Swift's *Directions to Servants, Prose Works,* 13: 57, contains the following instructions for the waiting maid: "You will have the Choice of three Lovers; the Chaplain, the Steward, and my Lord's Gentleman. I would first advise you to chuse the Steward; but, if you happen to be young with Child by my Lord, you must take up with the Chaplain." Richard Reynolds, "Swift's 'Humble Petition' from a Pregnant Frances Harris?" *Scriblerian* 5 (1972): 38–39, conjectures accordingly. The sexual innuendo in the poem is inconclusive, and given Swift's position in the Berkeley household at the time the poem was written, it seems unlikely that he would have been quite so sportive if Mrs. Harris were pregnant.

12. The phrase occurs in a description of some of the Market Hill poems in Swift's letter to Pope, February 13, 1728–29, *Corres.,* 3: 311. His next letter to Pope (March 6, 1728–29) elaborates: "I told you some time ago, that I was dwindled to a writer of libels on the lady of the family where I lived, and upon myself. . . . They were sometimes shewn to intimate friends, to occasion mirth, and that was all" (ibid., pp. 313–14). In spite of the deprecatory reference and the assertion that the poems were written for intimate friends, Swift eventually allowed most of them to be published.

13. Actually, each of Swift's three visits to Market Hill lasted for a period of months, and according to his correspondence, the time was pleasantly spent: "Sir A-- . . . pressed me to stay longer. . . . I hate *Dublin,* and love the Retirement here, and the Civility of my Hosts" (Swift to Thomas Sheridan, August 2, 1728, *Corres.,* 3: 296).

14. The experience that occasioned this poem is described in a letter to Pope, February 13, 1728–29, *Corres.,* 3: 311: "She is perfectly well bred, and desirous to improve her understanding, which is very good, but cultivated too much like a fine Lady. She was my pupil there, and severely chid when she read wrong."

15. *Prose Works,* 4: 213.

16. Reproduced in *Poems,* p. 888, n.61. Emphasis removed.

17. *Prose Works.* 4:221.

18. Ibid., 13: 23.

19. David M. Vieth, "The Mystery of Personal Identity: Swift's Verses on His Own Death," *The Author in His Work,* ed. Louis L. Martz and Aubrey Williams (New Haven, Conn.: Yale University Press, 1978), p. 250.

20. Thomas R. Edwards, *Imagination and Power* (New York: Oxford University Press, 1971), p. 6.

21. Letter of July 3, 1714, *Corres.,* 2:44.

22. *Prose Works,* 5:214.

23. Cf. "An Apology to the Lady Carteret," which develops from a similar misunderstanding and with a similar portrait of Swift as comically inept vis-à-vis a social superior.

24. Peter J. Schakel, *The Poetry of Jonathan Swift: Allusion and the Development of a Poetic Style* (Madison: University of Wisconsin Press, 1978), p. 75.

25. Oliver W. Ferguson remarks one conspicuous exception to Swift's persistent attacks on Ireland's foreign imports: "He strenuously opposed . . . all efforts to increase the tax on French and Spanish wines." *Jonathan Swift and Ireland* (Urbana: University of Illinois Press, 1962), p. 156. Swift's unconvincing argument was that the few men of fortune who lived in Ireland did so primarily because good foreign wine could be obtained cheaply there.

26. Cf. Swift to Archbishop King, October 10, 1710, *Corres.*, 1: 185; "I have known some great Ministers who would seem to discover the very inside of their Hearts, when I was sure they did not value whether I had proclaimed all they had said, at Charing cross." A similar contrast structures "The Discovery," where Lord Berkeley and his secretary Arthur Bushe are seen conferring, presumably about affairs of state. When someone eavesdrops on them, he finds the discussion to be about the price of oats and hay at the local market.

27. Until very recently "A Libel on Doctor Delany and a Certain Great Lord" and "A Panegyric on the Reverend Dean Swift" seemed to constitute a similar pairing. At the 1977 MLA session on Swift's poetry Aubrey Williams persuasively questioned the attribution of the "Panegyric" to Swift on the basis of internal evidence. Since then James Woolley has uncovered evidence to support Williams's contention that James Arbuckle is the probable author of the "Panegyric." Williams's essay, " 'A Vile Encomium': That 'Panegyric on the Reverend D--n S---t' " and Woolley's "Arbuckle's *Panegyric* and Swift's Scrub Libel: The Documentary Evidence" appear in *Contemporary Studies of Swift's Poetry*, ed. Donald C. Mell and John Irwin Fischer (University of Delaware Press, 1981), pp. 178–209.

28. *Poems*, p. 551; my translation.

29. Letter of May 27, 1713, *Corres.*, 1: 359.

30. Swift to Pope, March 25, 1736, *Corres.*, 4: 472.

31. Letter of May 12, 1735, ibid., p. 334.

32. Swift to Pope, January, 1732–33, ibid., p. 103.

33. Letter of August 19, 1727, *Corres.*, 3: 233.

34. Letter of February 9, 1736–37, *Corres.*, 5: 4.

35. Ronald Paulson suggests a relation to the maxim—untenably, I think—when he describes the anti-Swift speaker as demonstrating "that men's attitudes toward someone like Swift are dictated by their private needs." *The Fictions of Satire* (Baltimore, Md.: Johns Hopkins Press, 1967), p. 190. Whatever the private needs of the anti-Swift speaker, he had no personal relationship with Swift and thus does not fall under the aegis of the maxim.

36. The few critics who have discussed the poem are in agreement on this point. Arthur H. Scouten and Robert D. Hume, "Pope and Swift: Text and Interpretation of Swift's Verses on His Own Death," *Philological Quarterly* 52 (1973): 215, comment: "As a personal defense, it is really very effective." See also John Middleton Murry, *Jonathan Swift* (London: Jonathan Cape, 1954), p. 460; Paulson, p. 190.

37. Scouten and Hume, "Pope and Swift," pp. 211–18, provide an illuminating analysis of the tone and technique of the apologia.

38. William King to Mrs. Whiteway, January 30, 1738–39, *Corres.*, 5: 136–37, refers to the editing "to which I consented in deference to Mr. *Pope*'s judgment, and the opinion of others of the Dean's friends. . . ."

39. *The Correspondence of Alexander Pope*, ed. G. Sherburn (Oxford: Clarendon Press, 1956), 4: 130.

40. *Corres.*, 5: 139; cf. Murry, *Jonathan Swift*, p. 459, for a more violent expression of this view: "In truth the latter part of this famous poem is unworthy in every way. It lacks the vitality and vividness, and above all the humour, of the former; and it is morally incongruous with it. The sardonic objectivity gives place to an extravagence of self-laudation."

41. Paulson, *Fictions of Satire*, p. 191.

42. Barry Slepian, "The Ironic Intention of Swift's Verses on his own Death," *Review of English Studies* n.s. 14 (1963): 249–56, has Swift making his own case an exemplum of the maxim, a final proof that all men are vain; Marshall Waingrow, "Verses on the Death of Dr. Swift," *Studies in English Literature* 5 (1965): 513–18, believes that on the contrary Swift rises above the maxim and thus can instruct others; John Irwin Fischer, "How to Die: Verses on the Death of Dr. Swift," *Review of English Studies* n.s. 21 (1970): 422–41, sees Swift as exemplifying the proper way to accept death.

43. Vieth, "Mystery of Personal Identity," pp. 247–48, distinguishes four different Swifts in the poem: Swift #1 is the real Swift; Swift #2, the poem's principal speaker; Swift #3, the idealized figure of the eulogy; and Swift #4, the author of the footnotes.

44. Swift's failure to receive a mitre is mentioned a number of times in his poetry, as well as in the poems of others. See "A Dialogue between an eminent Lawyer and DR. SWIFT," "To Doctor Delany," and Jonathan Smedley's "Epistle to his Grace the Duke of GRAFTON."

45. "Personae," *Restoration and Eighteenth Century Literature*, ed. Carroll Camden (Chicago: University of Chicago Press, 1963), p. 34.

46. Schakel, *Poetry of Jonathan Swift*, p. 143, and p. 203, n.37, offers evidence that the Rose Tavern was a disreputable political meeting place in Swift's time.

47. Biographical references in Swift's poetry—in the Market Hill and Stella poems, for example—are often more private than this, but whenever Swift's public career is the subject, he seems to work with common knowledge. This does not, of course, preclude other levels of meaning accessible only to those of more intimate acquaintance.

48. There are subtler jokes, in addition. Several recent commentators have drawn attention to George Birkbeck Hill's discovery that the line "But what he writ was all his own" was taken from Denham's elegy on Cowley. Samuel Johnson, *Lives of the English Poets*, ed. George Birkbeck Hill (Oxford: Clarendon Press, 1905), 3: 66, n.2.

49. Another echo of the maxim occurs in 11. 403–6:

> "When, *ev'n his own familiar Friends*
> "Intent upon their private Ends;
> "Like Renegadoes now he feels,
> *"Against him lifting up their Heels."*

50. Herbert Davis, "The Poetry of Jonathan Swift," *College English* 2 (1940): 115.

51. Slepian, "Ironic Intention," p. 256, lists thirteen people satirized by name in the poem, although he unaccountably omits Lintot.

52. Review of Slepian, *Philological Quarterly* 64 (1964): 392.

53. Edward W. Said, "Swift's Tory Anarchy," *Eighteenth-Century Studies* 3 (1969): 62.

54. Donald C. Mell similarly finds this creation to be a defense against time and death, but without the emphasis that my interpretation places on egotism. "Elegiac Design and Satiric Intention in 'Verses on the Death of Dr. Swift,' " *Concerning Poetry* 6 (1973): 19.

Notes to Chapter 2: The Vulnerable Self

1. The condition Swift presents as a joke in the poem was apparently true to his real condition. See Swift to William Richardson, April 30, 1737: "When the deafness comes on, I can hear with neither ear, except it be a woman with a treble, and a man with a counter-tenor" (*Corres.*, 5: 38).

2. Letter of July 20, 1726, *Corres.*, 3: 145.

3. Letter of July 15, 1726, ibid., pp. 141–42.

4. See *Corres.* 3, passim, for Swift's apprehensions that Stella would die during 1726 and 1727. She died on January 28, 1728.

5. Holyhead Journal, September 26, 1727, *Prose Works*, 5: 204.

6. Swift wrote this to Stella's prospective suitor, William Tisdale, April 20, 1704, *Corres.*, 1: 46.

7. John Middleton Murry, *Jonathan Swift* (London: Jonathan Cape, 1954), p. 295, sees an underlying concern with both Stella and Vanessa: "One feels that the idea of splitting his worship in twain was too close to his actual condition to have been pure accident."

8. Swift was always somewhat inaccurate about Stella's age in the poems. She was forty in 1721, but the poem describes her as thirty-six and later has her rival, Chloe, "prate / Of thirty-six, and thirty-eight."

9. Swift later added the words "now deaf 1740" next to these lines in the margin of his copy of the *Miscellanies* (*Poems*, 2: 758n).

10. Swift to Sheridan, September 2, 1727, *Corres.*, 3: 236: "I long knew that our dear Friend had not the *Stamina Vitae*; but my Friendship could not arm me against this Accident altho' I foresaw it."

11. John I. Fischer, "The Uses of Virtue: Swift's Last Poem to Stella," comments: "By offering himself to Stella as an object for her pity, he provided her both an occasion for and a model of that practical virtue which he believed would 'guide [her] to a better state.' " *Essays in Honor of Esmond Linworth Marilla*, ed. Thomas Austin Kirby and William John Olive (Baton Rouge: Louisiana State University Press, 1970), p. 209. The distastefulness of Swift's deliberately trying the virtue of his dying friend does not rule out the possibility, but I find the concluding speech more effective as an unintentional test, an outcry of desperation rather than the preacher's calculated attempt to save a soul. "Me, surely me" strikes too forcefully as the poet's dominant concern in these emotional last lines.

12. *Corres.*, 3: 147.

13. Letter of July 5, 1721, *Corres.*, 2: 392.

14. *Prose Works*, 9: 89.

Notes to Chapter 3: The Verbal Universe

1. Samuel Johnson, *The Lives of the Poets*, ed. George Birkbeck Hill, 3 vols. (Oxford: Clarendon Press, 1905), 3: 65.

2. William K. Wimsatt, "Rhetoric and Poems: The Example of Swift," *The Author in His Work: Essays on a Problem in Criticism*, ed. Louis L. Martz and Aubrey Williams (New Haven, Conn.: Yale University Press, 1978), pp. 229–44, is an excellent discussion of some of Swift's poetic techniques.

3. "Dick" is Richard Tighe, a privy councillor and member of the Irish Parliament long disliked by Swift. See *Poems*, 2: 772–73 for a history of their relations.

4. Abraham Cowley, "Clad All in White" (10–12), *The Complete Works in Verse and Prose*, ed. Alexander B. Grosart, 2 vols. (Hildesheim: Georg Olms, 1969), 1: 107.

5. George Gordon, Lord Byron, *His Very Self and Voice: Collected Conversations of Lord Byron*, ed. Ernest J. Lovell, Jr. (New York: Macmillan, 1954), p. 268.

6. William Gass, *On Being Blue* (Boston: David R. Godine, 1976), p. 32.

7. *Gulliver's Travels, Prose Works*, 11: 240.

8. Ibid.

9. Smedley's poem is printed in *Poems*, 2: 357–60.

10. A factor in the different responses is Swift's friendship for Delany and enmity toward Smedley, who attacked him in print on a number of occasions. "An Epistle upon an Epistle" seeks to instruct Delany while "His Grace's Answer to Jonathan" intends to ridicule Smedley.

11. "To quibble" here has the obsolete meaning of "to pun, to play on words" *(OED)*.

12. Swift's *filthy froth* and *spue* are neutral words in Pliny: *sanies*, venom or poison, and *saliva*, spittle or saliva. *Natural History*, trans. H. Rackham, Loeb Classical Library, 10 vols. (London: William Heinemann, 1940), 3: 412 and 8: 232.

13. As Alan S. Fisher has commented: "The poem's interest in concepts is to destroy the false, but not necessarily to build up true ones in their place." "Swift's Verse Portraits: A Study in his Originality as an Augustan Satirist," *Studies in English Literature* 14 (1974): 345.

14. See George Orwell, "Politics and the English Language," *A Collection of Essays* (New York: Harcourt, Brace, Jovanovich, 1946), p. 167.

15. Petronius, *The Satyricon and the Fragments*, trans. John Sullivan (Baltimore, Md.: Penguin Books, 1965), p. 174.

16. Orwell, *A Collection of Essays*, p. 167.

17. Swift to the Rev. Henry Clarke, December 12, 1734, *Corres.*, 4: 274.

18. A good refutation of the anti-poetry school can be found in Robert W. Uphaus, "Swift's Poetry: The Making of Meaning," *Eighteenth-Century Studies* 5 (1972): 569–86.

19. Herbert Davis, "Swift's View of Poetry," *Fair Liberty Was All His Cry*, ed. Norman Jeffares (New York: St. Martin's Press, 1967), p. 89.

20. Letter of April 12, 1735, *Corres.*, 4: 320.

21. Swift was deeply grieved over the death of Lady Ashburnham; nevertheless, after seeing her mother and sister weeping together, he wrote: "There is something of Farce in all these Mournings let them be ever so serious. People will pretend to grieve more than they really do, & that takes off from their true Grief." *Journal to Stella*, 2: 602. Cf. ibid., 1: 69: "Mrs. Temple, the widow, died last Saturday, which, I suppose, is much to the outward grief and inward joy of the family."

22. *Prose Works*, 12: 24.

23. Ibid., p. 25.

24. "An Elegy on Mr. *Patrige*" (1708), "An Elegy on the much lamented Death of Mr. *Demar*" (1720), "A quibbling Elegy on the Worshipful Judge Boat" (1721), "Satirical Elegy on the Death of a Late Famous General" (1722), and "An Elegy on Dicky and Dolly" (1728).

25. Uphaus, "Swift's Poetry," p. 574, describes the poem as "an inverted elegy in which Swift contrasts Marlborough's military greatness (a fact Swift seems willing to concede) with the mundane circumstances of Marlborough's unheroic death." Such a conventional contrast would be less powerful than the picture Swift insistently draws of unworthiness unjustly rewarded by the world.

26. Swift's sentiments are similar to Dr. Johnson's on *Lycidas*: "Its [pastoral's] inherent improbability always forces dissatisfaction on the mind" (1: 163).

27. Marius Bewley, *Masks and Mirrors* (New York: Atheneum, 1970), p. 99.

28. "Swift's Description of the Morning," *Jonathan Swift: A Critical Anthology*, ed. Denis Donoghue (Cambridge: Cambridge University Press, 1971), p. 271.

29. David M. Vieth, *"Fiat Lux:* Logos versus Chaos in Swift's 'A Description of the Morning,' " *Papers on Language and Literature* 8 (1972): 306. Vieth's description of the prisoners' activities itself suggests a routinized cooperation between supposedly antithetical forces: "The criminal inmates (disorder), ostensibly confined by the prison (order), are let out to 'Steal' (disorder) according to a scheme of 'Fees' levied by the turnkey (order)."

30. Ralph Cohen, "The Augustan Mode in English Poetry," *Eighteenth-Century Studies* 1 (1967–68): 7.

31. Brendan O Hehir, "Meaning of Swift's 'Description of a City Shower,' " *ELH* 27 (1960): 206.

32. Swift's epic simile (11. 47–52) works like those in *The Rape of the Lock*, to emphasize the unheroic littleness of the characters described.

33. Denis Donoghue, *Jonathan Swift: A Critical Introduction* (Cambridge: Cambridge University Press, 1969), p. 44.

34. Swift's original version is more satirical. Philemon says: "I'm good for little at my days; / Make me the Parson if you please" (163–64).

35. Irvin Ehrenpreis, *Dr. Swift* (Cambridge, Mass.: Harvard University Press, 1967), pp. 243–48, has a good discussion of Addison's influence on the poem. As he observes: "It is through this Chaucerian excess, as in the strain he [Swift] imposes upon the tetrameters, that one feels the humorous conflict between reality and literary form. This fundamental virtue is what Addison attacked . . ." (p. 245). Eric Rothstein, "Jonathan Swift as Jupiter: 'Baucis and Philemon,' " *The Augustan Milieu*, ed. Henry Knight Miller, Eric Rothstein, and G. S. Rousseau (Oxford: Clarendon Press, 1970), pp. 205–24, provides a persuasive poetic rationale for the changes attributed to Addison's influence.

36. The other tree's grieving is Swift's only reference to the Ovidian motif of the couple's devotion.

37. Maurice Johnson, *The Sin of Wit* (Syracuse, N.Y.: Syracuse University Press, 1950), p. 91.

38. Williams, *Poems*, 1: 78, discusses the history of the two versions of "Vanbrug's House." The first poem, written in 1703 and published by Williams, will be referred to here as the manuscript poem. The second or revised version, probably written in 1708, was first published in 1710.

39. Ronald Paulson, *The Fictions of Satire* (Baltimore, Md.: Johns Hopkins Press, 1967), p. 200.

40. Cf. Swift's "Pastoral Dialogue Between *Richmond-Lodge* and *Marble-Hill*," where the two houses discuss their future. Marble-Hill predicts:

> Some *South Sea* Broker from the City,
> Will purchase me, the more's the Pity,
> Lay all my fine Plantations waste,
> To fit them to his Vulgar Taste;
> Chang'd for the Worse in ev'ry Part,
> My Master *Pope* will break his Heart.

(67–72)

Although she surprisingly fails to discuss the Vanbrugh poems, Carole Fabricant, "The Garden as City: Swift's Landscape of Alienation," provides a number of other examples of Swift's "increasingly somber perceptions of the land and its structures." *ELH*, 42 (1975): 536.

41. The attraction of the subject evidently overrode the awkwardness of Swift's friendly acquaintance with the playwright. Writing to Stella in November 1710, he recounts Vanbrugh's resentment: "Vanbrug [*sic*] I believe I told you, had a long quarrel with me about those Verses on his House; but we were very civil and cold" (*Journal to Stella*, 1: 84–85). The preface to the 1727 edition of the *Miscellanies,* jointly written by Pope and Swift, contains the following retraction: "In regard to two Persons only, we wish our Raillery, though ever so tender, or Resentment, though ever so just, had not been indulged. We speak of Sir *John Vanbrugh,* who was a Man of Wit and of Honour; and of Mr. Addison. . . ." *Miscellanies in Prose and Verse* (London: Benjamin Motte, 1727), 1: 9. In a list of "Men famous for their learning, wit, or great employments of quality, who are dead" (February 19, 1728–29), Swift included Vanbrugh (Appendix 31, *Corres.*, 5: 271).

42. When building Thebes, Amphion played his lyre so beautifully that the stones formed themselves into walls of their own accord. N. G. L. Hammond and H. H. Scullard, eds., *The Oxford Classical Dictionary*, 2d. ed. (Oxford: Clarendon Press, 1970), p. 54.

43. See "To Doctor Delany, on the Libels Writ against him," 11. 137–44, and "On Poetry: A Rapsody," 11. 335–44. Paul Fussell, *The Rhetorical World of Augustan Humanism* (Oxford: Clarendon Press, 1965), p. 234, notes that in an age where bugs were a constant annoyance, "the Augustan conservative imagination delights to image the contemptible by recourse to insects."

44. *Prose Works*, 1: 149 (emphasis removed).

45. See also "On the Little House by the Church Yard of *Castleknock*," for a similarly playful treatment of a small building without the larger implications of the Vanbrugh poems.

46. In this respect Vanbrugh joins Partridge, similarly satirized in Swift's "Elegy on Mr. *Patrige*," for his strange conjunction of trades, cobbling and astrology.

47. F. Elrington Ball, *Swift's Verse* (London: John Murray, 1929), pp. 66–67, attributes the change between first and second versions to Addison. Sir Henry Craik and John Forster are both cited in support of this view, but this seems to be a misreading of their remarks about "Baucis and Philemon."

48. Swift undoubtedly intends an ironic interplay between this meaning and the common meaning of *pile*, "a large building or edifice" *(OED).*

49. None of the meanings of *rhapsody* in Swift's time is totally appropriate to the poem. The most common, an epic poem or part of one, may be intended, for "On Poetry" stands as one of Swift's most ambitious and comprehensive ventures. To think of it as a "miscellaneous collection," the second meaning given by the *OED*, is to denigrate the poem's coherence. The least usual meaning is perhaps the most likely in an ironic sense: an exalted or enthusiastic expression of sentiment or feeling."

50. The effect is oddly similar to the conclusion of Herman Melville's satiric novel, *The Confidence-Man:* "Something further may follow of this Masquerade." Both endings invite continuation and allow for some hope thereby, but each work has created a closed universe of disvalue in which any possible sequel can only be more of the same folly and knavery.

51. Hugh Kenner, "James Joyce: Comedian of the Inventory," in *Jonathan Swift: A Critical Anthology*, pp. 264–65.

52. A. B. England, *Byron's Don Juan and Eighteenth-Century Literature* (Lewisburg, Pa.: Bucknell University Press, 1975), p. 133. Louis Tonko Milic, *A Quantitative Approach to the Style of Jonathan Swift* (The Hague: Mouton, 1967), p. 87, notes that Swift's use of prose seriation differs from that of other eighteenth-century writers: "There is a crucial distinction between Swift's undisciplined or informal method and Addison's or Johnson's careful and formal adherence to customary models."

53. The ironic *Letter of Advice to a Young Poet* contains the following comments about the relationship between poetry and religion: "I am not yet convinc'd, that it is at all necessary for a modern Poet to *believe in God*, or have any serious sense of Religion. . . . For *Poetry*, as it has been manag'd for some Years past . . . has been altogether disengag'd from the narrow notions of Virtue and Piety, because it has been found by Experience of our Professors, that the smallest quantity of Religion, like a single drop of Malt-Liquor in Claret, will muddy and discompose the brightest Poetical Genius" (*Prose Works*, 9: 328–29).

54. *Prose Works*, 4: 8.

55. George Orwell, "Politics and the English Language," p. 167. Although he discussed Swift in an essay entitled "Politics vs. Literature: An Examination of *Gulliver's Travels*," Orwell failed to see the resemblance between Swift's view of the politicizing of poetry and his own sense of the relationship between bad writing and bad politics. Much of Orwell's "Politics and the English Language" can be read as a twentieth-century prose version of "On Poetry: A Rapsody."

56. *Prose Works*, 5: 96.

57. Williams, *Poems*, p. 640, quotes Dr. William King, *Political and Literary Anecdotes* (1818), p. 15.

58. *Prose Works*, 11: 240.

Notes to Chapter 4: "Foppery, Affectation, Vanity, Folly, or Vice": The Disordered World of the Gentlewoman

1. *Prose Works*, 9: 88. Further page references will appear parenthetically in the text.

2. Letter to Vanessa (Esther Vanhomrigh), May 12, 1719, *Corres.*, 2: 326: "Quelles bestes en juppes sont les plus excellentes de celles que je vois semeès dans le monde au prix de vous; en les voyant, en les entendant je dis cent fois le

jour—ne parle, ne regarde, ne pense, ne fait rien comme ces miserables, sont ce de meme Sexe—du meme espece de Creatures?"

3. C. J. Rawson, *Gulliver and the Gentle Reader* (London and Boston: Routledge & Kegan Paul, 1973), p. 34.

4. Ronald Paulson, *The Fictions of Satire* (Baltimore, Md.: Johns Hopkins Press, 1967), p. 10.

5. See also Swift's commendations of Stella's courage in "To Stella, Visiting me in my Sickness," 11. 65–78, and in his prose memorial, *On the Death of Mrs. Johnson, Prose Works*, 5: 229–30.

6. Cf. "A Discourse Concerning the Mechanical Operation of the Spirit," *Prose Works*, 1: 167–90, where Swift examines "an Effect grown from *Art* into *Nature*" and "one which has only a natural Foundation, but where the Superstructure is entirely Artificial" (p. 176).

7. Gareth Jones describes Vanessa as a comic figure whose perfection is the " 'good child's' perfection—untried and potential." "Swift's *Cadenus and Vanessa*: A Question of 'Positives,' " *Essays in Criticism* 20 (1970): 434, James L. Tyne sees her as "satirized for the same either/or mentality of Strephons and Gulliver." "Vanessa and the Houyhnhnms: A Reading of *Cadenus and Vanessa*," *Studies in English Literature* 11 (1971): 521. My interpretation of Vanessa agrees with that of Peter J. Schakel, "Swift's 'dapper Clerk' and the Matrix of Allusions in *Cadenus and Vanessa*," *Criticism* 17 (1975): 246–61. Schakel finds that Vanessa "can be satirized in section four without loss of the admirable qualities which make her fully worthy of Cadenus" (p. 254).

8. Tyne, "Vanessa," p. 533. Swift gives numerous examples in the poem of pupil-teacher infatuation.

9. Irvin Ehrenpreis, *Dr. Swift* (Cambridge, Mass.: Harvard University Press, 1967), p. 651.

10. *Prose Works*, 4: 227.

11. Ibid., p. 263.

12. See my earlier discussion of "Cadenus and Vanessa," pp. 107–11.

13. According to Williams, both poems were probably written in 1720.

14. Rawson, *Gulliver and the Gentle Reader*, p. 36.

15. Cf. Swift on self-love: "The self-love of some men, inclines them to please others; and the self-love of others is wholly employed in pleasing themselves. This makes the great distinction between virtue and vice" (*Prose Works*, 4: 243).

Notes to Chapter 5: Poetry of Excess: The Body and the Body Politic

1. Thomas Sheridan, *The Life of the Rev. Dr. Jonathan Swift, Dean of St. Patrick's, Dublin*, 2d ed. (London: J. F. & C. Rivington, 1787), p. 393.

2. Ibid., p. 394.

3. Among present-day critics who see uncertainty or failure in the scatological poems are A. B. England, "World without Order: Some Thoughts on the Poetry of Swift," *Essays in Criticism* 16 (1966): 36; Maurice Johnson, *The Sin of Wit* (Syracuse, N.Y.: Syracuse University Press, 1950), pp. 118–19; C. J. Rawson, *Gulliver and the Gentle Reader* (London and Boston: Routledge & Kegan Paul, 1973), p. 34; and Peter J. Schakel, *The Poetry of Jonathan Swift: Allusion and the*

Development of a Poetic Style (Madison: University of Wisconsin Press, 1977), pp. 109–19.

4. Oswald Johnson, "Swift and the Common Reader," *In Defense of Reading*, ed. Reuben A. Brower and Richard Poirier (New York: E. P. Dutton, 1962), p. 187.

5. Herbert Davis, "Swift's View of Poetry," *Fair Liberty Was All His Cry*, ed. A. Norman Jeffares (London: Macmillan, 1967), p. 81, remarks in this conclusion "a gay little note, unusual in Swift."

6. Rawson, *Gulliver and the Gentle Reader*, p. 37.

7. John M. Aden, "Those Gaudy Tulips: Swift's 'Unprintables,' " *Quick Springs of Sense*, ed. Larry S. Champion (Athens: University of Georgia Press, 1974), p. 29, describes "A Beautiful Young Nymph" as "comic and pathetic *by turns*" [emphasis added]. This suggests a mechanical alternation, whereas the two are usually inseparable, as I have tried to demonstrate in reading lines 29–32. Even "levels" of comedy and pathos would fail to convey accurately the kind of effect the lines have.

8. Thomas B. Gilmore, Jr., "The Comedy of Swift's Scatological Poems," *PMLA* 91 (1976): 42, n. 8, makes a distinction between satiric and nonsatiric comedy in his discussion of the poem; however, satiric comedy need not be harsh, and all of the poem's comic effects tend to be satiric, that is, to reduce and ridicule Corinna.

9. Murray Krieger, *The Classic Vision* (Baltimore and London: Johns Hopkins Press, 1971), pp. 264, 265. Gilmore, "Comedy of Swift's Scatological Poems," p. 35, is in substantial agreement. John M. Aden, "Corinna and the Sterner Muse of Swift," *English Language Notes* 4 (1966): 28, uses the term *fierce sympathy*, which similarly will not work.

10. *Language as Symbolic Action* (Berkeley: University of California Press, 1966), p. 308.

11. Donald Greene, "On Swift's 'Scatological' Poems," *Sewanee Review* 75 (1967): 687.

12. A. B. England, "World without Order," p. 36, has commented: "Swift makes his exposure with vigorous clarity, but he is not sure what attitude to take towards it." Christine Rees, "Gay, Swift, and the Nymphs of Drury-Lane," *Essays in Criticism* 23 (1973): 15, finds the narrator's position "no more tenable" than Strephon's.

13. Among those identifying Swift's view with the speaker's are Maurice Johnson, *Sin of Wit*, p. 118; Denis Donoghue, *Jonathan Swift: A Critical Introduction* (Cambridge: Cambridge University Press, 1969), p. 209; Norman O. Brown, *Life against Death* (Middletown, Conn.: Wesleyan University Press, 1959), p. 188; Greene, "On Swift's 'Scatological' Poems," pp. 679–80; Krieger, *Classic Vision*, pp. 263–64; Aden, "Those Gaudy Tulips," p. 21; and Gilmore, "Comedy of Swift's Scatological Poems," p. 37.

14. David M. Vieth in *Notes & Queries* 220 (1975): 562–63, has suggested that *"Satira,"* a misprint for *Statira*, probably refers to the virtuous queen in Nathaniel Lee's popular play *The Rival Queens*.

15. Aden, "Those Gaudy Tulips," p. 28.

16. By political poetry I mean those poems devoted primarily to political issues and figures.

17. See also "Prometheus," "The Fable of Midas," "The Faggot," "The Storm," "On Mr. Pulteney being put out of the Council," "Wood, an Insect," and "A Simile, on Our Want of Silver."

18. Patricia Meyer Spacks, *An Argument of Images: The Poetry of Alexander Pope* (Cambridge, Mass.: Harvard University Press, 1971), p. 219.

19. Or again, it might not. According to Harold Williams, Montague "was a general patron of letters, and Swift's comment on him is hardly justified" (*Poems,* 2: 164). Swift's enmities are an idiosyncratic mixture of personal affront and political difference that may never be fully illuminated by scholarship. Even where Swift is on record with a deprecatory remark about someone he satirizes, there is often no explanation, or merely a speculation, to account for his dislike.

20. The device is used for a different purpose in Swift's letter to Pope, November 26, 1725: "I wish there were an Hospital built for it's [the world's] despisers, where one might act with safety" (*Corres.,* 3: 117).

21. W. B. Carnochan, "Swift's *Tale:* On Satire, Negation, and the Uses of Irony," *Eighteenth-Century Studies* 5 (1971): 136.

22. Michel Foucault, *Madness and Civilization,* trans. Richard Howard (New York: Random House, 1965), p. 74.

23. See Peter J. Schakel, "Virgil and the Dean: Christian and Classical Allusion in *The Legion Club,*" *Studies in Philology* 70 (1973): 427–38.

24. *On Swift's Poetry* (Gainesville: University of Florida Press, 1978), p. 201.

Notes to Conclusion

1. Ehrenpreis writes: "In childhood he had . . . suffered continually the bitter sensation of powerlessness to resist the will of those who took charge of him." "Swift and the Comedy of Evil," *The World of Jonathan Swift,* ed. Brian Vickers (Oxford: Basil Blackwell, 1968), p. 217.

2. Swift to Pope, April 28, 1739, *Corres.,* 5: 150.

3. *Prose Works,* 5: 192. Further examples in the next paragraph are also taken from the "Family of Swift," pp. 192–95.

4. Louis A. Landa, "Jonathan Swift: 'Not the Gravest of Divines,' " *Jonathan Swift 1667–1967: A Dublin Tercentenary Tribute,* ed. Roger McHugh and Philip Edwards (Dublin: Dufour Editions, 1968), p. 42.

5. Swift to Bolingbroke and Pope, April 5, 1729, *Corres.,* 3: 329.

6. John, Earl of Orrery, *Remarks on the Life and Writings of Dr. Jonathan Swift* (London: A. Millar, 1752), p. 4, writes: "His views were checked in his younger years, and the anxiety of that disappointment had a visible effect upon all his actions." Similar statements are made by Patrick Delany, *Observations upon Lord Orrery's Remarks* (London: W. Reeve, 1754), pp. 48, 56, and by Thomas Sheridan, *The Life of the Rev. Dr. Jonathan Swift* (London: J. F. & C. Rivington, 1787), pp. 2–3.

7. For a cogent and detailed account of Swift's prolonged efforts to secure the First Fruits for the Irish clergy, see Irvin Ehrenpreis, *Dr. Swift* (Cambridge, Mass.: Harvard University Press, 1967), pp. 131–33, 323–26, and 394–405. Swift wrote bitterly to Archbishop King, November 13, 1716: "It seemeth more reasonable to give Bishops Money for doing nothing, than a private Clergyman Thanks for succeeding where Bishops have failed" (*Corres.,* 2: 221).

8. Letter of October 20, 1713, *Corres.,* 1: 394. Cf. Swift to Archbishop King, May 18, 1727: "From the very moment of the Queen's death, your Grace hath thought fit to take every opportunity of giving me all sorts of uneasiness, without ever giving me, in my whole life, one single mark of your favour, beyond common

civilities. And, if it were not below a man of spirit to make complaints, I could date them from six and twenty years past" (*Corres.*, 3: 210).

9. Letter of January 29, 1725–26, *Corres.*, 3: 126.

10. Alvin B. Kernan, "Aggression and Satire: Art Considered as a Form of Biological Adaptation," *Literary Theory and Structure,* ed. Frank Brady, John Palmer, and Martin Price (New Haven, Conn.: Yale University Press, 1973), p. 126.

11. *Journal to Stella,* 2: 595. Similar sentiments appear frequently in Swift's letters of condolence; cf. Swift to Mrs. Whiteway, February 25, 1735–36: "He never intended any thing like perfect happiness in the present life" (*Corres.*, 4: 463); and to John Gay, November 10, 1730: "God hath taken care . . . to prevent any progress towards real happyness here, which would make life more desirable & death too dreadfull" (*Corres.*, 3: 417–18).

Works Cited

Adams, Percy G. *Graces of Harmony*. Athens, Ga.: University of Georgia Press, 1977.

Aden, John M. "Corinna and the Sterner Muse of Swift." *English Language Notes* 4 (1966): 23–31.

———. "Those Gaudy Tulips: Swift's 'Unprintables.' " In *Quick Springs of Sense,* edited by Larry S. Champion, pp. 15–32. Athens, Ga.: University of Georgia Press, 1974.

Ball, F. Elrington. *Swift's Verse*. London: John Murray, 1929.

Bateson, F. W. "Swift's *Description of the Morning.*" In *Jonathan Swift: A Critical Anthology,* edited by Denis Donoghue, pp. 269–73. Cambridge: Cambridge University Press, 1969.

Bergson, Henri. *Le Rire*. Paris: Presses Universitaires de France, 1962.

Bewley, Marius. *Masks and Mirrors*. New York: Atheneum, 1970.

Brown, Norman O. *Life against Death*. Middletown, Conn.: Wesleyan University Press, 1959.

Burke, Kenneth. *Language as Symbolic Action*. Berkeley: University of California Press, 1966.

Byron, George Gordon, Lord. *His Very Self and Voice: Collected Conversations of Lord Byron*. Edited by Ernest J. Lovell, Jr. New York: Macmillan, 1954.

Carnochan, W. B. "Swift's *Tale:* On Satire, Negation, and the Uses of Irony." *Eighteenth-Century Studies* 5 (1971): 122–44.

Cohen, Ralph. "The Augustan Mode in English Poetry." *Eighteenth-Century Studies* 1 (1967–68): 3–32.

Cowley, Abraham. *The Complete Works in Verse and Prose*. Edited by Alexander B. Grosart. 2 vols. Hildesheim: Georg Olms, 1969.

Davis, Herbert. "The Poetry of Jonathan Swift," *College English* 2 (1940): 102–15.

————. "Swift's View of Poetry." In *Fair Liberty Was All His Cry: A Tercentenary Tribute to Jonathan Swift 1667–1745*, edited by A. Norman Jeffares, pp. 62–97. London: Macmillan, 1967.

Delany, Patrick. *Observations upon Lord Orrery's Remarks on the Life and Writings of Dr. Jonathan Swift*. London: W. Reeve, 1794.

Dobrée, Bonamy. *English Literature in the Early Eighteenth Century, 1700–1740*. Oxford: Clarendon Press, 1959.

Donoghue, Denis. *Jonathan Swift: A Critical Introduction*. Cambridge: Cambridge University Press, 1969.

Dryden, John. *The Poems and Fables of John Dryden*. Edited by James Kinsley. 4 vols. London: Oxford University Press, 1958.

Edwards, Thomas R. *Imagination and Power*. New York: Oxford University Press, 1971.

Ehrenpreis, Irvin. "Personae." In *Restoration and Eighteenth-Century Literature*, edited by Carroll Camden, pp. 25–37. Chicago: University of Chicago Press, 1963.

————. *The Personality of Jonathan Swift*. Cambridge, Mass.: Harvard University Press, 1958.

————. "Swift and the Comedy of Evil." In *The World of Jonathan Swift: Essays for the Tercentenary*, edited by Brian Vickers, pp. 213–19. Oxford: Basil Blackwell, 1968.

————. *Swift: The Man, His Works, and the Age*. 2 vols. Cambridge, Mass.: Harvard University Press, 1962, 1967.

————. "Swift's Letters." In *Focus*, edited by C. J. Rawson, pp. 197–215. London: Sphere Books, 1971.

Elliott, Robert C. *The Power of Satire: Magic, Ritual, Art*. Princeton, N.J.: Princeton University Press, 1960.

————. "Swift's 'I.' " *The Yale Review* 62 (1973): 372–91.

England, A. B. *Byron's Don Juan and Eighteenth-Century Literature*. Lewisburg, Pa.: Bucknell University Press, 1975.

————. "World without Order: Some Thoughts on the Poetry of Swift." *Essays in Criticism* 16 (1966): 32–43.

Fabricant, Carole. "The Garden as City: Swift's Landscape of Alienation." *ELH* 42 (1975): 531–55.

Ferguson, Oliver W. *Jonathan Swift and Ireland*. Urbana: University of Illinois Press, 1962.

Fischer, John Irwin. "How to Die: Verses on the Death of Dr. Swift." *Review of English Studies* n.s. 21 (1970): 422–41.

———. *On Swift's Poetry.* Gainesville: The University Presses of Florida, 1978.

———. "The Uses of Virtue: Swift's Last Poem to Stella." In *Essays in Honor of Esmond Linworth Marilla,* edited by Thomas Austin Kirby and William John Olive, pp. 201–9. Baton Rouge: Louisiana State University Press, 1970.

Fisher, Alan S. "Swift's Verse Portraits: A Study of his Originality as an Augustan Satirist." *Studies in English Literature* 14 (1974): 343–56.

Foucault, Michel. *Madness and Civilization.* Translated by Richard Howard. New York: Random House, 1965.

Fussell, Paul. *The Rhetorical World of Augustan Humanism.* Oxford: Clarendon Press, 1965.

Gass, William. *On Being Blue.* Boston: David R. Godine, 1976.

Gilmore, Thomas B., Jr. "The Comedy of Swift's Scatological Poems." *PMLA* 91 (1976): 33–43.

Greene, Donald. "On Swift's 'Scatological' Poems." *Sewanee Review* 75 (1967): 672–89.

Guillén, Claudio. *Literature as System.* Princeton, N.J.: Princeton University Press, 1971.

Harris, Kathryn Montgomery. " 'Occasions so Few': Satire as a Strategy of Praise in Swift's Early Odes." *Modern Language Quarterly* 31 (1970): 22–37.

Hill, Geoffrey. "Jonathan Swift: The Poetry of 'Reaction.' " In *The World of Jonathan Swift: Essays for the Tercentenary,* edited by Brian Vickers, pp. 195–212. Oxford: Basil Blackwell, 1968.

Huxley, Aldous. *Do What You Will.* London: Chatto & Windus, 1929.

Irwin, W. R. "Swift the Verse Man." *Philological Quarterly* 54 (1975): 222–38.

Jaffe, Nora Crow. *The Poet Swift.* Hanover, N.H.: The University Press of New England, 1977.

Johnson, Maurice. *The Sin of Wit: Jonathan Swift as a Poet.* Syracuse, N.Y.: Syracuse University Press, 1950.

———. "Swift's Poetry Reconsidered." In *English Writers of the Eighteenth Century,* edited by John H. Middendorf, pp. 233–48. New York and London: Columbia University Press, 1971.

Johnson, Oswald. "Swift and the Common Reader." In *In*

Defense of Reading, edited by Reuben A. Brower and Richard Poirier, pp. 174–90. New York: E. P. Dutton, 1962.

Johnson, Samuel. *Lives of the English Poets.* Edited by George Birkbeck Hill. 3 vols. Oxford: Clarendon Press, 1905.

Jones, Gareth. "Swift's *Cadenus and Vanessa:* A Question of 'Positives.' " *Essays in Criticism* 20 (1970): 424–40.

Kenner, Hugh. "James Joyce: Comedian of the Inventory." In *Jonathan Swift: A Critical Anthology,* edited by Denis Donoghue, pp. 264–68. Cambridge: Cambridge University Press, 1969.

Kernan. Alvin B. "Aggression and Satire: Art Considered as a Form of Biological Adaptation." In *Literary Theory and Structure,* edited by Frank Brady, John Palmer, and Martin Price, pp. 115–29. New Haven: Yale University Press, 1973.

Krieger, Murray. *The Classic Vision.* Baltimore and London: Johns Hopkins Press, 1971.

Landa, Louis A. "Jonathan Swift: 'Not the Gravest of Divines.' " In *Jonathan Swift, 1667–1967: A Dublin Tercentenary Tribute,* edited by Roger McHugh and Philip Edwards, pp. 38–60. Dublin: Dufour Editions, 1968.

Lawrence, D. H. *Phoenix: The Posthumous Papers of D. H. Lawrence.* Edited by Edward D. McDonald. London: William Heinemann, 1936.

Leavis, F. R. *Determinations.* London: Chatto & Windus, 1934.

Mack, Maynard. "The Muse of Satire." *The Yale Review* 41 (1951): 80–92.

Mayhew, George P. "Recent Swift Scholarship." In *Jonathan Swift, 1667–1967: A Dublin Tercentenary Tribute,* edited by Roger McHugh and Philip Edwards, pp. 187–97. Dublin: Dufour Editions, 1968.

Mell, Donald C. "Elegiac Design and Satiric Intention in 'Verses on the Death of Dr. Swift.' " *Concerning Poetry* 6 (1973): 15–24.

Milic, Louis Tonko. *A Quantitative Approach to the Style of Jonathan Swift.* The Hague: Mouton, 1967.

Murry, John Middleton. *Jonathan Swift.* London: Jonathan Cape, 1954.

O Hehir, Brendan. "Meaning of Swift's 'Description of a City Shower.' " *ELH* 27 (1960): 194–207.

Orrery, John Boyle, Earl of. *Remarks on the Life and Writings of Dr. Jonathan Swift*. London: A. Millar, 1752.

Orwell, George. *A Collection of Essays*. New York: Harcourt, Brace, Jovanovich, 1946.

Paulson, Ronald. *The Fictions of Satire*. Baltimore, Md.: Johns Hopkins Press, 1967.

Petronius. *The Satyricon and the Fragments*. Translated by John Sullivan. Baltimore, Md.: Penguin Books, 1965.

Pliny. *Natural History*. Translated H. Rackham. 10 vols. Loeb Classical Library. London: William Heinemann, 1940.

Pope, Alexander. *The Correspondence of Alexander Pope*. Edited by G. Sherburn. 5 vols. Oxford: Clarendon Press, 1956.

———. *Imitations of Horace*. Edited by John Butt. London: Methuen, 1939.

Rawson, C. J. *Gulliver and the Gentle Reader*. Boston and London: Routledge & Kegan Paul, 1973.

———. "The Nightmares of Strephon: Nymphs of the City in the Poems of Swift, Baudelaire, Eliot." In *English Literature in the Age of Disguise,* edited by Maximillian E. Novak, pp. 57–99. Berkeley: University of California Press, 1977.

Rees, Christine. "Gay, Swift, and the Nymphs of Drury-Lane." *Essays in Criticism* 23 (1973): 1–21.

Reichard, Hugo M. "The Self-Praise Abounding in Swift's Verses." *Tennessee Studies in Literature* 18 (1973): 105–12.

Reynolds, Richard. "Swift's 'Humble Petition' from a Pregnant Frances Harris?" *Scriblerian* 5 (1972): 38–9.

Roberts, Philip. "Swift's Poetry." In *Swift,* edited by W. A. Speck, pp. 49–72. New York: Arco, 1970.

Rothstein, Eric. "Jonathan Swift as Jupiter: 'Baucis and Philemon.' " In *The Augustan Milieu,* edited by Henry Knight Miller, Eric Rothstein, G. S. Rousseau, pp. 205–24. Oxford: Clarendon Press, 1970.

Said, Edward W. "Swift's Tory Anarchy." *Eighteenth-Century Studies* 3 (1969): 48–66.

Schakel, Peter J. *The Poetry of Jonathan Swift: Allusion and the Development of a Poetic Style*. Madison: University of Wisconsin Press, 1978.

———. "The Politics of Opposition in 'Verses on the Death of Dr. Swift.' " *Modern Language Quarterly* 35 (1974): 246–56.

_____. "Swift's 'dapper Clerk' and the Matrix of Allusions in *Cadenus and Vanessa.*" *Criticism* 17 (1975): 246–61.

_____. "Virgil and the Dean: Christian and Classical Allusion in *The Legion Club.*" *Studies in Philology* 70 (1973): 427–38.

Scouten, Arthur H., and Hume, Robert D. "Pope and Swift: Text and Interpretation of Swift's Verses on His Own Death." *Philological Quarterly* 52 (1973): 205–31.

Sheridan, Thomas. *The Life of the Rev. Dr. Jonathan Swift, Dean of St. Patrick's, Dublin.* 2d ed. London: J. F. & C. Rivington, et al., 1787.

Shinagel, Michael. *A Concordance to the Poems of Jonathan Swift.* Ithaca and London: Cornell University Press, 1972.

Slepian, Barry. "The Ironic Intention of Swift's Verses on his own Death." *Review of English Studies* n.s. 14 (1963): 249–56.

Spacks, Patricia Meyer. *An Argument of Images.* Cambridge, Mass.: Harvard University Press, 1971.

Sutherland, James. *English Satire.* Cambridge: Cambridge University Press, 1958.

Swift, Jonathan. *The Correspondence of Jonathan Swift.* Edited by Harold Williams. Oxford: Clarendon Press, 1963–65.

_____. *Journal to Stella.* Edited by Harold Williams. 2 vols. Oxford: Clarendon Press, 1948.

_____. *The Poems of Jonathan Swift.* Edited by Harold Williams. 3 vols. Oxford: Clarendon Press, 1958.

_____. *The Prose Works of Jonathan Swift.* Edited by Herbert Davis. 14 vols. Oxford: Clarendon Press, 1937–68.

_____. *Swift's Poetical Works.* Edited by Herbert Davis. London: Oxford University Press, 1967.

_____. *A Tale of a Tub.* Edited by A. C. Guthkelch and D. Nichol Smith. Oxford: Clarendon Press, 1920.

_____, and Pope, Alexander. *Miscellanies in Prose and Verse.* London; Benjamin Motte, 1727.

Trickett, Rachel. *The Honest Muse: A Study in Augustan Verse.* Oxford: Clarendon Press, 1967.

Tyne, James L. "Vanessa and the Houyhnhnms: A Reading of *Cadenus and Vanessa.*" *Studies in English Literature* 11 (1971): 517–34.

Uphaus, Robert W. "From Panegyric to Satire: Swift's Early Odes and *A Tale of a Tub*." *Texas Studies in Literature and Language* 13 (1971): 55–70.

———. "Swift's Poetry: The Making of Meaning." *Eighteenth-Century Studies* 5 (1972): 569–86.

Vieth, David M. *"Fiat Lux:* Logos versus Chaos in Swift's 'A Description of the Morning.' " *Papers on Language and Literature* 8 (1972): 302–7.

———. "The Mystery of Personal Identity: Swift's Verses on His Own Death." In *The Author in His Work: Essays on a Problem in Criticism,* edited by Louis L. Martz and Aubrey Williams, pp. 245–62. New Haven, Conn.: Yale University Press, 1978.

———. "Swift's Poetical Works." *Notes & Queries* 220 (1975): 562–63.

Voigt, Milton. *Swift and the Twentieth Century*. Detroit, Mich.: Wayne State University Press, 1964.

Waingrow, Marshall. "Verses on the Death of Dr. Swift." *Studies in English Literature* 5 (1965): 513–18.

West, Nathanael. *Miss Lonelyhearts*. New York: New Directions, 1962.

Williams, Aubrey L. " 'A vile Encomium': That 'Panegyric on the Reverend D--n S---t.' " In *Contemporary Studies of Swift's Poetry,* edited by Donald C. Mell and John Irwin Fischer, pp. 178–90. Newark: University of Delaware Press, 1981.

Williams, Kathleen. *Jonathan Swift and the Age of Compromise*. Lawrence: University of Kansas Press, 1958.

Wilson, Edmund. *The Shores of Light*. New York: Farrar, Straus & Young, 1952.

Wimsatt, William K. "Rhetoric and Poems: The Example of Swift." In *The Author in His Work: Essays on a Problem in Criticism,* edited by Louis L. Martz and Aubrey Williams, pp. 229–44. New Haven, Conn.: Yale University Press, 1978.

Woolley, James. "Arbuckle's 'Panegyric' and Swift's Scrub Libel: The Documentary Evidence." In *Contemporary Studies of Swift's Poetry,* edited by Donald C. Mell and John Irwin Fischer, pp. 191–209. Newark: University of Delaware Press, 1981.

Index

Acheson, Lady Anne, 22, 25, 48, 57, 58, 59, 60, 61, 62, 63, 64, 65, 66. *See also* Swift, Jonathan, Market Hill poems; *individual titles*
Acheson, Sir Arthur, 57, 61, 65
Achesons, 59, 62, 64, 66, 67
Adams, Percy G., 198 n
Addison, Joseph, 133, 207 n, 208 n, 209 n
Aden, John M., 211 n
Allen, Joshua, second Viscount, 183, 186
Amphion, 136, 208 n
Anchises, 192
Anne, Queen, 73, 80, 87, 195
Apollo, 32, 33, 100, 113
Arbuckle, James, 203 n
Arbuthnot, Dr. John, 77, 92
Archilochus, 31
Ashburnham, Lady Mary, 197, 206 n
Atterbury, Dr. Francis, bishop of Rochester, 201 n
Augustus, 146

Ball, F. Elrington, 208 n
Bateson, F. W., 129, 130
Bathurst, Allen, first Baron and Earl, 199 n
Beach, Thomas, 126
Beatrice, 192
Bergson, Henri, 38, 39, 201 n
Berkeley, Lady Betty, 56
Berkeley, Charles, 194, 203 n
Berkeley household, 57, 67, 202 n
Bettesworth, Richard, 31, 40, 122, 196, 201 n
Bewley, Marius, 129, 130, 207 n
Boate, Judge Godfrey, 117, 127
Bolingbroke, Henry St. John, Viscount, 24, 28, 73, 195, 212 n

Bolton, Charles Paulett, second duke of, 187
Brown, Norman O., 211 n
Browning, Robert: monologues, 58
Burke, Kenneth, 176
Burnet, Gilbert, bishop of Salisbury, 200 n
Bushe, Arthur, 203 n
Byron, George Gordon, sixth Lord, 113

Carnochan, W. B., 190
Caroline, Queen, 148
Carteret, John, second Lord, 68, 76
Chaucer, Chaucerian, 133
Cherbury, Herbert, lord of: *The Life and Raigne of Henry VIII*, 29
Chetwode, Knightley, 47, 201 n
Cholmondeley, Hugh, first earl of, 187
Cibber, Colley, 84
Clarke, Henry, 206 n
Clemens, Samuel L., 112
Cleveland, Charles Fitzroy, 187
Clio, 192
Cohen, Ralph, 131
Cowley, Abraham, 113, 204 n
Craik, Sir Henry, 208 n
Cutts, John, Baron Cutts of Gowran, 196

Dante, 182; *Inferno*, 192
Davis, Herbert, 16, 89, 211 n
Delany, Dr. Patrick, 117, 144, 195, 206 n, 212 n. *See also* Swift, Jonathan, poetry, *individual titles*
Demar, John, 127
Denham, Sir John, 27, 204 n
Dobrée, Bonamy, 17
Donoghue, Denis, 132, 211 n
Dryden, John, 51, 52, 133, 164, 165,

221

187, 198 n, 201 n; *Absalom and Achitophel*, 187–88; *Honour'd Kinsman, John Driden, To my*, 51. *See also* Swift, Jonathan, panegyric, in Dryden
Duck, Stephen, 84

Edwards, Thomas R., 67
Ehrenpreis, Irvin, 15, 17, 86, 162, 194, 207 n, 212 n
Elliott, Robert C., 26, 48
England, A. B., 210 n, 211 n

Fabricant, Carole, 208 n
Faulkner, George, 25, 63, 199 n
Ferguson, Oliver W., 203 n
Finch, Daniel, second earl of Nottingham. *See* Nottingham, Daniel Finch
Fischer, John Irwin, 18, 193, 199 n, 201 n, 203 n, 204 n, 205 n
Fisher, Alan S., 206 n
Fleury, Cardinal, 182
Ford, Charles, 30
Foster, John, 208 n
Foucault, Michel, 191
Fussell, Paul, 208 n

Gass, William, 113, 114
Gay, John, 77, 213 n
George II, King, 146
Gilmore, Thomas B., Jr., 211 n
Golding, William, 133
Greene, Donald, 178
Guillén, Claudio, 20

Harris, Kathryn Montgomery, 201 n
Henry VIII, King, 29
Hervey, John, Lord, 148
Hill, Geoffrey, 26
Hill, George Birkbeck, 204 n
Horace, 22, 24, 32, 200 n
Howard, Henrietta, 76, 77
Hume, Robert D., 203 n
Huxley, Aldous, 16, 17

Irwin, W. R., 16

Jaffe, Nora Crow, 18, 199 n
James, Henry, 90
Johnson, Esther (Stella), 93, 97, 106, 210; approaching death, 94, 95, 96,

104, 106, 107, 205 n; birthday, 22, 92; compatibility with Swift, 97, 98, 99, 100, 102, 103, 105, 106; Swift's feelings for, 91, 94, 95, 96, 105, 150; Swift's letters to, 37, 208 n; Swift's poems for, 18, 23, 91, 94–95, 97, 98–106, 113, 139–40, 164–70, 197. *See also* Swift, Jonathan, poetry, Stella poems; *individual titles*
Johnson, Maurice, 15, 22, 210 n, 211 n
Johnson, Oswald, 16, 17
Johnson, Samuel, 15, 112, 207 n, 209 n
Jones, Gareth, 210 n
Juvenal, Juvenalian, 35, 200 n

Kenner, Hugh, 144
Kernan, Alvin B., 196
King, Dr. William, archbishop of Dublin, 203 n, 212 n
King, Dr. William, principal of St. Mary's Hall, Oxford, 82, 203 n, 209 n

Landa, Louis A., 194
La Rochefoucauld, François, duc de: maxim of, 76, 78, 79, 80, 82, 83, 88, 92
Lawrence, D. H., 16
Leavis, F. R., 16, 17
Lee, Nathaniel, 211 n
Lewis, Erasmus, 22
Lincoln, Henry Clinton, seventh earl of, 187
Lintot, Barnaby Bernard, 84–85, 204 n

Mack, Maynard, 21, 31
Marlborough, John Churchill, first duke of, 126, 128, 196, 207 n
Mayhew, George P., 198 n
Mell, Donald C., 203 n, 205 n
Melville, Herman, 209 n
Milic, Louis Tonko, 209 n
Milton, John: *Paradise Lost*, 141
Montague, Ralph, first duke of, 187, 212 n
Murry, John Middleton, 203 n, 204 n, 205 n

Neville, Sir John, 29
Nottingham, Daniel Finch, second earl of, 73

O Hehir, Brendan, 131, 132
Orrery, John Boyle, earl of, 82, 212 n
Orwell, George, 120, 125, 147, 209 n
Ovid, Ovidian, 114, 132, 133, 139, 207 n
Oxford, Robert Harley, first earl of, 22, 24, 40, 48, 68, 70–71, 73, 75, 76, 80, 195

Palmerston, Henry Temple, first Viscount, 195
Panegyric. *See* Swift, Jonathan, panegyric
Partridge, John, 21, 112, 127, 135, 172, 196
Paulson, Ronald, 38, 82, 135–36, 154, 203 n
Petrarch, Petrarchan, 99, 101–2, 167, 173; anti-Petrarchan, 102, 106
Petronius, 123
Pindar, Pindaric, 49
Pliny, 119, 120, 206 n
Pope, Alexander, 23, 82, 84, 89, 160, 182, 198 n, 199 n, 200 n, 203 n, 208 n; satiric persona, 21, 31, 33; Swift's letters to, 24, 28, 34, 47, 77, 194, 200 n. WORKS: *The Dunciad,* 141; *Imitations of Horace,* 32, 200 n; *The Rape of the Lock,* 207 n.
Portland, William Bentinck, first earl of, 187
Prendergast, Sir Thomas, 190, 191
Prometheus, 166

Rawson, C. J., 35, 39, 152, 168, 174
Rees, Christine, 211 n
Reichard, Hugo, 199 n
Reynolds, Richard, 202 n
Richardson, William, 205 n
Romney, Henry Sidney, first earl of, 194
Rosenheim, Edward W., 89
Rothstein, Eric, 207 n

Saeva indignatio, 18, 19, 28, 88, 183, 200 n
Said, Edward W., 89
Salmoneus, 183
Sancroft, Dr. William, 52, 53
Satire, satirist, 28–41, 152, 154, 196–97.

See also Swift, Jonathan, satiric poetry
Scatological poetry. *See* Swift, Jonathan, scatological poetry
Schakel, Peter J., 18, 70, 199 n, 204 n, 210 n, 212 n
Scouten, Arthur H., 203 n
Sheridan,Dr. Thomas, 106, 171, 200 n, 202 n, 205 n, 212 n
Shinagel, Michael, 199 n
Sibyl, 192
Singleton, Henry, Lord Chief Justice, 122
Slepian, Barry, 204 n
Smedley, Jonathan, Dean of Clogher and Killala, 135, 172, 206 n; *Epistle to his Grace the Duke of Grafton, An,* 116–17, 135, 204 n
Somerset, Elizabeth Seymour, duchess of, 73
Spacks, Patricia Meyer, 184
Steele, Sir Richard, 77
Stella. *See* Johnson, Esther
Stopford, James, bishop of Cloyne, 94
Sutherland, James, 200 n
Swift, Deane, 194
Swift, Jonathan: the Drapier, 33, 86, 89; early odes, 19, 22, 49, 50–56; life, 26, 31, 194–95; Market Hill poems, 19, 23, 25, 57–67, 202 n, 204 n; panegyric, dislike of, 126, 201 n, in Dryden, 51, 164–65, in early odes, 22, 49, 50, 51, 52, 53, 54, 55, in Market Hill poems, 62, 64, in *On Poetry: A Rapsody,* 141, 146, 147, in Stella poems, 101, 168–69; poetry of fictive self-portraiture, 19, 21–28, 45–111; political poems, 20, 140–49, 182–93, 197, 211 n, poems of Swift's political career, 24, 67–76; satiric poetry, 19–20, 28–41, 50–53; scatological poetry, 15, 16, 17, 20, 39, 40, 171–82, 193, 197, 201 n, 210 n; Stella poems, 19, 20, 21, 22, 23, 92, 94–95, 97–106, 107, 113, 164–70, 197, 204 n. WORKS: POEMS, "Advice to a Parson," 196; "Apology to the Lady Carteret, An," 202 n; "Author upon Himself, The," 22, 24, 49, 69, 71–74, 75; "Ballad on the Game of Traffick, A," 56; "Baucis and Philemon,"

133–35, 136, 148, 208 n; "Beautiful Young Nymph Going to Bed, A," 104, 174–76, 178, 182, 211 n; "Cadenus and Vanessa," 91, 106–111, 154, 161–64, 165, 166, 210 n; "Cassinus and Peter, A Tragical Elegy," 16, 176, 177–78; "Character of Sir Robert Walpole, The," 182; "Character, Panegyric, and Description of The Legion Club, A," 18, 20, 183, 185, 187, 188, 189–93, 201 n; "Clad all in Brown," 113; "Congreve, To Mr.," 55, 137; "Day of Judgement, The," 196; "Description of a City Shower, A," 17, 129, 130–32; "Description of a Salamander, The," 118–20; "Description of the Morning, A," 17, 129–30; "Dialogue between an eminent Lawyer and Dr. Swift, A," 32, 204 n; "Discovery, The," 203 n; "Doctor Delany, To," 37, 81, 142–43, 144, 147, 195–96, 204 n, 208 n; "Drapier's Hill," 27–28; "Elegy on Demar, An," 207n; "Elegy on Dicky and Dolly, An," 207 n; "Elegy on Mr. Patrige, An," 113, 135, 148, 207 n, 208 n; "Epigram Inscribed to The Honourable Sergeant Kite, An," 200 n, "Epistle to a Lady, An," 31, 33–36, 169, 182, 200 n; "Epistle upon an Epistle, An," 206 n; "Fable of Midas, The," 211 n; "Faggot, The," 211 n; "Friend who had been much abused in many inveterate Libels, To a," 48, 81; "Furniture of a Woman's Mind, The," 154, 155–58; "Grand Question debated, the," 64–65; "Harris's Petition, Mrs. Frances," 56–57; "Helter Skelter," 188–89; "His Grace's Answer to Jonathan," 116–17, 135, 206 n; "History of Vanbrug's House, The," 138–39; "Holyhead. Sept. 25, 1727," 21, 91, 95–97, 106; "Horace, Part of the Sixth Satire of the Second Book imitated," 24, 49, 71, 74–75; "Horace, Seventh Epistle of the First Book imitated," 22, 68, 71; "Journal of a Modern Lady, The," 158–61; "Lady Acheson weary of the Dean," 58–60; "Lady Betty Berkeley," 56; "Lady's Dressing Room, The," 151, 176, 177, 178–80, 181; "Libel on Doctor Delany and a Certain Great Lord, A," 203 n; "Life and Genuine Character of Doctor Swift, The," 20, 49, 76, 78–82, 83, 85, 89; "My Lady's Lamentation and Complaint against the Dean," 49, 60, 62; "Occasioned by Sir William Temple's late Illness and Recovery," 55; "Ode to Dr. William Sancroft," 52, 53; "Ode to the Athenian Society," 26, 45; "Ode to the Honourable Sir William Temple," 31, 34, 53–54; "On Censure," 81, 201 n; "On Dreams," 123–24; "On his own Deafness," 91, 92, 93–94; "On Mr. Pulteney," 211 n; "On Poetry: A Rapsody," 18, 30–31, 114, 140–49, 208 n, 209 n; "On the Little House by the Church Yard of Castleknock," 208 n; "On the Words—Brother Protestants and Fellow Christians," 121–22; "Panegyrick on the Dean in the Person of a Lady in the North, A," 22, 25, 49, 60, 62–64; "Pastoral Dialogue, A," 115–16; "Pastoral Dialogue between Richmond-Lodge and Marble-Hill, A," 208 n; "Pethox the Great," 113; "Place of the Damn'd, The," 124–25, 196; "Progress of Beauty, The," 104, 115, 172–74, 177; "Progress of Love, The," 150–51; "Prometheus," 211 n; "Quibbling Elegy on . . . Judge Boat, A," 117–18, 207 n; "Satirical Elegy on the Death of a late Famous General, A," 127–29, 207 n; "Sickness, In," 91, 92–93; "Simile on our Want of Silver, A," 211 n; "Stella, To, 1719," 98–99; "Stella, To, 1724," 95; "Stella on her Birth-Day, To, 1721," 99–100; "Stella's Birth-Day, 1720," 99; "Stella's Birth-Day, 1723," 100, 113; "Stella's Birth-Day, 1725," 102–104; "Stella's Birth-Day, 1727," 104–106, 112; "Stella, Visiting me in my Sickness, To," 98, 139, 164, 165–67, 210 n; "Stella, Who collected and transcribed his Poems, To," 164, 167–70; "Storm, The," 211 n; "Strephon and Chloe," 21, 110, 151, 171, 176, 178, 180–81; "Toland's

Invitation to Dismal," 187; "Traulus. The first Part," 40, 183–86, 200 n; "Traulus. The second Part," 183, 186; "Vanbrug's House," ms., 136–37, 207 n, 208 n; "Vanbrug's House Built from the Ruins of White-Hall," 136, 138, 207 n, 208 n, "Verses on the Death of Dr. Swift," 18, 25, 28, 31, 49, 76, 82–90, 199 n, 204 n, 205 n; "Verses to Vanessa," 110; "Verses wrote on a Lady's Ivory Table-Book," 155, 158; "Whitshed's Motto on his Coach," 120–21; "Wood, an Insect," 211 n.; "Yahoo's Overthrow, The," 201 n. PROSE WORKS, Battle of the Books, The, 137; Character of Mrs. Howard, The, 68; Directions to Servants, 63, 202 n; Discourse concerning the Mechanical Operation of the Spirit, 210 n; Drapier's Letters, The, 80; Education of Ladies, Of the, 163; Examiner, The, 30; Family of Swift, 194–95, 212 n; Good-Manners and Good Breeding, 61; Gulliver's Travels, 16, 114–15; Hints on Good-Manners, 63; Holyhead Journal, The, 96; Intelligencer, The, 200 n; Journal to Stella, The, 200 n, 207 n, 213 n; Letter of Advice to a Young Poet, 209 n; Letters, 28, 37, 47, 68, 77, 82, 94, 106, 107, 125, 194, 195, 200 n, 201 n, 202 n, 203 n, 205 n, 209–210 n, 212 n, 213 n; Letter to a Young Lady, on her Marriage, A, 110, 151–53, 154, 156, 164; Letter to the Writer of the Occasional Paper, A, 147; Marginalia, 200 n; Miscellanies, The, 199 n, 205 n, 208 n; Modest Proposal, A, 118, 188; On the Death of Mrs. Johnson, 210 n; Proposal for Correcting, Improving, and Ascertaining the English Tongue, A, 125, 147; Tale of a Tub, A, 17, 37, 87, 144, 152, 168, 174, 190; Thoughts on Religion, 164; Thoughts on Various Subjects, 199 n, 210 n

Temple, Mrs. Mary, 206 n
Temple, Sir William, 53, 54
Thomson, James, 198 n

Tighe, the Right Honourable Richard, 183, 196, 206 n
Tisdale, William, 205 n
Trelawney, Edward John, 113
Trickett, Rachel, 15–16
Twain, Mark. See Clemens, Samuel L.
Tyne, James L., 161, 210 n

Uphaus, Robert W., 201 n, 206 n, 207 n

Vanbrugh, Sir John, 135, 136, 137, 138, 139, 208 n
Vanessa. See Vanhomrigh, Esther
Vanhomrigh, Esther (Vanessa), 106, 107, 165, 166, 205 n, 209 n, 210 n. See also Swift, Jonathan, poetry, Cadenus and Vanessa, Verses to Vanessa
Venus, 163
Vieth, David M., 199 n, 204 n, 207 n, 211 n
Virgil: Aeneid, 146, 192
Vitruvius, 139
Voigt, Milton, 198 n

Waingrow, Marshall, 204 n
Walls, Archdeacon Thomas, vicar of Castleknock, 195
Walpole, Sir Robert, 20, 30, 40, 80, 200 n
West, Nathanael, 200 n
Whitehall, 135, 136, 137, 138, 139
Whiteway, Mrs. Martha, 82, 203 n, 213 n
Whitshed, William, Lord Chief Justice in Ireland, 120–21, 124, 127
William III, 195
Williams, Aubrey, 17
Williams, Sir Harold, 18, 31, 198 n, 207 n, 209 n, 210 n, 212 n
Williams, Kathleen, 201 n
Wilson, Edmund, 17
Wimsatt, William K., 206 n
Wood, William, 20, 196; Wood's Patent (Halfpence), 22, 86, 135, 183, 188
Woolley, James, 203 n
Woolston, Thomas, 84–85
Worrall, John, Dean's Vicar at St. Patrick's, 95

Yeats, William Butler: Sailing to Byzantium, 28